"At last, a real book by a real risk-taking practitioner. You cannot afford not to read this!"
—**Nassim Nicholas Taleb**, Author of *The Black Swan*

"Investors of all kinds will find immeasurable value in this convincing and thoroughly researched book where Mark champions the *roundabout* of Austrian capital theory. Using thought-provoking examples from both the natural world and the historical world, *The Dao of Capital* shows how a seemingly difficult immediate loss becomes an advantageous intermediate step for greater future gain, and thus why we must become 'patient now and strategically impatient later.'"
—**Paul Tudor Jones II**, Founder, Tudor Investment Corporation

"A timely, original, right-economic principles and history-based approach to investing. Drawing on impressive philosophical building blocks, *The Dao of Capital* illuminates the wellsprings of capital creation, innovation and economic progress. It also makes the point that government intervention to 'help' the economy is as destructive as the now-discredited policy of suppressing forest fires. Dazzling!"
—**Steve Forbes**, Chairman and Editor-in-Chief, Forbes Media

"This is a magnificent, scintillating book that I will read over and over again. It provides a theoretic and practical framework for understanding the insights of all the greats that a student of markets will encounter—Soros, Baldwin, Klipp, Buffett, Cooperman (albeit these greats might not realize or acknowledge it). It teaches you things about war, trees, martial arts, opera, baseball, board games. Every page is eye-opening, with numerous areas for testing and profits in every chapter. I will share the book with all my traders, friends, and circles of influence. Here's an unqualified, total, heartfelt recommendation, which coming from me is a rarity, and possibly unique."
—**Victor Niederhoffer**, Author of *The Education of a Speculator*

"*The Dao of Capital* is an impressive work. Spitznagel's approach is refreshing—scholarly without being tedious. What a broad look at economic history it provides!"
—**Byron Wien**, Vice Chairman, Blackstone Advisory Partners LP

"Wall Street gamblers who believe the Fed has their back need to read this book. Mark Spitznagel provides a brilliant demonstration that the gang of money printers currently resident in the Eccles Building have not repealed the laws of sound money nor have they rescinded the historical lessons on which they are based."
—**David Stockman**, Former U.S. Congressman, Budget Director under Ronald Reagan, and Author of *The Great Deformation*

"We live in a world warped by faulty assumptions and bad policies. Conventional wisdom explains very little because it's more convention than wisdom. Mark Spitznagel assembles the best insights in human nature and economics to bring order out of the chaos. Economists, investors and lay persons alike will find abundant treasures in *The Dao of Capital*, one remarkably useful and exciting book!"

—**Lawrence Reed**, President, Foundation for Economic Education and President Emeritus, Mackinac Center for Public Policy

"Spitznagel's excellent book is a powerful presentation of how monetary policy deceives entrepreneurs and investors into making poor investing decisions. I highly recommend *The Dao of Capital* as a guide to avoiding these deceptions and thus to better investment results. As Mark says, in my native tongue, '*Wir sind jetzt alle Österreicher.*'"

—**Marc Faber**, Publisher of *The Gloom, Boom & Doom Report*

"In *The Dao of Capital*, Mark Spitznagel stresses sound analytical foundations combined with shrewd strategic thinking to provide the reader with a broad philosophy of investing, where understanding the process that puts you in a position to win is more important than simply stating the goal of winning. The Austrian economics he employs unlocks not only the mystery of market coordination, but explains clearly the distortionary consequences of the manipulation of money and credit. Spitznagel guides the reader, not with point predictions, but with pattern predictions and strategic positioning for long run success in wealth creation. I greatly recommend this book."

—**Peter Boettke**, Professor of Economics and Philosophy, George Mason University

"Mark Spitznagel has done a remarkable job summarizing, synthesizing, and extending the great Austrian tradition, and weaving it into a wonderful set of practical lessons. What's more, he is a great writer and storyteller in the tradition of Bastiat, Hazlitt, and Rothbard, bringing subtle and sometimes complex ideas to life with memorable examples and sparkling prose. Highly recommended!"

—**Peter Klein**, Professor of Applied Economics, University of Missouri and Carl Menger Fellow, Ludwig von Mises Institute

"In *The Dao of Capital*, Mark Spitznagel has undertaken a sweeping study of the Austrian School and its correlative thought throughout history. A highly successful investor, Mark brings Austrian economics from the ivory tower to the investment portfolio, by demonstrating that its principles of capital, roundabout production, and free markets can and indeed should be applied to entrepreneurial investment."

—**Ron Paul**, Former U.S. Congressman (from the Foreword)

THE DAO
OF CAPITAL

THE DAO OF CAPITAL

AUSTRIAN INVESTING IN A DISTORTED WORLD

MARK SPITZNAGEL

WILEY

To my Kinder,
Edward and Silja—
My Grand Shi Strategy

Contents

Chapter Three:
SHI
The Intertemporal Strategy

Chapter Four:
THE SEEN AND THE FORESEEN
The Roots of the Austrian Tradition

Chapter Five:
UMWEG
The Roundabout Path of the Unternehmer

Epilogue:
THE *SISU* OF THE BOREAL FOREST 277

Foreword

In 1971, in the midst of a busy day in my medical practice, I took a long lunch to drive 60 miles to the University of Houston to hear one of the last formal lectures given by the great Austrian School economist Ludwig von Mises. He was 90 at the time, but still as passionate and articulate as ever. Here was the man whose writings had been my main inspiration to absorb and champion Austrian economics, which has dominated my thinking ever since.

I had been first introduced to the Austrians while I was a medical student at Duke University and came across a copy of F. A. Hayek's *The Road to Serfdom*. After that, I spent much of my free time reading everything I could find from the Austrian School. Along with Hayek and Mises, the works of Murray Rothbard and Hans Sennholz gave me a "new" view of economics.

Before discovering the Austrian School, I did not fully understand the process of how free markets work. The Austrians illustrated for me the benefits of free market economies relative to interventionist, centrally planned economies. The more I read, the clearer it became to me that this was how truly free individuals living in a truly free society should interact with one another. Austrian economists were also arguing for free markets at a time when the majority of intellectuals were praising collectivism and socialism. To this day, I owe the Austrians a debt of gratitude.

What I had thought were new ideas about the relationship between economic and personal liberties had, in fact, been around long before I discovered them for myself. Rothbard stated in his work *An Austrian Perspective on the History of Economic Thought* that the ancient Daoists "were the world's first libertarians,"[1] making Daoism and Austrian economics two bookends, spanning over two millennia, in the history of liberal economic and political thought. In *The Dao of Capital*, my friend and fellow Austrian Mark Spitznagel makes Rothbard's insightful connection a uniquely important theme.

More recently, the Austrian School's central principles—of private property, free markets, sound money, and liberal society in general—can be traced back centuries to classical liberalism, centered on the simplest tenets of all free societies. As economist Ralph Raico wrote:

> Classical liberalism—which we shall call here simply liberalism—is based on the conception of civil society as, by and large, self-regulating when its members are free to act within very wide bounds of their individual rights. Among these, the right to private property, including freedom of contract and free disposition of one's own labor, is given a very high priority . . . Austrian economics is the name given to the school . . . (that) has often been linked—both by adherents and opponents—to the liberal doctrine.[2]

Over the years, I became closely associated with many friends and students of Mises, and to all of us his example remained paramount. He never attempted to soften his stance nor mute his philosophy to become more acceptable to the conventional economic community. If he had chosen to do so, no doubt he would have received greater recognition during his lifetime. But rather than recognition, his goal was the pursuit of economic truth.

Mises was also a gentleman, kind and considerate, and in many ways I have tried to emulate him. I have always turned to Mises's wise words whenever the world (and economists in particular) seemed the most insane: "No one should expect that any logical argument or any experience could shake the almost religious fervor of those who believe in salvation through spending and credit expansion."[3]

The core of the Austrian School is the unpredictability of human action and the enormous influence individual choice wields in how economics works. It recognizes the subjectivity of value, the role of the entrepreneur, and the pursuit of capital creation to advance society itself. These truths are as essential to grasp today, and perhaps even more so, as they were when the school first emerged in the mid-nineteenth century.

In *The Dao of Capital*, Mark Spitznagel has undertaken a sweeping study of the Austrian School and its correlative thought throughout history. A highly successful investor, Mark brings Austrian economics from the ivory tower to the investment portfolio, by demonstrating that its principles of capital, roundabout production, and free markets can and indeed should be applied to entrepreneurial investment. Mark's "Austrian investing" is fascinating in its clarity and practicality, and points out just how difficult it is to go against the grain of interventionism, mainstream economics, and Wall Street culture.

As an adherent of the Austrian School, I have been frustrated by constantly being forced to watch what the centralizers and government planners have been doing to our economy—contriving recipe after recipe for disaster. We must understand that markets are naturally resilient. As *The Dao of Capital* illustrates, without the distorting effects of central planning and interventionism, natural market forces achieve homeostasis on their own—an idea anathema to today's bailout culture.

Rather than calming the markets by their actions, central banks create ever-mounting levels of distortion. Grasping at straws, they believe that flooding the world with money will somehow solve the very problems that such interventionism created in the first place.

People deserve better than this. Let capitalism function as it should without the manipulation of bureaucrats. As a doctor who practiced for a total of nearly 35 years, I abided by the *Hippocratic Oath* that charged me to do no harm and not get in the way of the body's natural ability to heal itself. The government must do the same and allow the market's natural homeostatic process to work. This goes to the heart of the message of *The Dao of Capital*, which shows people how to achieve harmony with the market process, distorted or not.

Over the years, deepening my understanding of the significance of free markets helped me see the need to fight for them through political action. Such action can take various forms, from education to revolution. In the United States it is possible to accomplish necessary change through education, persuasion, and the democratic process. Our rights of free speech, assembly, religion, petition, and privacy remain essentially intact. But before our rights are lost, we must change the policies born of decades of government interventionism.

I always believed deeply that the Founding Fathers got it right— certainly more so than their successors, who have worked feverishly against individual rights since the day our Constitution was ratified. Our nation was founded on the value of liberty, and I have never needed to be convinced of the merits of individual freedom. Other forces challenged my natural instincts toward freedom—an education establishment, the media, and government. They constantly preached that we need government to protect us from virtually everything, including ourselves. But I never wavered in my conviction that only an unhampered market is consonant with individual liberty.

This liberty goes hand in hand with sound money, a concept that is fundamental to Austrian economics. Mainstream economists continue to downplay or dismiss its importance. The continual and never-ending bad results of these dominant economic "experts" speak for themselves.

Money, according to Mises, must originate in the market as a useful commodity in order to function properly. The most important role money plays is that of a medium of exchange. It also serves as a measurement and store of value.

Unfortunately, politicians hold the conviction that money growth gives us economic growth. They are blind to the fact that government cannot create anything. *Government cannot make man richer, but it can make him poorer.* It is extremely naïve to think otherwise. We should all heed the lesson of "That Which Is Seen, and That Which Is Not Seen," the keen essay by nineteenth-century economist Frédéric Bastiat, to look beyond the immediate to the less direct results that can and should be foreseen—another of Mark's big themes in *The Dao of Capital.*

The Federal Reserve can intervene in the market and meddle with interest rates, but ultimately cannot escape the immutable nature of free market economics. Politicians may warp a monetary system to their liking but they cannot repeal economic laws that determine the nature of money. As I have said in the past and stand by today, distortion and corruption through monopoly control can benefit the few at the expense of the many for long periods of time, but eventually the irrefutable laws of nature will win. Free choice in the market is the only way economic calculation can come about.

Money had always been viewed as neutral. The supply of money was not thought to play a critical part in determining specific prices. Rather, it was accepted as fact that the price of a product depended only on the supply and the demand of the goods sold. This was tacitly accepted by even the early Austrian economists, but it took Mises to prove the nonneutrality of money. As he wrote in his masterful book, *Human Action*:

> As money can never be neutral and stable in purchasing power, a government's plan concerning the determination of the quantity can never be impartial and fair to all members of society. Whatever a government does in the pursuit of aims to influence the height of purchasing power depends necessarily upon the ruler's personal value judgments. It always furthers the interest of some groups of peoples at the expense of other groups. It never serves what is called the common wheel or the public welfare.[4]

To tamper with a nation's money is to tamper with every economic aspect of people's lives: earnings, savings, how much one pays in nominal terms for every purchase made. When money is manipulated at will by politicians, it always leads to chaos, unemployment, and political upheaval. For this reason it is imperative that we identify a money that cannot be abused, that prohibits inflation, and allows responsible working citizens to prosper.

As *The Dao of Capital* clearly shows, with an inflating fiat currency, capital investment in a market economy becomes very difficult. As money is destroyed, there is an increase in government power and interference in the markets to attempt to maintain order. Government officials throughout history have refused to admit that economic planning does not work until it's too late. And then when governments have tried to compensate for "printing too much money" it has only made things worse. This should sound all too familiar to Americans concerning the functions of the Federal Reserve.

Ironically, there is a consensus in America against government price controls in favor of free markets, until it comes to the most important price of all—the price of time, or interest rates. This is how the government controls the value of money. Through this price control, the government also distorts the market's elaborate coordinating function between consumers and producers. Thanks to the work of the Austrian economists, we know that the loss of this coordination gives us boom and bust cycles—due solely to the manipulation of the supply of money and credit by the central bank. Therefore, the rate of unemployment and the general standard of living are all a reflection in large part of the monetary policy a nation pursues.

Mises understood how money becomes as much a political issue as an economic one. His insights helped me to oppose excuses for deficits coming from both the left and the right. Regardless of their rhetoric, both factions depend on a fiat money system and inflation to continue government financing while serving their respective special interests.

The Austrians explain thoroughly why government intervention is the enemy and why individual liberty is key to realizing true freedom. The assurances I gained from these ideas and the example of Mises's character have enabled me to tolerate my time in Washington, DC and in Congress.

The phrase "Austrian economics" is not something I ever expected to come into widespread use. But since 2008, it has permeated our political vocabulary at a popular level that continues to thrill me as a longtime student of the Austrian School. Although these teachings have gloomy implications for today, we have much reason to be optimistic— namely the traction and potential gained among the younger generation. It has given me tremendous pride to see the thousands of young people who come to my rallies, a reflection of how the youth of America are embracing freedom, economic and otherwise.

To the degree that these principles become even more popular and others discover the economic truths espoused by Mises and his students, including through *The Dao of Capital*, we will finally be able to put our country on sound financial footing.

Freedom is indeed popular. But fully realizing it also means fully embracing Austrian economics.

RON PAUL

Introduction

At the outset, we must think of capital in a new way, as a verb, not a noun. Rather than an inanimate asset or piece of property, it constitutes an action, a means to an end—to build, to advance, to deploy the tools and instruments of a progressing economy. Indeed, capital is a *process*, or a method or path—what the ancient Chinese called the *Dao*.

Capital has an intertemporal dimension: Its positioning and advantage at different points in the future is central. Time is its *milieu*—defines it, shapes it, helps it and hinders it. As we think of capital in a new way, we also must think of time in a new way as we engage this process—our path, our *Dao of Capital*.

This path is notable in that it is exceedingly and purposefully circuitous—the keyword throughout this book is *roundabout*—the "going right in order to then go left" that leads first to the *means*, those strategic intermediate waypoints from which it becomes all the more possible and effective to arrive at the ultimate *ends*. As evident and ubiquitous as this process is all around us, from the natural world of the boreal forest to the business world of the entrepreneur, all too often we fail to perceive it. We tend to see the destination, but somehow often miss the path. So, we end up playing the wrong game.

This is a lesson that runs deep through many areas of life's strategic thinking and decision making. But this is a book about investing and, as such, this is my focus. Though I hope to make the point clearly in these pages that investing is an innate human action not distinct from others, nonetheless investing is perhaps where the lesson is most acute. The flashing lights of Bloomberg terminals and brokerage screens, with their allure of immediate profits, distract us such that they are all we can see. Unseen are the teleological mechanisms behind what is seen, the "engines of the world" as it were, churning away with time. Even Wall Street, that great sideshow with its temporal constraints shackling it to the urgent present, is blind to these mechanisms of the economy and can only chase the shadows of what is actually happening.

The good news, however, is that these mechanisms are very simple at their core; moreover, they have been clearly revealed by a tradition of economic thought known as the Austrian (or Viennese) School of economics, named (somewhat pejoratively) for its birthplace, the cultural and intellectual nexus of the nineteenth century, where founders Carl Menger and Eugen von Böhm-Bawerk established a new way of thinking about capital as roundabout means to more productive ends. Their intellectual progeny, the great Ludwig von Mises, did more to advance the Austrian School than any other and in whose name the torch is still carried today.

The Austrians, though, are not our only forebears. Indeed, in the roundabout we find a pillar of strategic thought that goes back some 25 centuries, to ancient China and the Daoists who in their concept of reversion saw everything as emerging from—and as a result of—its opposite: hard from soft, advancing from retreating. From these roots, both eastern and western, we learn to intertemporalize across slices of time, never focusing solely on the objective of our desire. In pursuit of circuitous means we assume a whole depth of fields.

The great strategists of the world did not need to be taught to train their attention on the means of their later advantages. The quintessential roundabout entrepreneur Henry Ford knew it in his gut. But as investors, we are completely separated from the means-ends process of production and economic progress, succumbing instead to what seems an endless complexity. Calling to mind the words of Finnish composer Jean Sibelius, rather than "manufacturing cocktails of every hue and description," I hope to offer here the "pure cold water" of this unadorned, archetypal approach.[1]

Following *The Dao of Capital*, we will build new habits of awareness regarding the mechanisms of capital and of capitalistic investing—the means and methodology of the market process itself. By aligning ourselves with these mechanisms, we find an intellectual and (far more importantly) practical discipline I call *Austrian Investing*, which does not directly pursue profits, but rather *the roundabout means of profits*.

When I was first approached by my publisher and finally convinced to write a book, I launched an arduous campaign of introspection and organization, and then eventually writing (the former was pure joy, the latter not at all—I am a professional investor, not a professional writer). In trying to explain and illustrate my central investment methodology I undertook a circuitous journey that spanned the coniferous boreal forests, Warring States China, Napoleonic Europe, burgeoning industrial America, and, of course, the great economic thinkers of nineteenth and twentieth century Austria. The common thread throughout was always orienting to means, not ends—seeking harmony with the market process, not profits. The result of my endeavors over the past two years, slipped in between, first and foremost, running hedge funds, is *The Dao of Capital*. (As a side note, I might observe that the worst thing about having written a book is ever being accused, quite literally—and fairly—of "talking your book." While I do describe here, in general terms, what I practice as an active investor and hedge fund manager, I hope to mitigate some of this first by stating that my partnerships are effectively closed and second by pledging any and all book profits to charity. And, think about it, anyone who writes an investment book and cannot say likewise should, in my view, be largely disregarded.)

This book offers, eventually, an introduction to Austrian Investing. I will marshal data to illustrate the effectiveness of my approach. However, these revelations will occur in the final two chapters of the book. The bulk of my discussion will focus on the all-important thinking behind Austrian Investing. It is fitting that I structure the book in this fashion, for as we'll see, the whole point of my approach to investing is that we must be willing to adopt the *indirect* route to achieve our goals.

Let me provide an overview of our journey. We begin in Chapter 1 with my own introduction to the market process through the careful tutelage of a wise old grain trader at the Chicago Board of Trade, Everett Klipp, whose teachings unknowingly echoed the ancient wisdom of the Daoists and the seminal book known as the *Laozi* (or *Daodejing*); I continue to learn from my recollections of "Klippisms" to this day. From there, we move to the natural world and central pedagogy that builds on nature's strategy and logic of productive and opportunistic growth—the *leitmotif* of the conifer that, as we will see in Chapter 2, is intergenerationally roundabout, by retreating first to the rocky, inhospitable places where competitors cannot grow, and from there seeds the

fertile areas cleared by wildfire. This strategy of the conifers was evident
in the canonical military strategists—the original strategic thinkers and
decision makers—as we will see in Chapter[3], starting with Sun Wu or
Master Sun, whose often superficially quoted teachings in the *Sunzi* provide us with the core concept of *shi*, which has multiple meanings but
can be thought of as strategic positional advantage. The same thinking is
also found within *Vom Kriege* (*On War*), the often misinterpreted writings of Carl von Clausewitz, who advocated going for the means of key
strategic points at which to weaken the enemy and thus better achieve
the final objectives of victory and peace more expediently. In Chapter 4,
we find roundabout strategic thinking in those who fought ideological
battles: proto-Austrian economist Frédéric Bastiat, who challenged the
Marxists and gave us the seen and the foreseen, and Austrian School
founder Menger, who took an *a priorist* stance as he jousted with the
German Historicists who held a slavish attachment to empiricism.

From Menger, we move in Chapter 5 to the man who put the
Austrian School on the map: Böhm-Bawerk, who gives us insights on
the relationship between saving, investment, and capital accumulation, thus providing today's investor with a theoretic understanding
of the market process. His capital theories illustrate the roundabout of
Produktionsumweg to amass deeper and increasingly efficient and productive capital structures (as exemplified by Ford, who turned coal and
steel into cars for the masses). The difficulty of the roundabout cannot
be underestimated, as we will see in Chapter 6, because of our inherent time preferences and myopic time inconsistencies (which might be
summed up here as impatience now/patience later). In the real world,
people seem to exhibit a much stronger discount (per unit of time) in the
immediate future, compared to the distant future, a phenomenon sometimes called "hyperbolic discounting." This feature of the world plays a
crucial role in my understanding of asset prices, but here Böhm-Bawerk
was a man ahead of his time, writing on these topics more than a century
ago. Because of the quirks of our human eagerness for the immediate
reward, we are forewarned that what seems easy and straightforward is
deceptively so; the roundabout is in practice a counterintuitive path—of
acquiring later stage advantage through an earlier stage disadvantage—
nearly impossible to follow. As the *Laozi* says, "The bright path seems
dim/Going forward seems like retreat/The easy way seems hard/The
highest Virtue seems empty . . . Great talents ripen late."[2]

In Chapter 7, the great Mises teaches us that "the market is a process," drawing from his insights from the early and mid-twentieth century when he explained real-world entrepreneurship and the booms and busts of the business cycle. Mises's work centered on the actions of the "acting man," reflecting, as Austrian economist Murray Rothbard observed, "the primordial fact that human beings have goals and purposes and act to attain them. And this fact is known not tentatively and hesitantly, but absolutely and apodictically."[3] It was Mises's focus on this crucial aspect of social affairs—that humans adopt means to achieve their subjective ends—that guided his interpretation of the market process as well as broader trends in history. Mises argued that without *first* constructing a solid body of economic understanding, the economic historian would be at a loss when analyzing empirical evidence, seeing spurious "relationships" everywhere.

As we will see in Chapter 8, the distortion of interventionism short-circuits the natural governors within systems, whether forests or markets; and yet, the forces that return the system to homeostasis persist and will eventually prevail, although reversions will be, almost by definition, extremely messy. Thus, we can view the market process as a grand "teleological" mechanism, which exhibits negative feedback loops as it gropes back toward a natural equilibrium after the central bank distorts its natural movements.

Across the span of these eight chapters, we establish the foundation of *The Dao of Capital*, the roundabout means toward our desired end. Only someone who is willing to defer the immediate objective, and read on topics that at first may seem only tenuously related, can benefit from the last two chapters and the discussion of capitalistic investment strategies known as Austrian Investing. This is new and important territory from an Austrian perspective. The Austrian tradition has confined itself largely to academic analysis of the economy and related policy recommendations, explaining what should be— and more to the point should not be—done to allow the free and full functioning of the entrepreneurial and market processes. In the last two chapters of this book, we move from government policy to investment practice, as we navigate a highly distorted and very real world. I call my approach Austrian Investing because it relies so heavily on the insights I have gleaned over the years from these great economists. A primary purpose of this book is to explain their importance to other investors so they, too, might benefit from the Austrian perspective.

Now more than ever, investors need to recognize the distortion in the system, which has reached near unprecedented proportions. Unhealthy growth of assets that would not exist without the deadly fertilizer of intervention is creating a tinderbox that will, in the not so distant future, erupt in massive wildfire. Given the visible distortion in the equity market (as I will discuss in Chapter 9) we should absolutely expect severe stock market losses to come—quite possibly within the next year or so. (That's an easy thing for me to flippantly say, and I spend a significant chunk of this book explaining, among other things, why it is so.) This urgency brings a somber yet critical note of warning to these pages.

In Austrian Investing I (Chapter 9), we learn how to gauge the distortion in the system using a measure I call the Misesian Stationarity index, after the principles of Mises, to protect ourselves from the distortion by knowing when to stay out of the market and when to stay in, or to profit from that distortion by using a sophisticated strategy (alas, well beyond the capability of retail investors, and even many professionals) known as "tail hedging." (Although I am known for this investment approach, let me tip my hand right now: When it comes to market events, there have been no impactful black swans—the so-called unexpected "tail events." What were unseen by most were, indeed, highly foreseeable.) In Austrian Investing II (Chapter 10), we employ Böhm-Bawerkian principles as we pursue roundabout capital structures in which to invest, looking at companies that are not part of the Wall Street shadow play because they exhibit promise though not immediately surging profits. (Austrian Investing is an older and more *gestalt* version of what has come to be known as value investing; Austrian Investing not only predates it, but also refines and focuses it.) In the Epilogue, I sum up the roundabout by homing in on a key ingredient in its arduous pursuit, a lesson straight from the boreal forest—*sisu*.

Besides incorporating Austrian theoretical insights into the nature of the market process, my approach mirrors the Austrian approach to economics itself. Unlike most mainstream economists, who desire to model their own discipline after the pattern of physicists, the Austrians in the tradition of Mises do *not* find much use in curve-fitting and econometric back-testing.

If we appreciate the power of Mises's arguments, we will understand that we can't just "let the facts speak for themselves" when it comes to understanding economic phenomena (such as the business cycle)—particularly in trying to predict the movements of stock prices. We need an antecedent theory to guide us, to pick out which facts are relevant and which can safely be ignored, to focus only on what matters. After our logical deductions lead us to an investment philosophy, we can of course use empirical investigation to "check our work"—and indeed we will do so.

In *The Dao of Capital*, I invite you into my process, not with a plug-and-play strategy, but, more importantly, with a way of thinking that can be applied to investing and, indeed, many other important activities in life in which one must choose wisely across slices of time so as not to jeopardize or bankrupt opportunities (often better ones) that arise later. Without the thinking, though, the acting is baseless. The reasoning is paramount, first and foremost.

When I was a young trader starting out in the pit (in fact the bond pit's youngest), Klipp made sure I understood why I was at the Chicago Board of Trade—which was not to learn how to make money (as I relate in Chapter 1). If that were the case, he told me, "you wouldn't even be in here. You'd be in a long line all the way down LaSalle Street, still waiting to get in." And so I say the same to you: If there were a book that could teach you how to make money, you would be at the end of a long line down the street from any bookstore (what few still exist).

The intention of this book is to teach you how to think and provide you the discipline of the roundabout. Like learning as an adult to swing a golf club or to ski, the intention is to understand the underlying mechanisms in order to coordinate our actions with them. With that foundation, you can engage in the necessary circuitous aspects required by this strategy and the intimately related roundabout process of capital. If and when we lose our way, we reorient ourselves with our Austrian compass that leads us right to go left, along a circuitous path as old as strategic thought itself.

In the words of the *Laozi*, "A journey of a thousand miles starts under one's feet."[4] And so we begin, with our first step along *The Dao of Capital*.

MARK SPITZNAGEL
Northport, Michigan
July 2013

**The Sage and the Apprentice—at the Chicago Board of Trade with
Everett Klipp (c. 1994)**

Chapter One

The Daoist Sage

Klipp's Paradox

"You've got to love to lose money, hate to make money, love to lose money, hate to make money. . . . But we are human beings, we love to make money, hate to lose money. So we must overcome that humanness about us."

This is "Klipp's Paradox"—repeated countless times by a sage old Chicago grain trader named Everett Klipp, and through which I first happened upon an archetypal investment approach, one that I would quickly make my own. This is the *roundabout* approach (what we will later call *shi* and *Umweg*, and ultimately *Austrian Investing*), indeed central to the very message of this book: Rather than pursue the direct route of immediate gain, we will seek the difficult and *roundabout* route of immediate loss, an intermediate step which begets an advantage for greater potential gain.

This is the age-old strategy of the military general and of the entrepreneur—of the destroyer and of the very creator of civilizations. It is, in fact, the logic of organic efficacious growth in our world. But when it is hastened or forced, it is ruined.

Because of its difficulty it will remain the circuitous road least traveled, so contrary to our wiring, to our perception of time (and virtually impossible on Wall Street). And this is why it is ultimately so effective. Yet, it is well within the capability of investors who are willing to change their thinking, to overcome that humanness about them, and follow *The Dao of Capital*.

How do we resolve this paradox? How is it that the detour could be somehow more effective than the direct route, that going right could be somehow the most effective way to go left? Is this merely meant to confuse; empty words meant to sound wise? Or does it conceal some universal truth?

The answers demand a deep reconsideration of time and how we perceive it. We must change dimensions, from the *immediate* to the *intermediate*, from the *atemporal* to the *intertemporal*. It requires a resolute, forward-looking orientation away from what is happening now, what can be seen, to what is to come, what cannot yet be seen. I will call this new perspective our *depth of field* (using the optics term in the temporal rather than the spatial), our ability to sharply perceive a long span of forward moments.

This is not about a shift in thinking from the short term to the long term, as some might suppose. Long term is something of a cliché, and often even internally inconsistent: Acting for the long term generally entails an immediate commitment, based on an immediate view of the available opportunity set, and waiting an extended period of time for the result—often without due consideration to or differentiation between intertemporal opportunities that may emerge during that extended period of time. (Moreover, saying that one is acting long term is very often a rationalization used to justify something that is currently not working out as planned.) Long term is telescopic, short term is myopic; depth of field retains focus between the two. So let's not think long term or short term. As Klipp's Paradox requires, let's think of time entirely differently, as *intertemporal*, comprised of a series of coordinated "now" moments, each providing for the next, one after the other, like a great piece of music, or beads on a string.

We can further peel away Klipp's Paradox to reveal a deeper paradox, at the very core of much of humanity's most seminal thought. Although Klipp did not know it, his paradox reached back in time more than two and a half millennia to a far distant age and culture, as the essential theme of the *Laozi* (known later as the *Daodejing*, but I will refer to it by its original title, after its purported author), an ancient political and military treatise, and the original text and summa of the Chinese philosophy of Daoism.

To the *Laozi*, the best path to anything lay through its opposite: One gains by losing and loses by gaining; victory comes not from waging the one decisive battle, but from the roundabout approach of waiting and preparing now in order to gain a greater advantage later. The *Laozi* professes a fundamental and universal process of succession and alternation between poles, between imbalance and balance; within every condition lies its opposite. "This is what is called the subtle within what is evident. The soft and weak vanquish the hard and strong."[1]

To both Klipp and the *Laozi*, time is not exogenous, but is an endogenous, primary factor of things—and patience the most precious treasure. Indeed, Klipp was the Daoist sage, with a simple archetypal message that encapsulated how he survived and thrived for more than five decades in the perilous futures markets of the Chicago Board of Trade.

THE OLD MASTER

Daoism emerged in ancient China during a time of heavy conflict and upheaval, nearly two centuries of warfare, from 403 to 221 BCE, known as the Warring States Period, when the central Chinese plains became killing fields awash in blood and tears. This was also a time of advancement in military techniques, strategy, and technology, such as efficient troop formations and the introduction of the cavalry and the standard-issue crossbow. With these new tools, armies breached walled cities and stormed over borders. War and death became a way of life; entire cities were often wiped out even after surrender,[2] and mothers who gave birth to sons never expected them to reach adulthood.[3]

The Warring States Period was also a formative phase in ancient Chinese civilization, when philosophical diversity flourished, what the Daoist scholar Zhuangzi termed "the doctrines of the hundred schools"; from this fertile age sprung illustrious Daoist texts such as the *Laozi* and the *Sunzi*, the former the most recognized from ancient China and one of the best known throughout the world today. Its attributed author, translated as "Master Lao" or "The Old Master," may or may not have even existed, and may have been one person or even a succession of contributors over time.

According to tradition, Laozi was the keeper of archival records for the ruling dynasty in the sixth century BCE, although some scholars and sinologists maintain that the Old Master emanated from the fourth century BCE. We know from legend that he was considered to have been a senior contemporary of Kongzi (Confucius), who lived from 551 to 479 BCE, and who was said to have consulted Laozi and (despite being ridiculed by Laozi as arrogant) praised him as "a dragon riding on the winds and clouds."[4] Furthermore, written forms of the *Laozi*, which scribes put down on bamboo scrolls (mostly for military strategists who advised feuding warlords), are likely to have been derivatives of an earlier oral tradition (as most of it is rhymed). Whether truth or legend, flesh and bones or quintessential myth, one person or many over time, the Old Master relinquished an enduring, timeless, and universal wisdom.

To most people, it seems, the *Laozi* is an overwhelmingly religious and even mystical text, and this interpretive bias has perhaps done it a disservice; in fact, the term "Laoism" has been used historically to distinguish the philosophical *Laozi* from the later religious Daoism. Recently, new and important translations have emerged, following the unearthing of archeological finds at *Mawangdui* in 1973 and *Guodian* in 1993 (which amounted to strips of silk and fragments of bamboo scrolls), providing evidence of its origins as a philosophical text[5]—not mystical, but imminently practical. And this practicality relates particularly to strategies of conflict (specifically political and military, the themes of its day), a way of gaining advantage without coercion or the always decisive head-on clash of opposing forces. *The Dao of Capital* stays true to these roots.

The *Laozi*, composed of only 5,000 Chinese characters and 81 chapters as short as verses, outlines the *Dao*—the way, path, method or "mode of doing a thing,"[6] or process toward harmony with the nature of things, with awareness of every step along the way. Sinologists Roger Ames and David Hall describe the *Dao* as "way-making," "processional" (what they call the "gerundive"), an intertemporal "focal awareness and field awareness"—a depth of field—by which we exploit the potential that lies within configurations, circumstances, and systems.[7]

The central concept permeating the *Laozi* is referred therein as *wuwei*, which translates literally as "not doing," but means so much more; rather than passivity, a common misperception, *wuwei* means noncoercive action—and here we see the overwhelming *laissez-faire*, libertarian, even anarchistic origins in the *Laozi*, thought by some to be the very first in world history[8] (as in "One should govern a country as one would fry a small fish; leave them alone and do not meddle with their affairs"[9]—a cardinal Laozi political credo most notably invoked in a State of the Union address by President Ronald Reagan). The *Laozi* also has been deemed a distinctive form of teleology, one that empha-sizes the individual's self-development free from the intervention of any external force. This leads to the paradox of what has come to be known as *wei wuwei* (literally "doing/not doing," or better yet "doing by not doing," or "do without ado"[10]). "One loses and again loses / To the point that one does everything noncoercively (*wuwei*). / One does things noncoercively / And yet nothing goes undone."[11]

In *wuwei* is the importance of waiting on an objective process, of suffering through loss for intertemporal opportunities. From the *Laozi*, "Who can wait quietly while the mud settles? Who can remain still until the moment of action?"[12] It appears as a lesson in humility and toler-ance, but, as we wait, we willingly sacrifice the first step for a greater later step. In its highest form, the whole point of waiting is to gain an advantage. Therefore, the apparent humility implied in the process is really a *false humility* that cloaks the art of manipulation; as French sinol-ogist François Jullien noted, "the sage merges with the manipulator," who, in Daoist terms, "humbles himself to be in a better position to rise; if he withdraws, he does so to be all the more certainly pulled forward; if he ostensibly drains away his 'self,' he does so to impose that 'self' all the more imperiously in the future."[13] This is the efficacy of circum-vention camouflaged as suppleness. And in this temporal configuration is, in the words of Ames and Hall, the *Laozi*'s "correlative relationship among antinomies":[14] With false humility we deliberately become soft and weak now in order to be hard and strong later—the very reason that, in the *Laozi*, "Those who are good at vanquishing their enemies do not join issue."[15]

In this sense, the *Laozi* can simply be seen as a manual on gaining advantage through indirection, or turning the force of an opponent against him, through "excess leading to its opposite."[16]

THE SOFT AND WEAK VANQUISH THE HARD AND STRONG

Perhaps the most tangible representation of *wuwei* can be seen in the interplay of softness and hardness in the Chinese martial art *taijiquan*—not surprising as it is a direct derivative of the *Laozi*. According to legend, *taijiquan* was created by a thirteenth-century Daoist priest, Zhangsanfeng. Cloistered on Wudang Mountain, he observed a clash between a magpie and a serpent, and suddenly fully grasped the Daoist truth of softness overcoming hardness.[17] The serpent moved with—indeed, complemented—the magpie, and thus avoided its repeated decisive attacks, allowing the snake to wait for and finally exploit an opening, an imbalance, with a lethal bite to the bird. In this sequential patience, retreating in order to eventually strike, was the *Laozi*'s profound and unconventional military art:

> There is a saying among soldiers:
> I dare not make the first move but would rather play the guest;
> I dare not advance an inch but would rather withdraw a foot.
>
> This is called marching without appearing to move,
> Rolling up your sleeves without showing your arm,
> Capturing the enemy without attacking,
> Being armed without weapons.[18]

Like Daoism itself, *taijiquan* has drifted into the more mystical and new age, but its roots remain in its martial application; this is clear today in the powerful blows of the original *Chen style taijiquan* form, as still practiced in Chen Village (located in Henan province in central China). According to Chen Xin (among the lineage of the eponymous Chen clan) in his seminal *Canon of Chen Family Taijiquan*, a deceptive rotational and circular force—known as "silk reeling"—is "the main objective of Taijiquan moves, which work on the centrifugal principles of a 'roundabout'."[19] The rotation is between retreating and advancing, between soft and hard. (When performed by a master, such as my teachers Qichen Guo and Jwing-Ming Yang, of whose *qinna* maneuvers I have oft found myself on the wrong end, it is most unsettling, almost deplorable in its artful deceitfulness.)

Taijiquan is a physical manifestation of the importance of waiting and exploiting another's urgency through softness in a clash. This is most apparent in the two-person *taijiquan* competitive exercise known as *tuishou*, or "push hands," in which two opponents engage in what looks to the casual observer like a choreographed series of synchronized movements. In actuality *tuishou* is a cunning contest with highly constrained rules, in which each tries to throw the other to the ground (or outside a boundary) during a sequence of subtle alternating feints and attacks. The real force is not in the pushing, but in the yielding. (In *tuishou* is an ideal roundabout and investing metaphor, one that I will return to again and again.)

The "Song of Push Hands," in its oral transfer of the art over centuries in Chen Village, instructs the competitor to "guide [the opponent's] power into emptiness, then immediately attack."[20] To guide or lure the opponent into emptiness and thus destroy his balance is the very

Tuishou: Zouhua and Niansui

indirect objective—to gain the position of advantage—to be followed by the direct objective of attack. This is the essential *tuishou* sequence of yielding, neutralizing, and sticking. Yielding and neutralizing—*zou* or *zouhua*, "leading by walking away"—is the sneaky retreating rout, followed by converting and redirecting a force to advantage; that advantage is exploited by sticking and following—*nian* or *niansui*—and thus eventually advancing back in a decisive counterattack. (Taken together, as we will see in Chapter 3, this sequence describes *shi*, the strategy of *wuwei*.)

The competition is a subtle interplay of delusive complementary—not opposing—forces between opponents, between hard and soft, each seeking the shrewd strategy of patiently attacking the balance rather than the force, of going right in order to ultimately go decisively left.

This is also the insidious strategy of guerilla warfare. While used effectively, for instance, by the scrappy American colonists against the British in the eighteenth century, it was later used deftly against the mighty United States by the far weaker and smaller Vietcong in the twentieth century, the very same alternating intertemporal softness and hardness: When the U.S. troops surged, the Vietcong retreated in a rout into the mountains (*zouhua*), drawing the U.S. troops out until overextended; then the Vietcong counterattacked, following the U.S. troops (*nian*) in a destructive counterrout. The great frustration—the unfairness—is that the harder you push, the harder you fall. Chairman Mao knew these words from the *Laozi*: "If a small country submits to a great country / It can conquer the great country. Therefore those who would conquer must yield / And those who conquer do so because they yield."[21] (We will encounter this again with the guerilla warriors of the north in the Epilogue.)

In the *wuwei* of *taijiquan*, the advantage comes not from applying force but from circular yielding, from directing the course of events rather than forcing them; from the *Laozi*, "Hence an unyielding army is destroyed. An unyielding tree breaks."[22] The patience of the intermediate steps of loss and advantage defeats the impatience of the immediate gain; the direct force is defeated by the counterforce. Thus there are always two games being played in time, one now and one later, against two different opponents. As the great *tuishou* practitioner Zheng Manqing observed, one must first "learn to invest in loss" by leading "an opponent's force away so that it is useless," and which will "polarize into its opposite and be transformed into the greatest profit."[23] In *taijiquan* is the essence of *The Dao of Capital.*

So much of waiting and ignoring present circumstances, of will-ingness to be in an uncomfortable place, is *understanding* the sequential instead of only *seeing* the immediate. There is a definite brand of epis-temology at the root of the *Laozi.* To the *Laozi,* much of the exterior world is but exterior diversion, much perception is a distraction from a hidden reality—though one which requires diligent attention. It states this most succinctly in "Venture not beyond your doors to know the world / Peer not outside your window to know the way-making. . . . The farther one goes / The less one knows."[24]

Paul Carus, in his definitive 1913 *The Canon of Reason and Virtue: Being Lao-tze's Tao Teh King,* went so far as to relate this epistemology of the *Laozi* to eighteenth-century German philosopher Immanuel Kant: The *Laozi* "endorses Kant's doctrine of the *a priori*, which means that certain truths can be stated *a priori*, viz., even before we make an actual experience. It is not the globe trotter who knows mankind, but the thinker. In order to know the sun's chemical composition we need not go to the sun; we can analyze the sun's light by spectrum analysis. We need not stretch a tape line to the moon to measure its distance from the earth, we can calculate it by the methods of an *a priori* science (trigonometry)."[25]

Indeed, there is an almost antiempirical vein to the *Laozi,* a stand against the *positivist* view of knowledge as exclusively flowing from sense perceptions. As Jacob Needleman interprets the *Laozi,* "We see only things, entities, events; we do not directly experience the forces and laws that govern nature."[26] Similarly, Ellen Chen says the *Laozi* "is not pro-science in spirit," "repudiating the knowledge of the many as not conducive to the knowledge of the one"[27] (thus invalidating *induction*). Truth is learned from understanding basic natural and logical construc-tions, a tree that bends to the force of a wind, pent-up water that eventu-ally destroys all in its path, the interplay between snake and bird. There is much deception in appearance, the tyranny of the senses, of empirical data—wisdom that gains particular context and meaning in investing.

INTO THE PIT

My exposure to investing came quite by accident. As a 16-year-old (whose only previous experience with markets was through a share in the Rochester Red Wings minor league baseball team, passed down proudly for three generations) I tagged along with my father when he paid a visit to his good friend (and corn futures trader, whatever that was) Everett Klipp at the Chicago Board of Trade. I stood in the visitors' gallery overlooking the grain trading pits, gaining a bird's-eye view over a kaleidoscope of bright trading jackets, flailing arms, and lurching bodies. I was expecting some kind of swanky casino (perhaps out of a James Bond film), but this was different than that. I was mesmerized. It reminded me of watching a flock of birds, a cloud of countless individual parts appearing as a single fuzzy organism, seemingly resting, hovering in midair, until something unseen starts to ripple through it like a pulse of energy, causing a sudden jolting turn in a burst of speed. The flock swoops and dives, rests, and then rises again, with a mechanical yet organic coordination and precision, while the outside observer can only marvel at its driver. In the pit was the same mystery, with pauses interrupted by sudden cascades of noise and energy driven by something imperceptible. It was a financial *Sturm und Drang*, but within it was an unmistakable, intricate communication and synchronization. In an instant, I scrapped my hard-won Juilliard plans (needless to say, my mother was horrified) and wanted nothing more than to be a pit trader.

After that fateful trip, I became obsessed with the grain futures markets. Price charts soon lined my bedroom walls and I constructed a potted corn and soybean plant laboratory (with seedlings lifted from local farms in the dark of night) for monitoring rainfall and crop progress. From then on, whenever I would see Klipp I always peppered him with questions (often with handy graphs and USDA reports in tow) on price trends, world grain supplies, Soviet demand, Midwest weather patterns—basically on where the markets were headed. His response was always a variation on: "The market is a completely *subjective* thing, it can do anything. And it is always right, yet always wrong!" His abject disdain for data and information left me bemused, even skeptical of this stubborn old Chicago grain man with the gravelly voice, ever speaking in fortune-cookie prose. How could he have done so well as a speculator without knowing—or even caring—where the market was heading? How could it be that "guys who know where the market is heading are no longer at the Board of Trade. They are either retired or broke. And I can't think of any that are retired." Classic Klipp.

If trading wasn't about predicting price movements, then what was it all about? After all, profiting was buying (or selling) at one price and then eventually selling (or buying) it back at a higher (or lower) price. How could this be done without any ability to forecast? The answer, which took this teenager some time to understand, was that the edge to pit trading was in the order flow—the succession of *mini-routs*, as I always called them—and in the discipline; it was in a patient response to someone else's impatience, someone else's urgency. The edge was a process—*an intertemporal process*—an intermediate step to gain an advantage, rather than any direct analytical acumen or information. And its monetization—its roundabout production—required time.

The bond pit was where the real action was (and where the average trader's age was perhaps twenty to thirty years below that in the corn pit). When it came time to ask Klipp what to study in college to best prepare me for a career in the bond pit, he advised, "Anything that won't make you think you know too much" (alas, my economics major would have to remain a dirty secret). During summers and over holiday breaks from college (where I can recall always carrying around a copy of the book *The Treasury Bond Basis*, still stubbornly trying to ready myself for trading) I worked as a lowly clerk for a few of Klipp's traders. Finally, after graduating, with backing from Gramma Spitznagel (my first and best investor) I leased a membership at the Chicago Board of Trade and took my place in the bond pit where, at age 22, I became its youngest trader.

The deliverable instrument of the bond futures contract is the 30-year U.S. Treasury bond (or a nearby "cheapest to deliver"), the benchmark interest rate (along with the 10-year) on which long-term debt is based. In the early-1990s, the bond futures pit was the center of the financial universe, the most actively traded contract and the locus of open outcry in all the world. The pit was where anyone with long-term dollar-denominated interest rate risk in the future converged to hedge their rates, whether savers worried about forward rates falling or borrowers concerned about forward rates rising.

Trading pits are configured like concentric rings (octagons, actually) that descend like a staircase, resembling an inverted tiered wedding cake. The very top, outer step of the bond pit was occupied by the biggest and baddest traders (as this was where the biggest brokers with the biggest order flow stood, as well as where the best sight lines were into the pit—an incalculable advantage). In my first month, I was decidedly not there. In fact, I was at the other extreme, at the very bottom of the pit where only the back month contracts sporadically traded.

For the first month or so, my day started and ended with Klipp standing next to me, feeding me trades and testing to see how I managed them. Klipp made it perfectly clear: "You're not here to make money, you're here to learn how to trade. If you could walk into the pit to make money, you wouldn't even be in here. You'd be in a long line all the way down LaSalle Street, still waiting to get in." This was an imminently roundabout start down a roundabout path.

THE PRIVILEGES OF A TRADER

Klipp's methodology was exceedingly simple—almost dubiously so—conveyed as a parent would to a child, not as principles, but as privileges: "As a pit trader, you have two privileges and two privileges only: One, you can demand the edge—buy at the bid price, sell at offer price; two, you can give up that edge when you've made a mistake."

The "edge" of Klipp's allotted privileges is that of the market makers, known as "locals" at the Chicago Board of Trade. (The bond pit was occupied by both locals, virtually all of whom, like me, traded independently for their own accounts, and brokers, whose job was to execute orders on their clients' behalf.) What locals do is provide *immediacy* to those who demand it, meaning they offer prices (a bid price and an ask price) at which they are willing to transact immediately, and in so doing they provide immediate liquidity. In exchange, the locals require a price concession, reflected in their bid and ask prices, a profit they expect to monetize as demands for immediacy flow in from both sides, from buyers as well as sellers. Locals stand in the pit all day waiting for that flow, specifically to trade against an impatient counterparty. It's not up to the locals to determine when they trade; rather, they wait and, if necessary, wait some more.

The price concessions, the "rents" extracted from urgent counterparties (who pay for not having to wait), are the local's ultimate edge. But, upon receiving such a price concession, the local's game is not over; he has the advantage, but he must act yet again, either by stepping aside (taking his loss) or following the market back. He accumulates inventory (a position) by transacting against urgent order flow, with the intention of closing out of that inventory profitably once the urgency subsides; thus, advancing seems to be receding, and the local advances by retreating. But, naturally, between these two steps is the potential for great loss—the cost of waiting and holding inventory. So the sooner he gets out the better, but in so doing his aim is to transact better than his urgent counterparty, from whom he received his position in the first place. The late legendary bond local Charlie DeFrancesca ("Charlie D.") put it best: "The question is: Can you be more efficient than the market?"[28]

Klipp liked to think about the local's role in more standard business terms, such as the inventory markup of the wholesaler or the retailer, or, more generally, the price spreads that exist in different phases of production for any economic good (including futures contracts). Both involve exploiting intertemporal imbalances between raw material and output, providing immediacy to end users, and the intermediation of waiting, carrying intermediate inventory (including capital goods and other factors of production), and providing a final good at just the right time and place (and, as we will see in Chapter 5, the more roundabout this process, typically the greater these spreads).

The second allotted privilege was "cruel," as Klipp would say, because it meant immediately closing out a trade once it turned negative (a "mistake"), what he called "always taking a one-tick loss." One could expect this to happen roughly half of the time, and much of the other half of the time (depending, of course, on how quickly any profits were grabbed, as we'll discuss) the price would find its way back to show a loss even then as well.

For instance, if the market was three bid, four offered (meaning 115 and 23/32nds bid, offered at 115 and 24/32nd), I had to buy at three or sell at four—"demand the edge"—without exception. If I managed to buy a one-lot (or one contract) at three, and then a big sell order came in and pushed the market down one tick to two bid, three offered, I was expected to immediately sell that one-lot to someone at two ("give up the edge," or "step out," preferably to a broker who would later return the favor), thus taking my one-tick loss (which amounted to $31.25 on one $100,000 bond contract). I was officially in Klipp's *Alpha School of Trading*, as everyone called it, after the name of his firm, Alpha Futures. (We were the guys in the aqua jackets who loved to lose money.)

Who could argue with this logic? If, as Klipp said, "There's only one thing that can hurt a trader at the Chicago Board of Trade, and that's a big loss," then, for God's sake, "never take a big loss." As his own mentor said to him some 40 years before, "Any time you can take a loss, do it, and you will always be at the Chicago Board of Trade." (To which Klipp always added with a smile, "Well, I've been losing money since 1954, but he was right, I'm still at the Chicago Board of Trade.") Naturally, this meant taking many small losses. Hence you had to "love to lose money," otherwise you'd just stop doing it.

Impatience and intolerance for many such small losses, as well as urgency for immediate profits, Klipp believed, dealt a death blow to traders, an easy and common one. The well-known *disposition effect* in finance, an observation that goes back at least a century, states that people naturally fall victim to these tendencies, and thus do the opposite of Klipp's approach: We sweat through large losses and take small profits quickly. Going for the immediate gain *feels* so right, while taking the immediate loss *feels* so wrong. The pressing need for consistent and immediate profits is hardwired into our brains; we humans have a shallow *depth of field* (as we will see in Chapter 6).

And nothing is better at amplifying this natural humanness about us than trading too big and having excessive carrying costs. These are the great external magnifying lenses on the immediate. All is decisive when all is at stake, whether through an excessive loss (because of too much leverage)—a loss that you can't afford to take immediately—or an insufficient gain (because of too much debt). No one trade need ever be decisive. As Klipp said, "One trade can ruin your day. One trade can ruin your week. One trade can ruin your month. One trade can ruin your year. One trade can ruin your career!"

It is not surprising, then, that Klipp's approach was not embraced by everyone, even by most; in fact, in many ways he was pit trading's greatest dissident (despite his title, bestowed by the futures industry, of *The Babe Ruth of the Chicago Board of Trade*). Among his greatest critics was none other than Charlie D.—the misinterpretation of whose criticism surely cost many an aspiring Charlie D. his shirt. (There will only ever be one Charlie D.) It was nearly impossible to follow and practice consistently—"brutal" was Klipp's term to describe the formidable challenge of looking beyond the immediate outcome—of retaining *depth of field*—a challenge that Klipp believed was essential to gaining an edge.

This was as it should be; indeed, if everyone accepted Klipp's Paradox, it would no longer be effective, no longer even be a paradox. From the *Laozi*, "The bright path seems dim / Going forward seems like retreat / The easy way seems hard / The highest Virtue seems empty."[29] Here are the favorite Daoist images of water and the valley, the *Laozi*'s "attitude of lowliness,"[30] which water always seeks.

This was Klipp's roundabout approach, and that of his mentor and perhaps his before: Expect to lose first, the first loss is a good loss; from that comes greater gain later. Call it playing good defense, embracing loss, biding one's time and using the present moment for later advantage, the advantage of then playing more effective offense. Or, as Klipp called it, "looking like a jerk, feeling like a jerk." Waiting must precede opportune action, by definition. Exploiting others' immediacy was the logic of the roundabout approach, the fundamental edge—the ultimate edge of trading and investing.

In baseball the difference between minor leaguer and major leaguer is generally thought to be in hitting the curve ball, as opposed to just a linearly extrapolated fast ball, and so too is the difference in investing in playing the curve, the roundabout intertemporal bends which deviate from the straight course. My mantra has always been like that of Milwaukee Braves pitcher Lew Burdette, who once said, "I earn my living from the hungriness of hitters."[31] I earn my living from the hungriness of investors, from their decisiveness, their forcefulness, from their great urge for immediacy. And this immediacy was not just the bid-ask spread; it was even more so, as we will see, in the larger routs.

ROBINSON CRUSOE IN THE BOND PIT

After about a month, Klipp released me into the wilds of the active bond contract, the upper steps. The discipline had to remain the same— I still had but two privileges—and, like a hawk, he kept an eye on me in the pit as well as on my daily trading statements, to make sure that it did.

The king of the bond pit, nay of all pits, was (and will forever be) Lucian Thomas Baldwin III (trading badge "BAL"), known for the largest trading size of any local—thousands of contracts a day—and his ability to single-handedly bully what was then the half-trillion-dollar government bond market. While I was still a teenager, at a time when most in Chicago idolized M.J., I idolized BAL. As a clerk in the pit, I intently studied his trading. He was a man possessed (which perhaps explained his unfortunate and notorious pencil-stabbing pit incident), but what was so astounding about him was his disciplined control in alternating between tremendous patience and overwhelming aggression.

So naturally I had to pick a spot in the pit near BAL's. He took one look at my fresh face and "SIZ" trading badge and branded me forever "The Sizzler," and made me his personal spitball target. But if I had to be hazed during my start as a pit trader, I was honored that it was by the greatest of all time (and it was something of a rite of passage when he stopped lobbing spitballs and started trading with me).

Venturing into the upper steps of the bond pit was like suddenly getting shipwrecked on a deserted island, all alone and with little access to order flow. I was the Robinson Crusoe of the bond pit. This apt metaphor (the solitary islander who devises a range of strategies for survival amid scarcity, the protagonist of Daniel Defoe's 1719 novel) runs deeper; it has become a quintessential economic parable—used most notably by the Austrian School economists, who focused so much on the actions of the individual in exchanging one state of affairs for another (what they called "autistic exchange"), but going back at least as far as Adam Smith, himself. (Crusoe's simple act of making a crude fishing pole and later sacrificing the time to construct a boat and net, tools by which he becomes more productive, will become integral to our roundabout concept in Chapter 5.)

Klipp had given me the equivalent of a pole with which to catch fish, but that was it. I endlessly cast my meager solitary line, bidding and offering one-lots, but cast after cast, more often than not the result was yet another one-tick loss (the fish stole the bait). Days sometimes passed with little to show for time spent standing and yelling in the pit; then I would hook a meal for a week.

Now, let's say Robinson Crusoe discovers, after exploring various fishing holes around his lonely island home, that at some, perhaps where the water is rather shallow, he can catch smaller fish with some frequency, and he has also discovered a few spots, perhaps where the water is very deep, where the fish are much larger, but fewer in number (and thus bite much less frequently). There is a natural trade-off for Crusoe, then, between size and frequency. This is of course a ubiquitous tradeoff in nature—and, when involving complex phenomena, is often described in terms of a "power law" of frequency along the size continuum (or "really small things are really common, really big things less so").

The question was: Where should Crusoe fish, or, in the trading pit, how big of a profit was I after—when to grab a winner? Answering this question was necessary to the second step in the roundabout process of pit trading.

While Klipp's methodology, his privileges, defined the edge and the downside of monetizing that edge, it left wide open the size of the profit to wait for. He explained the size of a "good loss," but said nothing about the size of a "good profit." He would always say, "While there's no such thing as taking a loss too quick, you *can* take a profit too quick—but I can't tell you when to take a profit." (The term "scalper" typically meant a local looking to make one tick on every trade. Klipp was the antiscalper.) With Klipp, there was no settling for minnows.

The question of profit size was, of course, not about trade size, which was a simple function of account size, and which, of course, would impact both losses and gains proportionately. This was about the size of profits *relative* to the size of losses, the *payoff*.

In Klipp's basic asymmetric strategy, the bigger the gain I waited for, the less frequently it would occur, and the more asymmetric (or "positively skewed") my payoff would be. For example, taking profits only after they reached ten ticks in my favor would naturally happen less frequently, and would be accompanied by more frequent losses, than after just three ticks. (I would often watch a profit of seven, eight, nine ticks come right back and become a one-tick loss. Not fun!) This could be extended to the absurd: I could shoot for hundreds of ticks, which might not happen for many years, perhaps never at all, with nothing but countless one-tick losses until then. On its own, a very potent strategy, but not necessarily very effective, in the end.

While Klipp was not a scalper, neither was his approach about hitting the jackpot on one lucky trade; it was about incremental gains, exploiting a systematic edge through time. But, indeed, as the profit objective increased, the trade became the equivalent of holding a basket of long option positions (or convex payoffs). Klipp had an intuitive understanding that the market tended to experience infrequent, large moves—what we call "fat tails," for mass in the extremes of the frequency distribution of market returns—and that replicating such a basket, in its simplest and most elegant form, was a good way to play it.

FISHING IN "McELLIGOT'S POOL"

As I experimented with moving from small fish to big, with decreasing frequency, I moved from the world of Defoe to that of another literary economic thinker, Theodor Geisel (otherwise known as "Dr. Seuss"). In his 1947 book *McElligot's Pool*, a young boy coincidentally named Marco imagines all sorts of wondrous fish that he can't see beneath a murky pond but intends to catch nonetheless. A disparaging old farmer repeatedly tells him that there are no fish in the pond, but Marco keeps trying. He casts and casts, undeterred. Marco's bet illustrates rather aptly the second and third century CE skeptic Sextus Empiricus's *problem of induction* (i.e., the "black swan" problem): All it would take would be one fish to prove that cynical old inductivist farmer wrong. (Marco says, defiantly, "It may be you're right. I've been here three hours / Without one single bite. There might be no fish. . . . But, again, Well, there might.") Although Marco can't see anything in that pond, and no one has ever caught anything there before, he patiently hopes to exploit the extreme unknown that he dreams up, described in Seussian rhyme, ". . . something bigger . . . some sort of a kind of a THING-A-MA-JIGGER!! A fish that's so big, if you know what I mean, that he makes a whale look like a tiny sardine!"[32]

As a young pit trader, ever squeezing my profits, indeed, I was Marco, waiting for the big unknown trophy. It turned out to be a rather productive approach for me (particularly from the limit down bond collapse of 1994), and such asymmetrical casting is a useful idea when the waters are murky, when you don't know anything (and you don't even know what you don't know). But it seemed to be conflating two edges, one systematic and one fuzzy, the local's edge and some kind of presumed underpriced tendency for large deviations. These were really very much the same, though on different scales. Indeed, all moves in the market, big and small, ultimately have immediacy at their source.

ENTER THE AUSTRIANS: A VON KARAJAN MOMENT

Klipp was convinced that nothing from academia would be useful in the real, gritty world of financial markets. But he was unaware of a particular old school of economic thought, where hidden within its formalized foundation was the very same foundation, not only for his Alpha School, but more broadly for a rigorous investment methodology predating and rivaling all others—though locked away by decades of neglect and never drawn out and applied. This was the great Austrian School of Economics, or the Vienna School (named after the origin of its founders), by most accounts nonexistent amid the vast majority of academic economic programs—and what better indication of the precedence of credentials over understanding the world in modern academia. So, Klipp was perhaps right in his expectation, as my collegiate exposure to the Austrians was truly the luckiest of breaks.

It started in a fortuitous economics course at Georgetown University taught by Professor George Viksnins ("Uncle George"). It is most fitting to gain the greatest insight about markets from those who fled antimarket regimes, in his case in Latvia. Uncle George's declared favorite economist was Joseph Schumpeter, a wavering Austrian, to be sure, but close enough to pique my interest. And from there I discovered a book by Henry Hazlitt titled *Economics in One Lesson*—and if I am able to get my children to read only one economics text in their lifetime, God forbid, it would be Hazlitt's. (In addition to the Austrian tradition's absence from most of the top universities, it should come as no surprise that, according to my diligent research, even Austrian-friendly texts are absent from virtually all the top preparatory schools in the United States—but for one, my favorite: Cranbrook Kingswood in Michigan, where Hazlitt's book is required reading.) *Economics in One Lesson* is an expansion on the essay, "That Which Is Seen, and That Which Is Not Seen," by nineteenth-century French economist Frédéric Bastiat (who plays a leading role in Chapter 4 of this book). Hazlitt's proclamation would become a central tenet for me (wherein I would equivalently swap the words "economics" with "investing" and "act or policy" with "capital and production process"): "The whole of economics can be reduced to a single lesson, and that lesson can be reduced to a single sentence: *The art of economics consists in looking not merely at the immediate but at the longer effects of any act or policy.*"[33] I could not put Hazlitt's book down (and it would even replace my dog-eared *Treasury Bond Basis*).

The closing verse of Hazlitt's book was an auspicious directive: "The reader who aims at a thorough understanding, and feels prepared for it, should next read *Human Action* by Ludwig von Mises."[34] Finally, as a pit trader, I got around to complying. So there I was, trading in the bond pit, likely the most competitive capital marketplace in the world, and being lectured to on my daily commute by its greatest acolyte (by way of the cassette version of *Human Action*).

Human Action is the *Laozi* of the Austrian School, the magnum opus of its central figure, a monumental economics treatise from 1949, which Mises wrote in English but which was based on his 1940 German-language *Nationalökonomie: Theorie des Handelns und Wirtschaftens*. (Mises is another case, like Uncle George, of one who evaded the destructive suppression of free markets, among other liberties, in his case the 1938 Nazi *Anschluss* in Austria.) In Mises's words, in his method, I instantly detected something unmistakably familiar, almost as if I'd heard them before. Hidden within this massive, dense, and formal work was the simplicity of Klipp's Paradox—the simplicity and elegance of the *Laozi*—yet articulated in a way that resolved it. It was a "von Karajan moment" for me, as I was struck by the same blow that the Austrian conductor Herbert von Karajan had described upon first hearing the great Arturo Toscanini conduct. (I would also gain my first understanding of roundaboutness—the circuitous pursuit of goals that is fundamental to *The Dao of Capital*—in the words of Karajan, who didn't achieve fame as a conductor until he was fifty and ultimately became the most renowned ever. In true Laozian style, Karajan secluded himself in the Austrian Alps for "quiet, concentrated study and meditation" and withdrew from the direct clash against his competitors—a feint that we will see in action with the conifers of Chapter 2. As he wrote in 1947, "For the moment, let the others decimate themselves in the Viennese battle of all against all—my time is sure to come and I await it, calm and confident"—and obsessively pouring over his tattered scores.[35]) Mises's lecture concluded, I immediately started over—over and over again (until my favorite sections became a tangled ball of magnetic tape).

What first stood out was the role of time in Mises's worldview. Time permeated everything; all action was a "temporal succession of events," always of steps and "fractions of time," the aim of which was "the removal of future uneasiness, be it only the future of the impending instant." Acting was to relieve our insatiable "impatience and the pains caused by waiting." And overcoming this natural urge was the necessary key to productivity—*roundabout production*—"the harvesting of the physically more abundant fruits of production processes consuming more time" and, thus, the significant "role played by taking account of waiting time."[36] (Mises rightfully credited this central notion of the roundabout to his predecessor, the great Austrian economist Eugen von Böhm-Bawerk, the subject of Chapter 5.) Degrees of impatience—what the Austrians call *time preference*, the singular source, in Mises's view, of interest rates—in waiting and forgoing immediate profits (or consumption) and even bleeding capital (such as through costly capital expenditures), was a logical part of our humanness—indeed, part of that humanness which we had to overcome to do certain propitious things (things which cumulatively amounted to the very progress of civilization). This was Klipp's Paradox, writ large, on the grandest scale, formalized and temporalized in the Austrian economic language.

Moreover, of most immediate concern for me (as a treasury bond trader during a period of immense monetary interventionism) was a fundamental result of Mises's framework: Taken to its logical conclusion, a society's time preference could not be repudiated, and the actual market rate of interest had to correspond to the underlying fundamental "originary" rate of interest. Any vain attempt to do otherwise, as when market interest rates are artificially set through monetary intervention, would mislead production and would result in an imbalance and distortion in the economy. Over time, forces would grow stronger and stronger to eliminate that imbalance, and would inevitably succeed in violently driving the artificial rate back to its natural level, and thus the scheme would come to a necessary end. This inevitable seeking of balance from an artificial imbalance, this reversion of opposites, was, to Mises, the very source of "the cyclical fluctuations of business," "the trade cycle," or, more precisely, the *boom and bust cycle* (the subject of Chapters 7 and 8).[37]

A STATE OF REST

Underlying Mises's observations throughout was the basic unruliness of market prices, of their inherent subjectivity—a subjectivity that stems from the perceptions, needs, tastes, and impatience of humans. As he wrote in *Human Action*, "No laboratory experiments can be performed with regard to human action. We are never in a position to observe the change in one element only, all other conditions of the event remaining unchanged. Historical experience as an experience of complex phenomena does not provide us with facts in the sense in which the natural sciences employ this term to signify isolated events tested in experiments. The information conveyed by historical experience cannot be used as building material for the construction of theories and the prediction of future events."[38] There it was, the illusory task of predicting markets using empirical data, explained as well as it ever could be.

This fundamental indeterminism led to "the method of economics," what Mises specifically called "the method of imaginary constructions." This was, for Mises, the singular method of *praxeology*, or the science of human action, which "cannot, like the natural sciences, base its teachings upon laboratory experiments and sensory perception of external objects."[39] It required the *a priori* deductive approach to knowledge (again, endorsing Kant) by way of well-crafted *gedanken* (or thought) experiments—a better description than "imaginary," as these constructions were often very real, just not easily observable or tractable. We might think of it as introspection as a source of knowledge in the study of human action. To Mises, these were the axiomatic building blocks of all economic insight.

Principal among Mises's praxeological precepts (in addition to the aforementioned *time preference*) was the notion of the market's *state of rest* (or what he called the *plain state of rest*). The state of rest is essentially an occurrence in a market when "the brokers have carried out all orders which could be executed at the market price. Only those potential sellers and buyers who consider the market price too low or too high respectively have not sold or bought."[40] It is a "lull" that will end with any new initiating order in the market, any new demand for immediacy, be it in response to news or perceptions of traders, and so forth. The state of rest is an intermittent end to all immediacy, a waypoint at which order flow is exhausted by mutually advantageous exchange, and it reoccurs in the markets over and over again.

Mises added another layer to this concept with the hypothetical continuous, yet ever elusive, aim of the market, the *final state of rest*. This was the price at which all transactions continually balanced and cleared, where no change ever occurred again in a particular market—truly an imaginary construction never attained, the intended destination never arrived at. Every state of rest was the result of a searching, bargaining process, a *Preiskampf*, or "price duel" as the Austrians called it, by which the markets were guided toward the final state of rest—though, naturally, something would change and it would never be reached. Mises's description of the market's ongoing "temporal succession of events,"[41] then, was of ever moving from one state of rest to another, ever estimating the inestimable final state of rest.

GUIDING INTO EMPTINESS . . .

At times, waves of orders would buffet the bond pit like a tornado, and you could literally feel their surge in the vibrations of scrambling brokers through the floor (before the market even moved—a moment when price swings were decidedly nonrandom in the pit). During those tumults, the prices no longer reflected a balance between buyers and sellers, or, in bond futures, between savers and borrowers.

Within the bond pit, as within all markets, is an elaborate heterogeneous temporal structure, with the urgent orders at the bottom and various degrees of less urgent orders—the least direct, the most patient, the most roundabout—at the top. The orders would swirl around the pit, intolerantly pushing prices as they moved, until finally finding a temporal home, a "fill"; the errors corrected, there was a brief eerie calm, a provisional state of rest, awaiting another swell in response. This was the messy process of price discovery in the pit (an experience that is today forever lost to the world, as such pit action described here no longer exists anywhere), a succession of failed balancing acts, with the locals as fulcrum. And in the futile search for the final state of rest is the market's grand homeostasis.

Here was Mises's whole description of the market process, "always disquieted by a striving after a definite state of rest,"[42] with each resulting price an error around the final state price; and these errors, what Mises called "false prices," were the local's edge. The local needed to perceive as quickly as possible these false prices, the wedges between each successive state of rest and the final state, visible only in the constant entrepreneurial urge to immediately modify and correct them—through an auction process that ultimately exhausted that urgency through overcorrection. Thus the local responded to a force by guiding the price to a new imbalance, a new and brief false state of rest.

Mises's market process made explicit what was implicit in the actions of the local, who certainly did not have to understand any

Austrian economics. (As the saying goes, the only PhD that counted in the pits was "papa has dough.") As Mises described, they had *Verstehen*, or an intuitive grasp (or "understanding") of entrepreneurial opportunism. What mattered to the local, their *raison d'être*, was avoiding a swelling inventory, the result of one-sided urgent order flow (as in only sell orders, for instance). In avoiding this, like birds in the flock that alter their course to avoid bumping into a neighboring bird, they thus create complex and efficient dynamics in the whole, from exceedingly simple program-like individual objectives.

Markets are necessarily asynchronous, and with each new asynchronous tidbit of transactional information everyone alters their plans. And it is in ignoring this most elementary of observations that so much of modern economics fails, focusing as it does on a hopeless single *ex ante* equilibrium state where all transacting will happen, free of time. Instead, the perfectly clearing *ex post* "Dutch-auction" price—where all transactions within a period of time, if done simultaneously, would match up— is the moving target that is being repeatedly estimated in the cumulative aggregation of false prices (resulting from the processional states of rest). (Indeed, so much of Austrian Investing is about understanding and recognizing how these estimates can be wildly distorted.)

All of this occurred in the bedlam of the pit, in a succession of *mini-routs* to a succession of states of rest, something which could take many months or even years to learn to decipher in the pit, though perfectly clarified by Mises. The market was not a casino game of flashing random variables (despite untold lives still spent studying their *stochastic* properties), but an intricate coordinating and balancing price-concession process. Indeed, in Mises's construct was that of the pit trader.

Oftentimes, this process could turn into a coordinated (certainly skirting cartel-like) manipulation, as large locals would nudge a market through and thus trigger anticipated "stop orders" (known as "running stops")—to their positional advantage. This was basically about flushing out the immediacy hiding in the market, like a covey of quail. It could be as simple as recognizing the urgency in an order from a broker's visible stress (and other "tells"), or just sensing the crescendos and decrescendos in the order flow as the market explored different price levels. (Here, Baldwin's "*coup d'œil*" in recognizing the decisive moment—and his ability to wait for it—rivaled Napoleon's.)

These are the basic machinations of market microstructure, and of any marketplace, whether human locals or high-frequency robots: an endless alternating procession of routs. And it is the art of pit trading, in leading the market into imbalance, a momentary false state of rest away from its final state. It could be subtle or violent, involving the slightest one-lot sell order at the bid price or thousands of contracts from one or many orders that send the market into a tailspin. It was the ducking and weaving of the flock, with no driver, no one in charge, only the search to exhaust and placate what was roiling it.

Here was the link between the market-maker's edge and the occasional huge moves of the market. The *major-routs* were identical to the *mini-routs*, only bigger (a property known in mathematics as *self-similarity*, or *fractal*). Specifically, they were both about imbalance seeking balance, of false prices seeking correct prices. The wedge was just bigger.

In the bond pit, order flow thus communicated and the locals thus balanced the immediate intentions expressed by marginal savers and borrowers. This meant that, in fact, when there were no urgent active orders, the economy would (when there was no artificial price setting) be in a state which Mises called *stationary* (another of his praxeological terms we will revisit in Chapter 7). (And a hypothetical final state of rest throughout an economy would provide what Mises called an *evenly rotating economy*—which we might think of as an economy in which nothing ever changes, a kind of economic Dark Ages.)

Understanding this process of liquidity is basically about understanding that any market exchange must be perceived as mutually beneficial to both parties. A failure to understand this, particularly in a market dislocation like a crash, is the source of much angst directed toward high-frequency traders, for instance, who cease their liquidity-providing activities (and thus create liquidity holes) when markets get too volatile. Why should we expect anything else? Why shouldn't the price of immediacy jump to infinity along with perceived demands for immediacy? Why should anyone be expected to accommodate a counterparty at prices that are strongly believed to be in error? After all, to assume anything else would be to assume that liquidity providers are charities.

Klipp's lectures to me as a teenager were spot-on (albeit, expressed in different terms): In ever searching for and finding a new state of rest, the market was always intermittently and provisionally right in correcting an error, though, in never arriving at a final state of rest, in never achieving a synchronized balance in all orders for immediacy, it was always wrong. And the greater the imbalance, the more wrong it was.

MOVING ON

Despite childhood dreams of becoming a pit trader finally realized, having moved up the steps from trading one-lots to tens and then hundreds of contracts, the time came to move on. I had been increasingly targeting larger bond price moves through options (flashed across the trading floor into the bond options pit from the bond futures pit), and my edge was increasingly moving away from that of the local. Moreover, it was early 1997, and the death knell for open outcry was being tolled by growing volume in the competing electronic trading (known at the Chicago Board of Trade as Project A).

And along with this new technology came a raging U.S. stock market, an unprecedented asset bubble clearly, from Mises, from an unprecedented monetary distortion—Greenspan had been on a loose monetary policy spree, following a Mexican debt crisis, and he inexplicably continued into President Bill Clinton's reelection.[43] It would end either through Greenspan applying the brakes (which seemed unlikely as he and Clinton had convinced themselves of a "New Economy" that was far from a bubble—not too hot, but just right, the "Goldilocks economy") or a capital and resource crunch applying them for him. Either way, the interest rate market was in extreme imbalance, an illusory temporary respite. Why plumb the murky depths of McElligot's Pool in the pit when whales were visible just under the surface?

I moved to Wall Street to become a proprietary trader at a primary government bond dealer (an investment house that participates directly in Federal Reserve transactions and Treasury auctions), and moved from bond futures and options to my new speciality, "midcurve" options on Eurodollar futures (or short-term options, expiring in less than a year, on forward three-month LIBOR contracts, expiring in more than a year). Naturally, the premiums for these options were then very low, and owning them allowed me to acquire a favorable position in the Eurodollar futures once the market woke up. It was just like being back in the pit: Option contracts are a means of gaining immediacy (though conditional on a price threshold, the "strike price"); owning them provides immediacy in the routs, and hedging them (what option traders call "long gamma hedging") can often pay for that privilege (and then some) by providing liquidity in the pit (thus earning back the price of immediacy).

It was the perfect setup for an *Austrian play*. What quickly became clear, however, was that the significance of the trade wasn't predominately in the hoped-for lump payout; it was in the advantage afforded by the timing of that payout. The interest rate shock I was targeting (either a surprise tightening, like 1994, or a surprise easing, from an inevitable credit bust) would be accompanied by a general market dislocation wherein immediacy would be in exceedingly high demand, and I would be essentially all alone in having the fresh capital to exploit it. As effective as the option trade was, it was but the prelude, an intermediate waypoint toward an even greater edge, an attack and counterattack of *tuishou*. In the option trade was the temporal coordination of capital with its most advantageous and opportune use. This was a chance encounter with roundabout investing, the key to Klipp's approach and paradox: Fishing most effectively by not even fishing at all, but rather by constructing a harpoon for later use—just in time for the appearance of a whale.

As it turned out, the markets did not rest in 1997 nor, especially, in the summer of 1998. The obvious counterattack, upon booking gains in the Eurodollar options trades, was to short the freshly blown-out "on-the-run-off-the-run" bond spread—and as it inevitably converged I would follow it right back to zero. This was a pure "flight to liquidity" distortion, as everyone demanded the more liquid bellwether bond over the off-the-run bond, amplified by the ill-fated hedge fund Long Term Capital Management paying anything to unwind that very same convergence trade. (It turns out their name was most apropos, as this spread was, with certainty, a perfectly profitable *long term* trade—a shame that profit was entirely usurped by the path, by their profoundly shallow *depth of field*.)

Of course, Greenspan continued his monetary distortion apace throughout the crises, which meant the insurgencies would continue. Indeed, the whales of '97 and '98 would be but a preparation for much bigger Thing-A-Ma-Jiggers to come. I joined Nassim Taleb in 1999 as he was launching Empirica Capital, a mutually obvious relationship from our shared pit trading background and a shared view on the certainty of an eventual collapse in the then-bubbly U.S. stock market (and to this day there is no one with whom I more enjoy and benefit from sparring about tails). We called ourselves "crisis hunters" (we were, indeed, the first formalized tail protection firm ever)—which we duly snagged in the 2000 equity collapse. This would be the highlight of an aggregate Empirica record that, while functioning well as a tail hedge, was the lowest return period in my career, before or since (though much has been learned along the way—representing a wonderful barrier to entry as competitors come and go.) We parted ways in 2005, and I went on to form my own investment firm Universa Investments, moving beyond the basic mandate at Empirica. (After I started, Nassim joined me again but in a strictly hands-off, passive capacity.) Nassim has since gone on to do voluminous and very significant work on uncertainty, specifically the "black swan problem" (as well as his neologism *antifragility*—the convexity of Marco), which has wonderful far-reaching consequences—albeit less straightforward, I believe, for capital investment.

I show in Chapter 9 how extreme uncertainty and *black swans* are not the stories of the big stock market busts of the past century in the United States (including those during my career), and how the effectiveness of exploiting such busts, or "tail hedging," is highly conditional on the particular environment of economic distortion. The real black swan problem of stock market busts is not about a remote event that is considered unforeseeable; it is rather about a foreseeable event that is considered remote—which I have spent the bulk of my career exploiting (and which explains the use of this moniker in some of my current partnerships).

Although I naturally employ positive-asymmetric, convex payoffs—a trite thing to say, as in the familiar "favorable risk/reward"—all the data clearly shows that most such "volatility loving" payoffs are and have been overpriced, *ex ante* (using power law tail and other rigorous valuation measures) and *ex post*; and this is why I do not apply what has come to be known as the *barbell strategy*. These bets are mostly the stuff of gamblers and financial salesmen, from nonlinear derivative securities to highly volatile equities to momentum strategies of all stripes; alone, they are a direct, frontal attack. Rather, to me, convexity is an efficient (low-risk) tool for exploiting routs of pent-up immediacy and distortion, but only under the right circumstances (as in the game of *tuishou*); and it is only a part of a roundabout strategy, an intermediate step (of *zouhua* and *nian*) toward the decisive end goal of productive capital investment (the counterattack)—not the game itself. It is a tool of Austrian Investing, but not its key; that belongs to the *roundabout*, a *depth of field*, and, of course, the Austrians.

Today one of my old aqua Alpha trading jackets (stained with ink and blood) is mounted on my office wall, like a skin from some Hemingway-esque safari. Draped over it is a tattered Adam Smith necktie. From day one at the Board of Trade my uniform included this tie. Gamblers' ticks have their place, and neckties were required on the floor, but mostly I was following the example set by Uncle George, who proudly wore his with such zeal. Smith was, of course, *the* free market apostle who radically asserted its organic coordinating function; Mises himself had declared the publication date of Smith's magnum opus (*An Inquiry into the Nature and Causes of the Wealth of Nations*), falling as it did on the same year as the United States' independence, "the dawn of freedom both political and economic."[44] That tie was and still remains an important reminder for me that the pits—and markets in general—are not a casino, but a purposeful force, the Misesian market process at the very heart of the progression of civilization.

It was a roundabout start along a roundabout path toward the methodology of Austrian Investing, from the pit to my current investment partnerships at Universa—which started constructing Thing-A-Ma-Jigger harpoons in 2008, conveniently (though not coincidentally) put to productive use at the end of that year and into the next—and at Dao Capital (respectively comprising Austrian Investing I and II, of Chapters 9 and 10). This is our path as we follow *The Dao of Capital*.

THE WISDOM OF THE SAGES

Legend has it that, during the Warring States Period in ancient China, as one of the seven states began to fall into decline, Laozi decided it was time to leave it behind and spend the rest of his days in solitude. As he made his way on an ox, he reached the border gate at Hangu Pass, the site of many a bloody battle; beyond was Laozi's unknown new home. As the story goes, the gatekeeper realized that Laozi was leaving for good, forever taking with him all the wisdom he possessed, and entreated the Old Master to write down his thoughts for

Laozi, "The Old Master," Retreats from the World, Leaving His Wisdom Behind

posterity. Laozi complied and wrote down a concise treatise of some 5,000 Chinese characters.

The story, we can surmise, is fictional, perhaps much like the author himself. What is undeniable, however, is the efficacy of the words that remained, which have lasted more than two thousand years, and still echo in the wisdom of the ages: a perception of time and the preeminence of patience, a depth of field and the roundabout way of doing by not doing, and the very illusory nature of historical experience—the wisdom of an old grain trader who loved to lose money and of a great school of economic thought that would change the world forever. All would be scorned, yet all would persist, and one day come together in an archetypal investment methodology.

Chapter Two

The Forest in the Pinecone

The Roundabout and the Logic of Growth

In Everett Klipp's last years, I made a point to visit him whenever I passed through Chicago. I would always try to bring him books, ranging from Austrian economics (for which he not surprisingly seemed to have a natural affinity) to probability (which often made no practical sense to this intuitive old grain trader). As we sat and talked (typically with his golf on in the background—for mood), our conversations were punctuated by his favorite sayings—the "Klippisms" that I had heard so many times before. Since leaving the pit, however, one adage in particular took on greater meaning and resonated more deeply with me, despite its banality: "Anyone can see the pinecones in the tree. None can see the trees, none can foresee the forest in the pinecone."

In this simplest of sayings, once again, was Klipp's great disdain for focusing only on the immediate, the tangible, the seen. And in it was also a dramatic story of struggle and conquest. Indeed, from the single cone to the finite numbers produced now, the immediate pales in comparison with all the trees to follow, and then all the pinecones produced by those new trees, and so forth. We shift our sights beyond only what is visible now—a pinecone—to the seedling, the seedpod-producing conifer, and eventually the forest of "look-ahead trees," over many iterative generations unfolding from countless changing environments and intertemporal ebbing and flowing of opportunities. Each seed is a solitary path or musical line with the potential for recursively branching into a raucous fugue. Some paths end abruptly, while others forge ahead far in time, to a great many trees. So how do some of those paths navigate past many an intertemporal twist and turn of forest fires, disease, and competition? If we could follow one of those paths, where would it take us? What would the route look like? Would it randomly ramble aimlessly? Or would it rather follow a purposeful, straightaway course? Somewhere in between, as it turns out, is the very roundabout way of the conifer.

The necessary focus to merely recognize this path and its temporal waypoints is the very depth of field of the Dao. What matters most is not just the existence of a single pinecone—the seedpod that gives the conifer its name ("cone-bearing")—but all the unfolding opportunities that the conifer somehow "perceives," whether the forest floor choked with overgrowth, the rocky outcroppings where competitors cannot thrive, or the fertile barrenness of a fire-cleared area, that affect how and where its seeds will grow.

As the *Laozi* tells us, nature is our greatest teacher; indeed a major Daoist theme, inseparable from the totality of its message, is to observe and learn from nature. This is a common approach, contained even in the most basic of elementary school lessons. In this axiomatic construct, too, is enduring wisdom, readily found in the ancient texts that embrace metaphors such as the tree yielding to the wind, as from the *Laozi*, "A tree as great as a man's embrace springs from a small shoot."[1] Another quintessential Daoist image is the uncarved block known as *pu*, a state of pure potential. In its uncarved state, the wood appears useless, and it takes tremendous imagination as well as patience to see what it can become; "When the block is carved, it becomes useful. When the sage uses it, he becomes the ruler."[2] Time bridges the two—the temporal aspect of means—after which the advantage emerges but the potential is gone. The *Laozi* advises, quite simply, to see the unappreciated uncarved block, unassuming as the humble pinecone, as being fully ripe with potential of what is yet to be.

For Klipp, who grew up on a dairy farm in Manteno, Illinois, and later became something of a gentleman farmer, such depth of field perspective came naturally. From planting to waiting for harvest, there is no coercing a crop from the ground, no ripening it more hastily. The appreciation of the potential in the uncarved block (*pu*) is perennial in the newly seeded field, returning with every spring. Thus the intertemporal positioning of fields (such as through crop and pasture rotation) has always been central to the strategy of farming. (Moreover, there is no better reflection of the collective agrarian understanding of waiting for the opportune moment for decisive action than the adage "make hay while the sun shines.") The temporal is embedded in the farmer's field, as expressed by no less than the great German writer Johann Wolfgang von Goethe in one of his most familiar couplets (which became his motto, and appeared in the first edition of his novel, *Wilhelm Meisters Wanderjahre*): "Mein Erbteil wie herrlich, weit und breit! Die Zeit ist mein Besitz, mein Acker ist die Zeit."—"My inheritance how lordly, wide and fair! Time is my fair seed-field, to Time I'm heir."

With Klipp's imagery of the pinecone, the conifer becomes emblematic, an evocative trope for *The Dao of Capital* and a pedagogical tool to better understand our archetypal roundabout strategy. We follow the example of the sages of the great Daoists' texts, who observed nature and drew from experiences, and tended to use mediums of "image, historical allusion, and analogy" to express complex ideas, theories, and concepts. As sinologist Roger Ames observed, "What constitutes evidence and makes things clear in the text is often an effectively focused image, not a theory; an inexpressible and inimitable experience, not an argument; an evocative metaphor, not a logically demonstrated truth."[3] The role of image, therefore, is as a vehicle for conveying knowledge and wisdom, while remaining subordinate to them, so that once a certain meaning or sense has been conveyed, the linguistic tools themselves no longer matter.[4]

Thus, we are not merely learning about the growth of conifers and how they opportunistically exploit available resources; we see beyond the forest and the trees to the fundamental and universal lessons they contain. We look to the conifer and its logic of growth, and we learn from one of the truly great success stories of natural history. Through its adaptive strategy that has allowed it to survive over hundreds of millions of years, the patient and persistent conifer teaches us that it is far better to avoid direct, head-on competition for scarce resources and, instead, to pursue the roundabout path toward an intermediate step that leads to its eventual position of advantage.

THE FOREST AND THE TREE

Among the conifers are the oldest species on the planet (known, collectively, as gymnosperms, meaning "naked seeds"), which first appeared some 300 million years ago and literally covered the earth by the time the dinosaurs took their first steps. Conifers are arguably the most successful members of the Kingdom Plantae and rank among the most enduring of all living things on earth (along with such other hoary examples as cockroaches and ferns). Eight families of early conifers still exist, including the *Pinaceae* family of pine, cedar, hemlock, spruce, and fir, with a fossil record dating back to the Cretaceous period 150 million to 65 million years ago. During the Jurassic and Early Cretaceous periods, 200 million to 150 million years ago, herbivorous dinosaurs, the likes of stegosaurs and sauropods, fed on conifers. Given their voracious appetites, these predators opened up large areas of fertile land, which had long been dominated by the conifers, to an emerging competitor— the flowering angiosperm (meaning "covered seeds"). After that, the world of the conifers was never the same.

By the end of the Cretaceous period, the angiosperms had staged an impressive rout of the conifers, such that, 65 million years ago, nine out of every ten vascular plant species were angiosperms. Today, angiosperms continue to dominate with plant life that spans some 250,000 varieties, from grasses to trees, among them the deciduous maple, oak, ash, birch, and willow. With advantages from fast growth to more efficient reproduction with the help of insects (which are attracted to the angiosperms' flowers, their signature trait), angiosperms have used their prolific and rapid colonization wherever and whenever possible to gain an upper hand over the conifers from which, no doubt, many descended. As a result, conifers are largely absent, for example, from lowland tropical and subtropical forests, because angiosperms can outcompete them in such temperate environments through faster seedling growth.

Yet, in certain times and places, conifers not only reach the development threshold needed to thrive, but can outgrow and outlive their angiosperm competitors. As Figure 2.1 shows, the conifers change their pace of growth in a deceptive coniferous "changeup": The growth rate of conifers in general lags that of the faster-growing angiosperms through the early phase of life. In fact this is a highly calculated move, as it were, as conifers fall behind early on because they are assembling their "assets," developing strong roots and thick bark, which allow them to become very efficient in resource use and to enjoy often impressive life spans. This also means that, over time, as the graph shows, the longer-living conifers can overtake angiosperms in biomass and height.

The needled conifers may lack some of the internal efficiencies of the broad-leaved angiosperms (such as in vascular fluid conduction). Nonetheless, conifers manage to be more productive than angiosperms, thanks to an edge that comes from their very roundaboutness—the slow accumulation of total surface of foliage. The evergreen conifer keeps several seasons of leaf growth (its needles last for multiple years, compared to the annual shedding of deciduous leaves), which eventually surpass even the most profuse angiosperm in total leaf surface area.[5]

For conifers, growth is a patient process that takes tenacity and grit, and most successful with (and even requiring) a roundabout strategy,

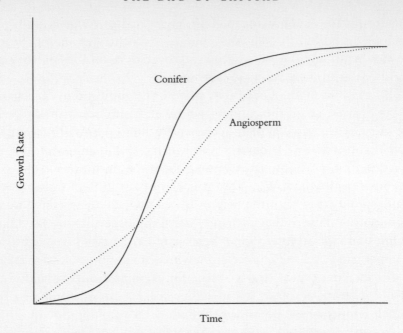

Figure 2.1   Growth Rate of Evergreen Conifers Eventually Catches Up with and Surpasses That of the Deciduous Angiosperms

Reprinted with permission from Biological Journal of the Linnean Society, *1989, 36:227–249: W. J. Bond, "The Tortoise and the Hare: Ecology of Angiosperm Dominance and Gymnosperm Persistence."*

with slow early stages that create the structure for subsequent fast and efficient development. The conifers' progress exhibits the teleology of purposeful "behavior" that shows a goal-oriented mechanism in action from their adaptation, as they retreat to the rocks as the means toward an end. In other words, conifers pay now for productivity gains later. In building efficiencies, they aim first toward means (step one), whereas the angiosperms, in their immediate fast growth, aim straight toward ends (the final step).

Such purposeful indirectness, focused on means to the attainment of a desired end, does not occur just within the growth of a single conifer. It also governs the growth patterns of conifer stands within the forest. (Of course, my intention is not to infer that conifers are capable of cognition; their strategy is but an optimized product of evolutionary adaptations.) In order to better their overall chances of survival, conifers cede to their competitors the immediate advantage in the most obvious areas, so that they can seed more opportunistically and effectively later on. For their nourishment and survival, conifers do not head directly to the source; rather, like Robinson Crusoe, they first head in the opposite direction, away from the sea of fish and fertile soils toward an interim step, in order to make a more effective and successful move to the source later on. To more fully appreciate the importance of this strategy, favoring the intermediate over the immediate, the circuitous over the direct (with metaphoric lessons for investors), we must first understand just how deadly the head-on clash can be.

THE SLOW SEEDLING

Interaction is a law of nature. When conifers and angiosperms grow in the same area, that interaction intensifies. In the local forest, amid a tangle of sunlight-hogging broad-leaved angiosperms, there is a riot of competition for scarce resources such as water, soil, and sunlight. In a direct clash for dominance (particularly in the most fertile, hospitable areas) the odds are usually stacked against the conifer, a continuous replay of the battle that dates back to the Cretaceous period. So what are their tactics? How do the two species compete?

For many years, it had been assumed that competition between angiosperms and conifers occurred mostly at a later stage of development, when a canopy was created as branches from adult trees overlapped. This late growth was accepted as the root of the causal relationship between angiosperm invasions and conifer extinctions within specific areas in which there is co-occurrence of the species. What had not been explored by botanists until more recently was the impact of competition right from the start. Now it is well understood that the battle begins as soon as conifer seedlings manage to put down roots in dappled patches of sunlight among faster-growing angiosperms, but then quickly lose the ability to compete for a sufficient share of resources.

The more densely populated a forested area, the more individual growth and performance become negatively impacted with competitive effects that include the number and size of neighboring plants and their proximity to each other. Plants that gain the first roothold or that encounter fewer competitors gain the edge of monopolizing local resources and, thus, grow more rapidly than those that are seeded later or that attempt to grow in more crowded areas.[6]

When deprived due to a resource crunch, young conifers become sickly and stunted, and all the more susceptible to insects, disease, harmful fungi, litterfall (leaves, bark, and twigs that cover the forest floor), grazing herbivores, and the most voracious of all predators—fire. In these conditions, suppressed conifer seedlings lose ground and fail to thrive, a scenario that has come to be known as the "slow seedling hypothesis."[7]

The Chiltern-Mt. Pilot National Park in northwestern Victoria, Australia, is home to a diverse mix of wildlife. What drew botany researchers to the park, from 2004 to 2010, was the opportunity to test the slow-seedling hypothesis in a unique laboratory-like environment with two distinct samples: a control group of conifers in a largely homogeneous stand and another comingled group of conifers and angiosperms seeded together. Specifically, botanists studied the interaction between a type of conifer known as callitris, related to cypress trees, and eucalyptus, the angiosperm that populates the park's extensive forests, both of which had reseeded in the park after a high-intensity fire in 2003. In areas in which seedlings from both species mixed, the callitris clearly lost to its faster-growing eucalyptus neighbors. Callitris seedlings were, on average, shorter and less healthy than the eucalyptus. In addition, seed cones were absent on the shorter callitris seedlings, preventing any propagation. In fact, seed cones were produced by only the tallest callitris, which grew most abundantly where the population was largely uniform, in patches of virtually all conifers except for a few angiosperms.[8]

As the field study demonstrated, young callitris trees were most often the losers in head-to-head competition; their very seeding was "mal-seeding" (producing plant growth that was inappropriate for the ecosystem) whose seedlings—due to "recruitment bottlenecks"—were constrained from ever reaching sufficient size and strength to thrive. Inevitably, they failed to even finish what they started. Stunted growth meant it took longer (if it occurred at all) for these young trees to hit the threshold beyond which they developed some fire-defense mechanisms.[9] (In some conifers, such traits include thicker bark and the ability to "self-prune" by shedding lower branches as they grow higher foliage to create a canopy.) When small conifers do not thrive, they can fall victim to even low-intensity grassfires that would not do much damage to a more mature tree, but which will scorch and burn seedlings that have not topped above the high grass.

WILDFIRE AND RESOURCE REALLOCATION

In the forest, the comingling of aggressive angiosperms and suppressed conifers results in an overgrown tinderbox, especially vulnerable to a spark such as a lightning strike. Or, as we might say, this is evidence of *malinvestment* that occurs unnaturally in the forest "economy" (where fire suppression is practiced) and the need for available resources to be reallocated to healthier growth. It is not the deadwood, not just the accumulation of a network of otherwise many small fires into one big one—the rationale that is cliché among the complexity types. Rather, it is artificial change in the ecosystem and the temporal structure of its growth patterns—a wearing-out without replacement—that makes the forest prone to fire. The failure of live trees to thrive—and the forest's failure to adapt as a result of internal competition—produce unhealthy, unwarranted, and unsustainable growth that upsets the balance of the system. Fire suppression leads to distortion as malinvestment continues, causing extensive overgrowth, as if there were more available resources than there really are. The forester fools the forest into reacting to a more benign, resource-laden environment for growth. The artificial environment of fire suppression collapses all the intertemporal strategies in the forest, as even the conifer's is morphed into a fight for immediate survival (an effect we will see again in Chapter 7). The irony, then, is that this eternal Garden of Eden mirage prompts only a desperate head-to-head mad dash to the finish—even by the conifers—as if there were no tomorrow. Yet even then, distortion will eventually be corrected as the system seeks homeostasis (the topic of Chapter 8). At some point, alternation must occur to redistribute resources, which is accomplished largely through predators, especially small, localized wildfires.

When a wildfire breaks out, everything is at risk, including the conifers that burn more quickly and easily because they are particularly combustible. (In a high-intensity fire, pine trees ignite like torches.) Smaller, naturally occurring fires, however, are nature's way of turning back the clock as resources are released and flow from trees that are not thriving to those that perhaps can. This is a crucial part of the discovery process and the control and communication within the system to determine the right mix and magnitude.

In particular, in lower altitudes and in more temperate areas, periodic wildfires act as mini-routs to manage the succession of the forest over time, searching for balance through constantly perturbed imbalance. Otherwise, angiosperms such as oaks and maples would dominate for extended periods of time, because they are more tolerant of each other at the seedling and sapling stages and can "shade out" their conifer competitors and rob them of sunlight. Smaller wildfires, though, can even the score by creating change within the forest system. These incremental blazes also help prevent the major-routs that prove deadly to the forest and are of benefit to no one. Thus, what might appear to be a destructive force is in actuality constructive, balancing the temporal structure of total growth in the forest.

It's not that the forest needs disorder to further its growth, nor does it want major fires such as the infamous inferno that ravaged Yellowstone National Park in 1988. Such massive destruction is as devastating to the forest as war is to civilization (and war is *never* good for a civilization). Civilizations advance through the accumulation of highly configured capital, which does not thrive amid extreme volatility and destruction; on the contrary, capitalism wants stability—but also the free competitive transferral of resources (through failures, bankruptcies, and the opportunity for profits) to where they are most suited to the needs of consumers. However, when there is a suppressed free market, then even a crash can indeed bring about good because it eliminates unhealthy "growth" or *malinvestment*. The parallel to the forest is an obvious one: smaller wildfires enable the turnover of resources, transferring them between competitors, from what we might view as a lower order of production (the fast-growing angiosperms) to more roundabout, higher-order production (the conifers). While small natural wildfires destroy with precision (by definition), great unnatural forest fires destroy indiscriminately. This is the unfortunate price paid for the necessary succession.

Seeing the configuration of the forest in this way requires an appreciation that it is not a uniform blob of vegetation, but a highly heterogeneous temporal structure. The efficacious growth of the conifers, then, is but a test case of the roundabout strategy in the process of capital deployment, *The Dao of Capital* and its destination of Austrian Investing.

THE CONIFER EFFECT

Nature takes a roundabout, intertemporal approach; indeed, this strategy is the conifers' singular advantage over the more aggressive angiosperms. The conifers can leave the more tangible and immediate gains from the fertile, sun-drenched areas to the angiosperms, and retreat (thanks to their wind-borne seeds) to the rocky, exposed areas where conditions are harsh, but sunlight is still plentiful. It is not that conifers prefer rocky, acidic, sandy, waterlogged, and other low-quality soils; indeed, when they are planted and cultivated in better climates with more fertile conditions, conifers thrive. However, in order to avoid the direct competition for scarce resources, conifers retreat to inferior soil, wind-battered ridges, and low-lying areas where water collects, leaving the prime site to the faster growers.[10] (A happy coincidence worth noting is that the Austrian pine, a subspecies of the European black pine, or *Pinus nigra*, seems particularly drawn to the craggiest of terrain, pushing into the most barren areas, just as the entrepreneur—the focus and hero of the Austrian tradition—pushes out to the areas overlooked and yet undiscovered by his brethren competitors.)

Conifers, obviously, cannot send their seeds to a specific place; however, their seeds are, in a sense, directed. For example, strong winds generated by wildfires suck the wind-borne seeds from trees on the periphery into the ravaged areas. Serotinous cones that open only after exposure to high heat and flame also provide seed to regenerate growth after a fire. Even the trees' intermittent seed dumps may be attuned to wildfire occurrences. All these factors point to the logic of nature. Although the conifer is a dominant metaphor in this chapter and throughout the book, in the real world of the forest a universal strategy is at work that makes these trees among the most successful forms of organic life.

In these less-than-desirable areas with thin, rocky, and nutrient-deficient soil that cannot sustain other species, conifers find a niche, thanks to a few adaptations that allow them to be highly efficient, making the most out of very little in exposed way stations en route to their ultimate gains. For example, *mycorrhiza*, a symbiotic association between conifers and fungi that colonize among their roots, helps the trees to absorb nutrients from the rocky soil. Other adaptations include the size and shape of conifer needles that reduce evapotranspiration to guard against moisture loss. (Conifers also possess such defense mechanisms as rough bark and spiky needles which discourage browsing herbivores, and even poisonousness in some varieties specific to their archnemeses the domesticated goats that will nonetheless devour them before exiting the gene pool—the "do not eat the conifers" rule *en force*.[11])

Conifers can furthermore tolerate significant temperature fluctuations, both intraday and seasonally, perhaps recalling their ancestors that survived extreme climatic change, tectonic shifts, and geologic upheavals. This plays out on a far grander scale in the great boreal forest, a northern biome also known as the *taiga*. The boreal forest wraps around the northern latitudes of the earth, like a monk's tonsure, covering most of Canada and Alaska, the extreme northern regions of the continental United States, Iceland, Sweden, much of Norway, Finland, reaching down into the Alpine regions of Europe, and much of Russia, northern Japan, and northern China. (It is largely the backdrop of the characters in this book.) In a harsh climate with thin soil and limited sunlight, where the competition cannot grow, conifers have carved out their domain: the world's largest terrestrial ecosystem.

At my home in northern Michigan (named "Nabatic"—Ojibwe for "within the trees"—almost a hundred years ago by its original owner, founder of the company that manufactured the first manual transmission and was a major supplier to Henry Ford, who is featured in Chapter 5), on the very cusp of the boreal forest, a large stand of eastern white pines (*pinus strobus*) lines the crest of a bluff overlooking a Lake Michigan bay. These hardy trees have thrived for countless decades, perhaps a century or more, despite rocky soil (we have unearthed huge boulders) and harsh elements, particularly during sometimes long, brutal winters. Each time I see them, I cannot help but admire their tenacity and efficiency, making the most out of conditions that stymie their competitors and, thus, allow these conifers to grow unimpeded.

During the Pleistocene Age, some 2.6 million to 11,700 years ago, a period of repeated glaciations, massive descending glaciers pushed the conifers southward, to areas more traditionally dominated by angiosperms. Yet each time the ice cap receded, the conifers followed it right back to recapture their enclave in the north, where they had an edge over the angiosperms. Again and again, the conifers yielded as the glaciers extended to the south with gouges that plowed out the fertile valleys and piled up higher elevations that became the fields for later battles with angiosperms. As a result, over millions of years, conquering armies of conifer species that survived a "great winnowing," which left only those species that could adapt to the harsh conditions and short growing season in the taiga, built vast empires in the permafrost of the northern climate in Eurasia and North America, the most extensive forests on earth.[12]

Despite such an unforgiving environment, conifers can conceivably exist forever, to the point that perhaps after 200 years they will dominate completely, edging out all but the occasional angiosperm. But that is not the conifer's only refuge. Outside of boreal and high-elevation montane regions, "islands" of conifers can even grow among a sea of angiosperms by taking advantage of pockets of poor soil or other spaces with unfavorable growing conditions.

The story, however, does not end there. It does not matter where one tree grows or what happens with one pinecone, which, as Klipp reminds us, is all that we can see. Rather, we focus on what none can see: a roundabout strategy unfolding intertemporally in the forest, through the reallocation of scarce available resources. Conifers are soft, highly flammable, highly fragile, but in their roundabout intertemporal strategy—in gaining by losing—they are strong. Here, again, we see our two-step process, a strategy of intermediate objectives attained by a group of individual trees in pursuit of an edge, an eventual gain for the species.

The conifer's indirect growth mirrors a central evolutionary mechanism of mate selection, in which the desirable objective sought is not for the direct material advantage of the parent, but rather to improve the fitness of the offspring. Indeed, conifers may be among the most indirect in all of nature when they forego direct material advantage by growing on the rocks, so that, following an intergenerational strategy, they might survive the competition and predators (especially fire) and thus enable their offspring to one day take advantage of better growing conditions (postwildfire). In fact, given the long history of conifers' evolution, the adaptations and genetic mutations that have enabled them to survive and thrive in the most desolate areas have been ultimately focused on progeny, the untold generations in the future, which one day will gain the advantage during the succession of the forest and seed in the choicest of fertile areas.

Thus it is the way of the conifer to forego the need for immediacy, the present state, and instead prepare for the counter-rout—as the *Laozi* states, "That which shrinks / Must first expand. That which fails / Must first be strong. That which is cast down / Must first be raised. Before receiving / There must be giving."[13] As Ames and David Hall wrote, "The moon that has waxed full will eventually wane; the stand of cypress that has grown old will gradually be renewed."[14] As nature shows us, that which can be defined as a singular, isolated event is not the focus, but rather what occurs within the context of a process. Here, too, the conifer blazes a trail for *The Dao of Capital:* "Insight into the 'wholeness' of the process that we discern in nature where everything in due course gives rise to its opposite can be instructive in guiding the human experience."[15] For the conifers, their roundabout strategy allows them to withdraw to inhospitable places, all the while producing innumerable pinecones loaded with seeds that can be expediently dispersed by the wind to other remote areas, giving rise to a phalanx of patient, long-living warriors awaiting the next rout in the ongoing battle between conifers and angiosperms.

Longevity among the conifers can reach some impressive extremes. It should come as no surprise that conifers are among the world's oldest known living things (along with some 250-million-year-old bacteria found in a kind of suspended animation in ancient sea salt beneath Carlsbad, New Mexico, and a patch of submerged seagrass that is an estimated 80,000 to 200,000 years old). Nor should we expect to find these conifers anywhere except in harsh conditions that provide refuge, reduce competition, and eliminate overgrowth that makes trees susceptible to fire. In tundra-like conditions in northern Sweden, where angiosperms cannot grow, lives an ancient Norway spruce that has thrived there for an unbelievable 9,550 years, dating back to the last Ice Age. (In actuality, it is the root system that has grown for nearly ten millennia, while the trees that sprout from these roots are considerably more recent—evidence of a very efficient, temporal structure.) This living relic is a testament to the adaptability and longevity of the conifer, not only outsurviving its nearest competitors, but nearly everything else on the planet, as well.

Other long-lived conifers include a stand of Alaskan yellow cedar on Vancouver Island, which has been growing for more than 4,000 years. In mountainous regions of California, Nevada, and Utah, the Great Basin bristlecone pine lives up to its scientific name of *Pinus longaeva* (literally, "ancient pine"), with one particular specimen, called the Methuselah Tree in the White Mountains of California, that is an estimated 4,800 years old. The coast redwoods of the Pacific Northwest include some that are more than 2,000 years old. Outside the window of my study in Los Angeles and lining my street, giant coast redwoods, many with a girth greater than my arms can span, provide a visible symbol and reminder of the universality of the roundabout strategy. (And when such notable reminders abound, how has California so emphatically disparaged its roundabout industrial past?)

While conifers growing on the rocks may appear to be nature's outcasts, theirs is truly the false humility of the Daoist manipulator-sage: They withdraw to where others cannot go and then act when conditions suddenly shift and an opportune moment arises, such as after a wildfire. Then we can see the *wei wuwei*—or what we might call here "seeding by not seeding"—of the conifers: By growing on the rocks they avoid mal-seeding in the fertile areas and thus establish a defensive position that, in time, becomes an offensive vantage point from which they can disperse seeds to be wind-borne to the fire-cleared areas—the same fertile ground from which they originally retreated. In nature's demonstration of *tuishou* (or "push hands"), conifers pose no resistance to the angiosperms in the obvious, fertile places, yielding to the rout that sends them up into the craggy, isolated places. But when the angiosperms extend too far and produce dense overgrowth that leads to wildfires, the conifer follows them back, dumping their seeds on the newly vacated ground.

As the ground cools, conifer seeds from cones that survived the heat and flames begin to germinate in soil that has been enriched by nutrients released by the fire, and are soon joined by seeds blown by the wind from trees on the periphery and growing in the rocky, isolated areas beyond the reach of the fire. (A few species of conifer produce resin-coated serotinous cones that open only during a forest fire—the greatest fire opportunists of them all. For example, the lodgepole pine is a particularly prolific seed producer with serotinous cones that are retained in the canopy for many years; mature trees may hold well over 1,000 closed cones, and the amount of stored seed may number in the millions per hectare.[16]) In this scenario of forested *Schadenfreude*, fire is friend, not foe, to the patient conifer—nature's greatest opportunist.

Although some angiosperms will also move into the cleared area and spring up quickly, conifers can often gain a roothold over this initial competition and, in time, develop into a largely homogeneous forested stand. Thus, as biologist and conifer expert Aljos Farjon wrote, it is the nature of the conifers "to outlive their neighbours and occupy their living space . . ."[17] The very strategy of their growth exploits opportunities brought about by shifting ecology, climate, and the system's mechanism of adaptation through internal adjustment and discovery, in pursuit of homeostasis.

Along the Porcupine River in Alaska, it is water, not fire, that creates opportunities for the conifers to spread. The slow, meandering river cuts back the forest on the outer bends and then deposits the sand, gravel, and clay on the inner bends, new soil for new growth. Fast-growing willows and poplars may seed first along the river, but eventually spruce trees native to the area make their way into the new ground. It is not that the climate is disadvantageous to the angiosperms. Rather, a slower rate of seedling establishment and growth results in favorable timing for the spruce, enabling these conifers to eventually gain an edge in the forest succession. The longer they live and the more numerous they become, the spruce alter the conditions of light and soil in their favor, and thus become dominant. Over time in this northern ecosystem, these conifers replicate the dense growth that can be found in the surrounding homogeneous forest.[18]

Some have compared the roundabout strategy of the conifers that eventually gain at the expense of the initially more aggressive and direct angiosperms to Aesop's fabled race between the tortoise and the hare. But it is really a refined version, call it the tortoise-that-morphs-into-a-hare; in our fable, the tortoise doesn't remain slow, but rather builds his strength and gradually accelerates—the strategy of the conifer. (An impressive example can be found among the giant sequoias of California that experience an *increased rate of growth* even after maturing to towering heights over 200 feet, compared to much younger trees in the species.) Another apt image is found in the *Laozi*, reminding us, once again, that "soft and weak vanquish hard and strong," with a highest efficacy that is like water.[19]

It is because water benefits everything . . .
Yet vies to dwell in places loathed by the crowd
That it comes nearest to proper way-making.
In dwelling, the question is where is the right place.[20]

A LOGIC OF GROWTH

As we have seen, it is not that the forest would somehow be better off with only conifers and no angiosperms. Rather, a give and take, a search and discovery process, an adapted alertness to opportunities—and always emanating from the imbalances of states of rest—must be allowed to unfold naturally in order to create the most efficient balance of available resources between them. In the forest system, advantages are not static, but emerge and change with time. Within parts of an established forest, angiosperms may take over for a certain period, while conifers become roundabout, thus losing and bearing the cost in the immediate of giving up the fertile, most desirable places ("loving to lose, hating to win"). Then wildfires or other disturbances stop the angiosperms' lead in the race, creating openings for the opportunist conifers, gaining by losing, followed eventually by even more sprinting angiosperms. In the alternation of the flow of resources as the ecosystem discovers the right mix over time there is a logic of growth.

Maladjustments result in a world of change; indeed, they lead naturally to that very change, setting in motion forces that will eventually eliminate and correct them. In the forest, maladjustments (overgrowth, susceptibility to predators) presage change in the system. Alternation in the search for balance is the rule of nature—neither order nor disorder—which we can grasp only by seeing the entire process, with its many interconnected intermediate steps.

The conifer's faster and more efficient later-stage growth is a tremendous productivity advantage; and it would be perhaps insurmountable were it not for the angiosperm's equally potent counteracting check—a progressive tax, as it were—on the time it takes the conifers to reach that later stage. In the productivity of the conifer's roundaboutness, of efficiencies gained at the expense of the immediate, is the logic of growth for the forest; its realization is in the forest's succession, which rewards the waiting game. Nature's progress, her secret, is in her depth of field, implied in the roundabout path of the conifer, the directional choices that lead right in order to proceed more effectively left.

Through this pedagogy from an ancient tree we best build our understanding of this central roundabout strategy, a universal lesson taking us from the boreal forests to, as we will see, the canonical military strategists stretching across 20 centuries from China to Prussia, and leading us to the great economic thinkers of late nineteenth-century Austria. But perhaps it will still be in the conifer that we see it at its most poignant, in the simple pinecone, and the forest yet to be.

Chapter Three

Shi

The Intertemporal Strategy

Across more than 2,000 years and 4,000 miles, two hideously violent yet highly creative epochs in human history—the Warring States Period of ancient China and the military conquests of Napoleonic Europe—shaped the political landscapes of their times and gave rise to what have become two canonical texts of a universal strategic methodology: the *Sunzi*, attributed to a Chinese general known as Sun Wu (or Master Sun), and *Vom Kriege* (*On War*) by the Prussian major general, Carl von Clausewitz.

Traditionally, but erroneously, they have been positioned as contrasts, completing each other "like a perfect couple formed of opposites,"[1] not only chronologically but philosophically. *Vom Kriege* has been typically viewed—particularly by its most vehement critic, English military historian Sir Basil Henry Liddell Hart—as advocating total war waged through the most deadly means of direct confrontation, while the *Sunzi* avoids destructive clashes whenever possible and, instead, subdues the enemy through indirect means such as manipulation and deception.

Within what is the greatest and most efficacious of human strategic thought is a common thread that, though winding and tangled, will lead us to an understanding of how it is applied in other realms of human endeavor with complex objectives—the most significant of which, I would argue, is capital investment (specifically the methodology of

Austrian Investing).The thread shows us a metasystem, perhaps obvious, though nonetheless difficult to implement, of intertemporal exchange, the pursuit of an intermediate state whose efficacy furthers the realization of a desired final state, instead of just charging ahead toward a final state alone.

Recent examinations of the two works reveal strategic commonalities between the voluminous *Vom Kriege*, whose meanings must be carefully extracted out of its convoluted prose, and the almost cipherlike, highly nuanced *Sunzi*. There are obvious connections: Both are about war, the deadly preoccupation of the human race and completely anathema to the advancement of civilization, and both carry their authors' unblinking realism about the bloody and destructive nature of warfare. Moreover, these two preeminent military strategists were products of their times. Neither armchair theorists nor instigators of conflict, they were nonetheless immersed in the warring culture that surrounded them. Not surprisingly, their works are required reading today at such institutions as the U.S. Military Academy at West Point. (Ask any student of military strategy what languages one must know to read the classics in the original and the answer will invariably be Chinese and German—the latter, I would also add, is singularly necessary for that of economics.)

Beyond these similarities, there is a deeper and far more important thread between Sun Wu and Clausewitz. Both recognize that not all battles are decisive; rather, it is far better to deploy the roundabout strategy—that which we have discussed thus far—of patiently achieving an intermediate *position of advantage*, the teleology of efficacious means toward realizing an eventual, final objective. Clausewitz used the framework of *Ziel, Mittel, und Zweck*—a strategically circuitous path from the intermediate aim (*Ziel*) of subordinate commanders as the means (*Mittel*) for the strategists to obtain the ultimate end (*Zweck*). Sun Wu employed the same intertemporal approach—indirect now in order to be direct later—summed up in a single word: *shi*, by which the wise general gained a strategic advantage over his enemy, "intervening upstream before the conflict unfolds and thus without having to join serious battle subsequently,"[2] as a means of ending and even avoiding battle. As the *Sunzi* states, "To win a hundred victories in a hundred battles is not the highest excellence; the highest excellence is to subdue the enemy's army without fighting at all."[3]

Ambiguous and imprecise, *shi* (pronounced like the affirmative "sure") has no formulaic translation into English, but rather is defined with a cluster of meanings; among them are potential, disposition, configuration, influence, and, most important to the military theorist, *strategic advantage*[4]—which can be extended to *positional advantage* or *advantageous deployment*. We might call it cultivating the influence of the present on the future. These multiple definitions are not choices from which to pick and choose, but rather parts of a much larger, complex whole. The etymology of the Chinese logogram for *shi* (势) is a pairing of what is thought to be a hand holding an object—meaning "to sow, to plant, to cultivate," including "the cultivation of artistic talents and skills,"[5] and in some interpretations what is held is seen as a clod of earth, indicating something being put in position—with that of force or *li* (力). A homonym for *shi* (in an oral tradition, they would essentially be the same word, and in fact are often used interchangeably) brings in a temporal association, as in "opportunity."[6]

The potential of concentrated energy is embodied in the image of the dragon, another *shi* motif that is also commonly used in Chinese symbolism. As *shi* imagery, the dragon dynamically and strategically morphs from water creature to sky dweller, able to take a concrete form and then diffuse into misty vapors.[7]

Although a rather common term in Chinese culture and not given any particular philosophical significance, *shi* is the defining concept of the *Sunzi* (not to mention, along with the analogous *Ziel, Mittel, und Zweck*, of this book). To the militarist, *shi* conveys the importance of gaining influence through "nonintervention" and "nondeployment"[8] to ultimately secure battle advantage. Thus, the circuitous *shi* is to the *Sunzi* as the roundabout *wuwei* is to the *Laozi*. Indeed, *shi* becomes the strategy of *wuwei*, as the *Laozi* states, "marching without appearing to move."[9]

Shi, as positional advantage, overlaps the concept of *hsing*, strategic positioning; or, as we might say, *shi* is the greater superiority gained through *hsing*. D. C. Lau, a leading translator of Daoist texts, has observed that there are passages in the *Sunzi* in which the two terms are near-synonyms.[10] The strategic positioning (*hsing*) of troops is most prominently compared in the *Sunzi* to the positioning of pent-up water in a mountain stream; in its potential is *shi*: eventually gushing downward, carrying boulders as it plunges in a powerful yet effortless surge, ultimately overcoming everything in its path. The sage acts by "positioning himself upstream from its full deployment."[11] (Paradoxically, water is one of the softest and yet strongest forces in nature.)

Shi can also serve as a tool in the same way that a handle makes an axe so much more effective.[12] The intermediate advantage is in both the tools and their assembly—their "purchase" (another meaning for *shi*)—the configuration of assets into the means of an ultimate objective. (An asset need not be physical or material; it can be a state, as in an advantageous readiness.)

Strategic positional advantage is never fixed, but emerges *intertemporally* through roundabout means amidst fluid and shifting factors—the enemy's strategic position, the rise and fall of the terrain, light and dark, cold and heat, sun and fog. With awareness of all these elements, the commander must move only when they are in optimal alignment—and actively seek a position of their optimal alignment.[13] The *shi* of Sun Wu was to "make the most of the strategic advantage" and "if there is no advantage, do not move into action."[14] This may mean "occupying the key passes and lying in ambush"; when there is no such terrain, one must "hide in the shadows and the mist" and "go by way of places that would never occur" to the enemy, and thus catch him off guard.[15] Just as in *tuishou* ("push hands"), the objective is to wait for the attainment of a position from which one can exploit an imbalance within one's opponent, which will make the ultimate rout all the more effective.

The central *shi* concept can also be found in *Vom Kriege*, in the deployment of military forces toward a *Ziel*, or aim, itself a *Mittel*, or means, along a roundabout path toward eventually reaching the *Zweck*, the ultimate end. For example, Clausewitz advocated weakening the enemy first at certain "focal points," instead of expending resources (especially one's soldiers) by battering against entrenched defenses in the all-out attack (*die Schlacht*, or "slaughter"). This common thread, therefore, effectively ends the debate that has raged across centuries, and alters perceptions that saw the *Sunzi* and *Vom Kriege* as polar opposites. The two generals, one Chinese and one Prussian, are not philosophical opponents, but strategic doppelgänger.

Clausewitz, certainly the greatest of all military strategists, provides us with further clues and perspective for studying the strategy of war to glean insight into other complex human pursuits. As he wrote in

Doppelgänger Sun Wu and Clausewitz

Vom Kriege, "We therefore conclude that war does not belong in the realm of arts and sciences; rather it is part of man's social existence. War is a clash between major interests, which is resolved by bloodshed—that is the only way in which it differs from other conflicts. Rather than comparing it to art we could more accurately compare it to commerce, which is also a conflict of human interests and activities; and it is *still* closer to politics, which in turn may be considered as a kind of commerce on a larger scale."[16]

The teleological means-end framework is indeed implied in the *shi* approach (and there are some, with a too-simplistic view, who would take issue with this) of accumulating upstream strategic and advantageous means, tangible and intangible, so that the final end can best be served. Thus, the overarching concepts and keywords are *shi*, the very manifestation of the *Dao*, and its German equivalents of *Ziel, Mittel, und Zweck*, all of which become central to *The Dao of Capital*.

To further our understanding, we must again travel back in time, first to ancient China and an era of philosophic diversity, during which emerged a Daoist general who rightly became one of the most celebrated military minds.

THE DAO OF SUN WU

From Qi on the Yellow Sea to Qin on the plains to the west, seven Chinese feudal states battled for dominion during the aptly named Warring States Period, from 403 to 221 BCE. Military service became obligatory for all men, and by 300 BCE, regional warlords mobilized armies numbering in the hundreds of thousands of drafted foot soldiers. As war raged among the semiautonomous states, traveling military strategists offered their expertise to the feudal rulers; among those itinerant experts was said to be a general from the state of Wu named Sun Wu, who later became known as Sunzi or Master Sun. The quintessential warrior-philosopher, Sun Wu personified his times when political survival was paramount and warfare, by necessity, became "applied philosophy."[17]

Like the *Laozi*, the *Sunzi* (also known as *The Art of War*) came from an oral tradition, which makes authorship cumulative over time, thus calling into question the historic validity of Sun Wu as the sole source of the text and spawning theories that there may have been more than one Master Sun. Translated first from Chinese into French by a Jesuit missionary in 1772, the *Sunzi* has since been published in most of the world's major languages. Its wide-reaching sphere of influence (along with that of *Vom Kriege*) spans Mao Zedong (though many attach his "guerilla strategy" to the *Sunzi*, he was actually closer to European strategists), Henry Kissinger, the Soviets, and the Vietcong. (And, of course, it had been superficially applied in business management in ways that quickly became cliché.)

With deep knowledge of highly effective military campaigns, Master Sun knew how to turn soldiers into a disciplined army, and an army into an efficient fighting machine. One story told about Sun Wu, although considered more legend than fact, tells of his service to a warlord from Wu state: Asked to demonstrate his skill as a military leader, Sun Wu agreed to train the ruler's harem of concubine as soldiers, and divided the 180 women into two battalions, appointing the two favorites as commanders.

But when his orders produced giggles instead of strict compliance, Sun Wu ordered the execution of the concubine-commanders. Although the warlord protested and suddenly lost interest in this war game, the rest of the harem began to follow Sun Wu's orders without question.[18] (Daoists are certainly not all pacifists.)

Sun Wu was the genesis of the indirect approach and demonstrated mastery of being *direct within the indirect*, constructing and seizing upon those opportune moments when it is, indeed, time to act. His was a strategic thought of inherent (though not explicit[19]) means and ends through the efficacy of the setup. Thus, who will win and who will lose are less a matter of chance. As the *Sunzi* states, "The task of a good general is to calculate in advance and with accuracy every factor, so that the situation develops in a way as beneficial as possible to him; victory is then simply a necessary consequence."[20]

Even better, though, in the eyes of Sun Wu is the wise commander who, in recognizing the destructiveness of war, establishes positional advantage and thus uses threat, manipulation, and deterrence to subdue the enemy and convince the opponent to withdraw or surrender without coercion. The commander "takes the enemy's walled cities without launching an attack, and crushes the enemy's state without a protracted war"[21]—winning without fighting. These words echo *wuwei* and the *Laozi* (itself a military and political treatise): "I dare not make the first move but would rather play the guest; I dare not advance an inch but would rather withdraw a foot."[22] Moreover, rather than ascribe war to the *Sunzi* and more philosophical matters to the *Laozi*, we recognize that warfare was the source of this philosophy, a response to this horrific period during which strategic thought sprouted from the fertile soil of the contemptible battlefield.

In his conduct of war, perhaps the Daoist (and thus the naturalist) Sun Wu drew inspiration from the conifers, which retreated to unwanted territory that then became their strategic outposts (marching "through territory where there is no enemy presence," attacking "what the enemy does not defend," and defending "where the enemy will not attack"[23]). And perhaps this reveals Sun Wu's call to see the "seed"—"even before it has grown."[24]

Yet, when the opportune moment to strike appeared, there was one weapon, one of the premier technological innovations of the age, which changed the way war was waged: the crossbow, which in its potential and intermittent force embodied *shi*.

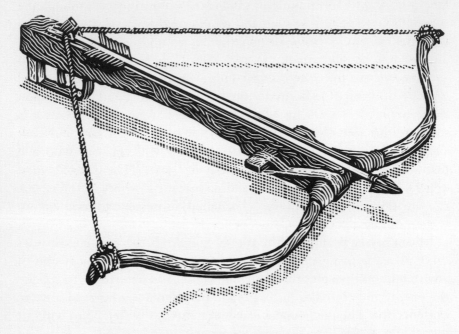

Crossbow, Introduced to China circa 500 BCE

SHI AND THE CROSSBOW

Most likely introduced into China by non-Han people as early as 500 BCE, the crossbow became widespread by 200 BCE. In Sun Wu's home state of Wu, elite troops wore heavy armor and helmets, strapped spears to their backs and a sword at their waists, and carried a crossbow and 50 arrows on their shoulders as they marched as many as 50 kilometers in a day.[25] The archers set their arrows on the horizontal stocks of their crossbows and drew the bowstrings taut (it is thought, using their legs and foot stirrups to brace the bow). Then, they were "at the ready," fingers on the trigger mechanisms, which would release the coiled energy, producing enough power and velocity to pierce the armor and shield of an enemy a hundred paces away, while the archers remained well beyond the reach of the opponent. With the crossbow, proximity became an important factor of battle, in both time and space, as one could suddenly kill effectively at a distance from out of nowhere, and thus the setup and its efficacy became the aim. As Sun Wu said, "That a bird of prey when it strikes can smash its victim to pieces is due to its timing. So it is with the expert at battle that his strategic advantage . . . is channeled and his timing is precise."[26]

No such advantage came from a head-to-head clash of swords, an aggressive face-off between opponents. *Shi*, though, was found in the loaded crossbow and was personified by the archer, who did not rush into action, but, instead, employed time and positioning until the optimal moment to unleash. (Here, again, as we saw with Zhangsanfeng and *taijiquan*, is explicit reference to the control and coordination of a predator with its intended target, the tactical feint and sudden strike of a snake.)

So important is an understanding of *shi* that the Pentagon, in reports to Congress just a few years ago on the People's Republic of China, used *shi* to explain that country's "grand strategy" of maintaining balance among competing priorities for sustaining momentum in economic development, and maintaining favorable trends in the security environment within which such development can occur (more evidence that the *shi* concept can be most confounding). A report from the Office of the U.S. Secretary of Defense, while noting a lack of a direct Western translation, defined *shi* as a "strategic configuration of power" and as roughly equivalent to an "alignment of forces," as well as potential and propensity, which "only a skilled strategist can exploit."[27]

To summarize, a *shi* strategy boils down to acquiring positional advantage and superiority for an easier, if not assured, victorious fight to follow. *Shi* is always focused more on the future than the current moment, an emphasis on "upstream," intermediate aims, or intermediate foci within the field, becoming means, and by which the ultimate ends can be more readily achieved. The path to victory, therefore, is reduced to the essential element of adhering to *shi*, an intertemporal advantage, instead of the headlong rush into conflict, an approach known as *li*.

LI—THE DIRECT PATH

Everything has its opposite; alternation occurs between distinct but complementary pairs. In the *Dao*, *yin* (unseen, hidden, passive) balances and is balanced by *yang* (seen, light, active). The antithesis to *shi*, the intermediate and circuitous, is *li*, the immediate and direct. As the "all or nothing" of a pitched battle, *li* seeks decisive victory in each and every engagement (the "false shortcuts" denounced by the *Laozi*[28])—a model of warfare "bequeathed to us by the Greeks,"[29] of Hannibal, the great Carthaginian commander, a perspective of finality that correlates closely with *li*'s attempt to win now (what some call a very Western world view).

In contrast, *shi* can be likened to a journey made up of many steps, across a depth of field, from one step to the next. It unfolds like a Daoist "scroll on which a path running up a mountainside (and thereby giving it consistency) appears at one point, then disappears around the hill, to reappear even further on."[30]

The forward-looking *shi* strategist takes the roundabout path toward subtle and even intangible intermediate steps, while the *li* strategist concentrates on the current step, the visible power, the direct, obvious route toward a tangible desired end, relying on force to decide the outcome of every battle. Simply stated, *li* goes for the immediate hit, while *shi* seeks first the positional advantage of the setup. The former is the aggressor racing against time and who in his directness risks becoming overextended, stretched too thin, and thus vulnerable to the counterattack. The latter, the nonaggressor, with no need to rush, puts time on his side, even to the point of ceding an unimportant clash now in order to come back all the stronger later on.

SHI AND *LI* AT THE *WEIQI* BOARD

Perhaps the clearest and most pedagogical example of the contrast between *shi* and *li* strategies is in *weiqi* (pronounced "way-chee"— roughly meaning "encircling game"), more commonly known as *igo* or simply *go* (its Japanese name). Originating as many as 4,000 years ago in China, making it the world's oldest existing board game, *weiqi* teaches lessons in strategy and geopolitical diplomacy. (According to legend, *weiqi* was invented by an emperor to enlighten his son on the same.) Just as the *Sunzi* advocates a *shi* strategy to overcome an enemy gradually, enabling victory without making every battle decisive—through softness rather than through hardness—the same approach is deployed

Shi versus Li

Shi	Li
Roundabout, intertemporal	Direct, atemporal
Emphasis on means	Emphasis on ends
Patient, nonaggressive	Impatient, aggressive
Seeks to secure future advantage through immediate objectives	Focuses on immediate results rather than accumulating means
Counterforce	Force
Subtle, intangible	Dramatic, tangible
Outcome of most battles immaterial	Outcome or every battle decisive
Progress is continuous	Progress is sequential
Focused more on cause	Focused more on effect
Ziel, Mittel	*Zweck*
Wuwei	*wei*

with great effectiveness in *weiqi*. Learning the game of *weiqi* instructs and practices the specific strategic and operational ideas of the *Sunzi*, and provides insight into its philosophy, stratagems, and tactics.

How the game of *weiqi* unfolds is illustrative of *shi* versus *li* thinking, which can even unintentionally set up an "east versus west" contrast in philosophy and in war and diplomacy. Author and *weiqi* expert Peter Shotwell notes that *li*, as a general term, "can mean a direct profit-oriented *yang* strategy," one that "gets things done," while *shi* "is a *yin* strategy that prefers to go for influence at the expense of immediate profit or advantage."[31] *Shi* is intertemporal; *li* is myopic.

Weiqi is played on a board marked with a 19 × 19 grid (smaller boards for beginners may be 9 × 9 or 13 × 13). Representative of the earth, then thought to be flat, the board has a square shape that symbolizes stability and four corners that stand for the seasons. Stones are used as game pieces, one set black and the other white; their round shape connotes mobility, while their uniform size shows them to be equal in power with no differentiation among them.[32] (The contrast with chess is obvious, from its complicated hierarchy of pieces to its relatively direct pursuit of total annihilation.)

In essence, *weiqi* is a simplistic game, yet out of that simplicity comes great complexity and sophistication. *Weiqi* is, in fact, the most calculated of games. The exponential explosion of possible permutations of future moves and scenarios in the "look-ahead tree" is yet too many for the best optimizing computer player to defeat the best human—unlike in chess; rather than sequentially thinking ahead many moves, in *weiqi* the best strategy comes through backtracking, inverting the problem from a decisive positional advantage at the end to the present means to that end.

The object of the game is to surround the most territory on the grid. At the start, the board is empty. The player with the black stones plays first, placing a piece on the board at any intersection where two lines cross. Players then take turns putting stones on any unoccupied intersection. If a player manages to occupy all the "liberties" or intersections around an opponent's stone or group of stones, that stone or group is captured. At the end of the game, the player whose stones encircle the most intersections, netted against stones captured by the opponent, wins.

Given the objective, an obvious initial strategy is to dive for the corners of the board, the quickest territory to surround (since the sides of the corners already provide half of the enclosure). Going for a solid, immediate gain, however, is typically suboptimal in *weiqi*; a *shi* strategy is the preferred approach, with the patient accumulation of influential positions that create future potential and relative advantage,[33] rarely obvious at first, but emerging slowly over time.

In Figure 3.1 (depicting the first 11 sequential moves in a game), both black (moves 1 and 3) and white (move 2) play a very standard "star-point" opening. The divergence in their strategies emerges when white (move 4) does not respond in kind to black's move with a stone in an open space on the board; instead, white remains in the same corner in hopes of establishing immediate points. With its subsequent plays (moves 6, 8, and 10), white seals off its corner, but in so doing allows black (with moves 5, 7, 9, and 11) to create enormous potential to eventually surround much of the vast territory in the middle of the board. Black, employing the indirect and circuitous *shi* strategy, seeks future opportunistic potential. They are truly playing two different games that are not even against each other; black competes not against the position of white's stones, but rather against a future position of white's stones.

Such advantage, however, will not be obvious at first. On a larger scale, it is in fact an exceedingly difficult intertemporal tradeoff: At first

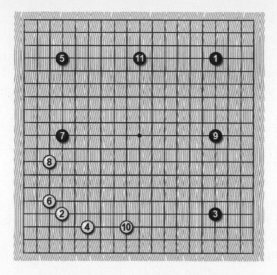

Figure 3.1 *Shi* **(Black) versus** *Li* **(White) on the** *Weiqi* **Board**

black will appear to have captured no territory at all and, indeed, at the end of this sequence has scored no sure points; white, though, has 30 unassailable points, which seems to validate its *li* approach—but the allure is only in the immediate, the tangible. Black's current position will likely eventually amount to 50 points, which would be an extraordinary lead. (Competitive *weiqi* matches typically come down to very low single-point spreads.) White's territory is far more assured, but black's is greater. This was the cost for black's lead: an immediate payment in exchange for the edge further down the road. Black has essentially husbanded his resources, withdrawn them in order to assert them more decisively later—when black's subsequent moves in the center will have much support. It is an intertemporal tradeoff of aiming at a means to a greater end, rather than directly at the end—it is the roundabout way.

We can see, too, in the *weiqi* match that the means of positional advantage provide for the opportunism of decisive blows that occur toward the end (in what might even appear as a surprising "tail event" to someone watching the scoreboard only—see Chapter 9). Indeed, it is the whole point of the *shi* approach, the whole point of the difficult sacrifice of the immediate. Within *shi* is *li* (just as within *shi*'s logogram is *li*). After being loaded and drawn, the crossbow must be fired (because if it were never fired, it would not be *shi*).

In the opening sequence in Figure 3.1, we see in the *weiqi* board perhaps the purest example of *shi* that I could ever imagine—*shi* in its perfection. Real-world examples are everywhere, but much subtler. What is clearest in this ideal is that *shi* actually requires *li* in the opposition in order to be effective; it is the hungriness and immediacy of the latter that provides the edge to the former (much like Lew Burdette from Chapter 1). A *weiqi* match between two opponents employing the same such strategy is a far different game altogether (and far more difficult, for black).

A COMMON THREAD, FROM EAST TO WEST

From the culture and philosophy of ancient China, we move on to Napoleonic Europe, which, like the Warring States Period, saw bitter battles for domination and advancements in the art and technology of warfare. And, like ancient China, this era in European history had an incomparable military scholar and scribe: Carl Philipp Gottlieb von Clausewitz. (There is confusion around the spelling of Clausewitz's names, but we will follow what is written on his tombstone.) Clausewitz was a child of war, born in 1780, at a time when revolutions reshaped the political landscape of Europe and North America and gave rise to despotic powers in the person of Napoleon Bonaparte. At the age of 13, Clausewitz entered the Prussian Army as a *Fahnenjunker* (cadet), and by 1793-1794 was part of the Prussian forces in the First Coalition against Napoleonic France. (The Prussian ruler Frederick the Great had kept the officer corps free of commoners, thus Clausewitz and his brothers could only be accepted as officer cadets after the king's death in 1786. Although born into a middle class family, as opposed to the aristocratic "Junkers," Clausewitz and his brothers eventually became generals and thus rightfully earned the nobiliary particle "von" that their father added to the family name, perhaps with a fictitious claim to some ancient noble tie. In 1826, the family's right to the claim of nobility was affirmed.[34]) In 1801, Clausewitz was admitted to the war academy in Berlin, from which he graduated at the top of his class in 1804 and was made an aide-de-camp to Prince August of Prussia. It was also during this time that he met his future wife, a noblewoman considered well above his station in life, Countess Marie von Brühl.

A lifelong military officer, Clausewitz followed in the boot steps of his father, Friedrich Gabriel Clausewitz, who had entered the Prussian Army as an officer-cadet in 1759 and fought in the Seven Years' War (1756–1763), which embroiled Prussia, Great Britain, and their allies on one side, and France, Spain, and their allies on the other. War spread over parts of Europe, Africa, India, North America (where it became known as the French and Indian War), South America, and the Philippines.

Upheaval and revolutions followed the Seven Years' War, as the established European powers suddenly appeared vulnerable to attack. The American colonies broke from Great Britain, thus inspiring the French Revolution; the overthrow of the French monarchy was a watershed event that forever changed Europe. Blood ran in French streets as the monarchs and their supporters were executed by *La Guillotine* before the crowds. Chaos and bloodlust created a vacuum into which strode a French military officer, a Corsican born of parents of noble Italian ancestry, who had successfully led military campaigns for the French— Napoleon Bonaparte. In 1799, Napoleon installed himself as first consul following a *coup d'état;* in 1804, he crowned himself emperor.

Despite his hatred of Napoleon, Clausewitz studied him and even admired his military tactics; Napoleonic battles would later serve as a centerpiece of Clausewitz's opus, *Vom Kriege*. But the defeat of Napoleon was nothing less than Clausewitz's life's work. (Ironically— since it might have saved him much trouble—it is safe to assume he never read the *Sunzi*, simply because Clausewitz despised all things French and refused to speak the language, the only one from Europe into which it had been translated by that time.)

Politically, in response to Napoleon's attempts to plant the French flag over much of Europe, alliances and empires were formed. In 1804, to counter Napoleon, the Austrian Empire (which had been preceded by the Habsburg dynasty's Holy Roman Empire) was born; it included all or parts of what are today Austria, Croatia, the Czech Republic, Hungary, Italy, Poland, Romania, Serbia, Slovakia, Slovenia, and the Ukraine. Austria and Prussia overcame a long-standing conflict over which should be recognized as the legitimate force among German-speaking people. Although they had opposed each other during the Seven Years' War, Austria and Prussia improved relations to the point that both countries were able to cooperate during the Napoleonic Wars. (Their common antipathy toward Napoleon's aggression was embodied in a one-time admirer, the inimitable Ludwig van Beethoven—from Prussia but residing in Austria—who originally dedicated his Third Symphony as the "Bonaparte Symphony," but became so enraged by Napoleon's self-coronation that he vigorously scraped the name from the title page of the score, and renamed it "Eroica.")

For the ever-decisive Napoleon, timing was everything in his conquests; as he reflected, "I may lose a battle, but I shall never lose a minute."[35] Napoleon's basic strategy was one of upsetting the enemy's balance so that once the equilibrium was broken, the opponent became an easy defeat. He plied this strategy against Austria, France's most determined opponent, by positioning northern Italy (termed "the junior partner") as the corridor to get to Austria ("the senior partner"); after that, Spain and Italy would then quickly follow. His plan worked: "By drawing Austria's forces into successive offensives against him in Italy, and defeating them there, he gained, 12 months later, an open road into Austria."[36]

Clausewitz received a firsthand view of Napoleon's strategy in a battle against French forces in 1806. Prussian soldiers were overpowered, and Clausewitz and Prince August were captured. Held in captivity in France and Switzerland, Clausewitz's imprisonment gave him time to write, deepening his understanding of what he recognized as the essential differences between the French and the Prussian armies as they waged war. He went so far as to level sharp criticism against his own country and its military leadership, while recognizing that Prussia had faced a formidable adversary in the strong Napoleonic army. Yet, Clausewitz could not help but conclude that French victory "was due less to modernity or numerical weight than to Napoleon's genius abetted by the 'intellectual poverty' and moral cowardice of his opposition."[37] (Clausewitz's criticisms of the Prussian military were considered so inflammatory that they were not published in Germany for nearly 70 years.)

Clausewitz's captivity lasted until 1808 when he returned to the Prussian Army as an assistant to General Gerhard von Scharnhorst, who is credited with the creation of the modern general staff system—and Clausewitz, in turn, was credited with helping to reorganize the army whose structure and leadership he had so pointedly criticized. In 1810, Clausewitz was appointed a professor at the academy of war in Berlin; also that year, he and Marie married, apparently having overcome her mother's reservations about the suitability of the match. Letters chronicling their courtship showed another side of Clausewitz, far different than the cold-hearted military strategist as he is sometimes seen to be. In love, Clausewitz became a poet, clearly influenced by the Romantic Era, which valued aesthetic experience, intuition, and emotion, rather than the rationality of the Age of Enlightenment that was associated with the French Revolution.

In war, though, Clausewitz became consumed with the art and science of the military campaign (*Feldzug*, as he called it), committing not only his intellect, but also his philosophical nature as well. He was clearly influenced by the German philosophers of his time, especially the great Immanuel Kant, from whom he learned two forms of truth: formal and material. In *Vom Kriege*, he brought both together and used logic to produce abstractions, while remaining very much opposed to learning from history—understanding that, particularly on the battlefield, no circumstances or events are ever the same. Thus, Clausewitz can be seen as Kantian (while in substance, perhaps, one should say he was more like Wilhelm Friedrich Hegel, who played a major role in establishing German Idealism).[38] As biographer Peter Paret wrote of Clausewitz, "German philosophy gave him the means of subjecting war to logical inquiry."[39]

In his conviction to put a stop to Napoleon's conquest for total control of Europe, Clausewitz was a man of action. When Prussia refused to fight France due to a short-term alliance between the two countries, a disgusted Clausewitz joined the Russian Army in 1812 (a foray that earned him a brief mention in Leo Tolstoy's *War and Peace*, about the French invasion of Russia). However, his actions took him forever out of favor of the Prussian king, Friedrich Wilhem III, who thenceforth viewed him as a mutineer and revolutionary, even after the alliance with France ended and Clausewitz was reinstated in the Prussian army in 1814.

When Prussia waged war against Napoleon, Clausewitz served under the command of General Johann von Thielmann at the Battle of Wavre of 1815, the last major military action of the Hundred Days' Campaign and the Napoleonic Wars, in which Prussian troops dealt a decisive blow to Napoleon's forces, thus preventing additional French soldiers from joining the fight at Waterloo.

After Waterloo, a defeated Napoleon was sent into final exile on the island of St. Helena in the south Atlantic, where he died in 1821. As for

Clausewitz, despite a promotion to the rank of major-general in 1818, he, too, faced a banishment of sorts as he failed to curry any favor with the king: He was assigned to a desk job at the war college, an administrative post he would occupy for the next 12 years, and was expressly forbidden by the king to make any changes in the curriculum of the academy. Thus, as one historian wrote of him, "Clausewitz, the man of fire, was reduced to tending embers."[40] (He would have most happily retired to a country farm to peacefully write, were it within his means.) Those long years at the war college, however, allowed Clausewitz to spend hours each day contemplating his boundless notes from the front and composing them (in many cases more than once) into an exhaustive, if perhaps sometimes discordant, compilation.

In 1830, Clausewitz finally saw military action again, with an appointment as chief of staff as the Prussian Army mobilized on the Polish border, in response to a crisis in Poland and unrest elsewhere in Europe that raised concerns of another major European conflict. When cholera broke out in the region in 1831, Clausewitz commanded the army's efforts to construct a sanitary zone to contain the deadly disease, but soon fell victim to it. Upon returning home, his spirits and his health seemed better for a short time, and he and his wife passed eight days together; on the ninth, he fell ill again, showing signs of cholera, and, at the age of 51, died after apparently suffering a heart attack. Following his death, Marie, assisted by her brother and two of Clausewitz's friends, arranged for the publication of his writings, with the first manuscripts appearing in 1832, and several more to follow before Marie's death in 1836. (Unfortunately, for all her devotion to her husband and his work, Marie was not a professional editor, as the uneven, disjointed, and incomplete manuscript attests.) Following Marie's death, the last two installments of Clausewitz's writings were published.

AN ATTACK OF MISUNDERSTANDING

Despite the genius of Clausewitz's insights (military historian Ralph Peters called *Vom Kriege* "one of the most enduring texts of the era, save only Goethe's *Faust*"[41]), in its unfinished state it became one of the most misunderstood books of the last two centuries. Quoted by many but read by few, *Vom Kriege* has been the target of misinterpretation and caustic attack. Clausewitz's most notable and vocal critic, Liddell Hart, waged a war of words against *Vom Kriege* with his own work, *Strategy: The Indirect Approach* (first published in 1954, 101 years after Clausewitz's death). An English infantry officer who had been gassed during World War I, Hart had retired from the army as a captain in 1927 and spent the rest of his career as a military writer. (At one point, he worked out for himself the plans for D-Day and wrote a critique of them, which he circulated among military officers and politicians, thus prompting Winston Churchill to call for his arrest for treason and suspicions of being a Nazi sympathizer. Instead, Hart was kept under surveillance, but later was exonerated and then knighted in 1966.)

In *Strategy*, Hart cast Clausewitz as an "apostle of total war,"[42] blaming him and his ideals for the carnage of the Western Front, asserting that European commanders had followed Clausewitz's dogma in the conduct of the Great War, which claimed more than 16 million military and civilian lives, making it one of the deadliest in human history. Such assertions against Clausewitz stemmed from his use of the word *Gewalt*, or force, (the German equivalent of *li*), giving the appearance that he advocated the use of direct assault in a pitched battle. As Hart asserted, "Accepting the Prussian philosopher of war, Clausewitz, as their master, they blindly swallowed his undigested aphorism such as—'The bloody solution of the crisis, the effort for the destruction of the enemy's forces, is the firstborn son of war.' 'Only great and general battles can produce great results.' 'Blood is the price of victory'."[43]

As a rebuttal to Clausewitz, Hart offered what he called the "indirect approach" to military strategy, believing it to be far superior to the direct assault that depletes the attacker and strengthens the resistance of the attacked. An indirect assault on a strategic point, Hart argued, weakens the opponent and thus avoids the high casualty rates that result from an all-out offensive against the enemy's entrenched positions. Hart's indirect approach was meant to discredit Clausewitz, whom he portrayed as advocating the "straight-ahead bashing of armies in battles to the death."[44] Hart's view, however, was skewed to the point of inaccuracy—and dare I say he got Clausewitz precisely wrong. In "Notice of 19 July 1827" in *Vom Kriege*, Clausewitz describes two kinds of war: one to overthrow the enemy and the other to occupy some frontier districts to be annexed or used for bargaining during peace negotiations. Hart also failed to recognize in *Vom Kriege* the "dual nature of war," on one hand "absolute" in its violent tendencies and, on the other, "limited" by the political aims of those who use war as a political tool. Such duality of linked but disparate concepts—strategic/tactical, absolute/limited, attack/defense, and so forth—were part of the philosophical arguments of Clausewitz's time.[45]

Thus we can side with Clausewitz's defenders and their more recent analyses; the blame for the massive armed clashes and carnage of the Great War (as well as even of the wretched Nazis, who also revered him) cannot be laid on Clausewitz, but rather on the generals and commanders who interpreted and applied his theories for their own purposes. (If Clausewitz is at fault at all, it is because of the difficulty of understanding his text.)

ON WAR—AN INDIRECT STRATEGY

Clausewitz's *Vom Kriege* is a dialectic approach to war, starting with the most basic premise, with a first chapter entitled "What is War?" In it, he rejected "the abstruse definitions of war used by publicists," and offered instead the image of two wrestlers. "Each strives by physical force to compel the other to submit to his will: his first object is to throw his adversary, and thus to render him incapable of further resistance."[46] (Was Clausewitz, too, using *tuishou* as his central metaphor?) He later describes military engagements—through *handeln*, which today refers to an exchange or trade—as preliminary, in order to acquire an advantageous position:

> Things which cannot be regarded as the destruction of enemy's force, but only leading up to it certainly by circuitous road, but with so much the greater effect. The possession of provinces, towns, fortresses, roads, bridges, magazines, &c., may be the *immediate* object of a battle, but never the ultimate one. Things of this description can never be looked upon otherwise than as means of gaining greater superiority, so as at last to offer battle to the enemy in such a way that it will be impossible for him to accept it. Therefore all these things must only be regarded as intermediate links, steps as it were, leading up to the effectual principle, but never as that principle itself. [47]

Handeln were the "building blocks" of war, both the immediate aims and the "springboards" toward the ends.[48] Thus war was conducted through the interplay of tactics and strategy. (In reading Clausewitz, it is often difficult to say where his tactics stop and strategy begins. Given the weighty oftentimes incoherence of the tome—Clausewitz used a type of German that favored the past tense and produced long, confusing sentences—it becomes impossible and even irrelevant to say.) In his study of strategic military history, he concluded that Swedish King Gustavus Adolphus, fighting in the Thirty Years War, 1618–1648, was the first to demarcate, in practice, strategy from tactics, making him the father of military strategy.[49] (Having never read the *Sunzi*, Clausewitz was wrong, of course.)

To Clausewitz, the method of war was the employment of the available means for the predetermined end,[50] an Aristotelian teleological framework made Clausewitzian with his additional concept of *Ziel*, the intermediate aim. Clausewitz's *Ziel* made clear that the very purpose of battle was not in achieving the ends of victory, the triumphant reward, but rather in acquiring the means to the ends. Thus, the aim of the battle was not absolute victory, not the ultimate end of peace; the aim of the battle was the means it afforded toward that ultimate objective. As these means are often far removed from the ends, both in time and space, they are often exceedingly indirect—the very paradoxical "indirect efficacy" of the *Sunzi*[51]—and the path to Clausewitz's decisive victory in war is a protracted, roundabout path. He understood what it meant to go right in order to go left more decisively. (One cannot help but think back to the conifers' withdrawal to the rocky, isolated places so that they might one day occupy the fertile land from which they retreated.)

Even ultimate ends identified by Clausewitz had a nested relationship, as the *Zweck* of winning the war was subordinate to a higher *Zweck* (the goal or end, also translated as "purpose") of a lasting peace. (Such higher-order ends were known as "Grand *shi*" to the Daoists.) When Clausewitz spoke of absolute war, it was not as an advocate for the bloody conquests of annihilation. Rather he cautioned that a final peace must be ever-present in the mind, moving backward from that end and focusing on the intermediate positioning to achieve it, *die Mittel* ("means," also translated as "instrument")—just as the *Sunzi* instructs to "go back" to the "subtle" earlier steps to determine that which "makes victory easy to win."[52] (Many translations have been less than rigorous in the distinctions between *Ziel* and *Zweck*, calling them aims, objects, ends, and goals. Thus, there has been ambiguity among these terms as presented by translators that Clausewitz never intended.)

Another concept of Clausewitz's roundabout approach (and also gravely misunderstood) is the *center of gravity* (or *Schwerpunkt*). The center of gravity can best be thought of in mechanical terms, using a physics analogy (which was Clausewitz's intent), as a "focal point." Such junctures become balance points; as modern military strategists have described, "providing a certain centripetal, or center-seeking, force" and thus perform a "centralizing function that holds power systems together and, in some cases, gives them purpose and direction."[53] The center of gravity strategy required the concentration of force in time and space, "at the right place and the right time," at the "decisive point"[54]—a major intertemporal theme of Clausewitz (like Sun Wu, "in the meantime, from a great distance, he arranges the conditions for success"[55]). This was Clausewitz's strategic end (leading to peace), the accumulated and pent-up military potential finally emitted in a torrent (or, better yet, not at all). He was very much against spreading forces thinly over a large area of engagement, preferring them to stay together, and instead aimed to separate the enemy's forces as a key positional advantage from which to strike its center of gravity. The *shi* in this approach should be obvious.

The source of confusion around Clausewitz's center of gravity concept stems from the interpretation of these focal points as sources of strength. However, in his original German text, it has been noted, Clausewitz did not refer to a source, or *Quelle*, of strength; rather he wrote about the *Gewicht*, or "full weight" of the enemy's force, that could be traced to as few centers of gravity as possible, and areas in the enemy's configuration where there was *Zusammenhang* (or interdependence) between various parts.[56] A decisive blow to the center of gravity would ostensibly cause the enemy's entire structure to collapse, lessening or even eliminating the need for further assault; thus Clausewitz (like Sun Wu) shows his preference for striking when the configuration is optimal, so decisively (or threateningly) that violence then becomes unnecessary.

An analogous concept was the Clausewitzian "balance of power," which emerges spontaneously and operates like a law of nature. In the balance of power, Clausewitz observed the interaction of war and politics, whereby an aggressor nation upsets the balance of power and then expends its resources, stretching them too thin in an assault on an entrenched opponent. Thus, aggression is actually a disadvantage, while nonaggression accrues a decided advantage, as the defender then "reaps where he has not sowed," as Clausewitz wrote, alluding to the Bible's "Parable of the Talents" from Matthew. "Every suspension of offensive action either from erroneous views, from fear or from indolence, is in favour of the side acting defensively."[57]

From aggressor to nonaggressor, offense to defense, war is not a continual siege, but a succession of movements between tension and "states of rest" (Clausewitzian terminology which anticipated verbatim the Misesian). During periods of tension, different gradations of immediacy exist between the aggressor who seeks to act now and the nonaggressor who gains by waiting. When the aggressor's movement has been exhausted, what follows is a "state of rest," a pause or equilibrium, which will lead to a new tension—"in most cases in the opposite direction."[58]

Clausewitz emphasized an intertemporal strategy, particularly in the deployment of troops to gain the all-important setup for the eventual "decisive point," concentrated in time and space. At the onset of battle, he advised, which begins with a "wearing-out exchange of fire" designed to inflict casualties, a general should seek to minimize early losses, "husbanding reserves" until the point when the balance shifts, and the battle escalates.[59] Clausewitz gave the example of two armies of 1,000 soldiers each. One side, however, sets aside 500 to deploy in a subsequent stage and sends 500 into immediate battle against the 1,000. Each side is assumed to suffer 200 casualties (the 1,000 are a bigger target, but fire more shots). But the smaller army gains the advantage when the 500 fresh troops it had "husbanded" in reserve enter the fight, facing a battle-weary, overextended opponent. Although the numbers of troops are now equal (each side has 800), it is now an uneven fight, as the previously smaller, yielding army emerges with the advantage. The nonaggressor becomes the aggressor, and nonaggression trumps aggression—later; the soft overcomes the hard. Gaining superior positions from which to subsequently fight more effectively was, in fact, his method, through "delayed riposte." It was a matter of intertemporalizing the fight into two phases of blow and counterblow: "waiting for a blow and then parrying it (*Abwehr*)."[60] He simplified it as "*Beati sunt possidentes*": Blessed are those in possession.[61] Clausewitz thus sums up the intertemporal tradeoff with a very effective argument for cultivating one's resources now (upstream)—even if it entails a retreat—for strategic advantage later (downstream): "In this way it becomes evident how the employment of too many forces in combat may be disadvantageous; for whatever advantages the superiority may even give in the first moment, we may have to pay dearly for in the next."[62]

Such was Napoleon's grave error in his invasion of Russia in 1812: the deployment of great masses of troops, the *li* without the *shi*. Instead of achieving victory, Napoleon's *Grand Armée* was routed.

SHI, ZIEL, MITTEL, UND ZWECK

As the two great masters of the battlefield, Sunzi and Clausewitz, teach us, victory lies at the very end of a roundabout path. In their now-snarled Chinese-German: It first aims for the positional advantage of *shi*, a *Ziel* that is the *Mittel* for an ultimate *Zweck*.

Here, too, we find the Austrians, with their singular focus on roundabout means (or "capital") that serve the attainment of a distant end. As Ludwig von Mises himself observed, "The result sought by an action is called its end, goal, or aim. One uses these terms in ordinary speech also to signify intermediate ends, goals, or aims; these are points which acting man wants to attain only because he believes that he will reach his ultimate end, goal or aim in passing beyond them."[63] The danger of not viewing things through this lens of means and ends is assigning an erroneous value on any given link in the chain. If we perceive things as separate—in essence, mistaking *Ziel* for *Zweck*—we focus only on the immediate, what can be seen, and we lose our depth of field. We lose any appreciation for that which cannot yet be seen.

Now, with our understanding of *shi* and of *Ziel, Mittel, und Zweck*, we are ready to exit this span of two millennia and the great strategists who marked it, and move from Prussia to emerging *fin-de-siècle* Vienna, Austria (with a detour through France), a stone's throw in distance and only a few decades hence, until we finally reach a great school of thought, whence Austrian Investing ultimately takes shape.

Chapter Four

The Seen and the Foreseen

The Roots of the Austrian Tradition

First there is the *seen*, visible and immediate, that which is most easily grasped. Then there is the *yet unseen*, what comes next as the consequence of the former, realized in the latter—which can, indeed, become the *foreseen*. Herein, we find a time sequence, a sequential seen and unseen—not to be confused with the concurrent seen and unseen, one visible and one hidden. To emphasize, our focus is on the temporal, on an extended depth of field from the immediate to the intermediate and beyond. With the foreseen—a key concept that comes to us from Frédéric Bastiat, a proto-Austrian economist and a key figure of this chapter—moving from proximate to ultimate, the future becomes clearer, even obvious, but not because of prediction, the stuff of naïve data analyses and mathematical models. One cannot learn from history, *a posteriori*, because causal relationships are deceptively veiled from our perception (what is unfortunately termed the "teleological fallacy"). Rather, in many cases the foreseen emerges through the logical rigor of deduction, based on what one knows (and, to some degree, what one observes and experiences) as a sentient human being.

The bridge from the seen to the foreseen is crossed purposefully, via a teleological path of means and ends—our familiar *Ziel* as *Mittel* to achieve a *Zweck*, the common thread of the Clausewitzian strategy. Means are teleological; that is to say, means are tools used in service of a *telos*, an end or goal. The more disparate these means and ends, the more roundabout and circuitous the route as opposed to direct, often the more efficient and efficacious—a fundamental conviction and investment theme of this book. In this thought paradigm of seen and unseen, and the teleology of means to a purposeful end, we find the Austrian School of Economics and its unique methodology that is grounded in deduction, *a priorism*, and the subjectivity of human preferences. The Austrian tradition, established in the late nineteenth century by Carl Menger, forever changed the map of economic thought; its intellectual epicenter was the University of Vienna (a position later tentatively assumed by New York University following an exodus of Austrian economists from Austria, as we will discuss in Chapter 7).

Before Menger, however, there were forerunners, the "pre-Austrians" who, while not entirely "Austrian" in their thinking (nor in their nationality), did help to lay its foundational, teleological roots. These precursors and early influencers include A. R. J. Turgot, who published his free-market views before Adam Smith's *Wealth of Nations* appeared, and Jean-Baptiste Say, who expounded upon Smith's ideas with clarity and readability, which made Say's works highly popular; Thomas Jefferson had the first English edition translated in 1821. Say, however, was more than just an interpreter of Smith's ideas. Notable differences exist between their views, and Say was critical of Smith and pointed out inconsistencies in his thinking. For example, Say brought the entrepreneur into the spotlight of economic thought (he is said to have invented the term, which literally means *undertaker*—which the Austrians call *Unternehmer*—with the connotation of one who undertakes an adventure[1]), whereas the entrepreneur had been absent in Smith. (Although the Austrians generally acknowledge Smith for his free-market stance, he has been rejected by some, most notably by Murray Rothbard, for unwittingly providing ammunition to the Marxists, who also hail Smith as a founding father. For many Austrians, the free-market lineage begins with Turgot and Say.)

Say also intersects our historical timeline that, in Chapter 3, brought us into Napoleonic Europe. Say served as a member of Napoleon's

100-member Tribunat assembly, until his criticism of government policies led to his ouster and the banning of his writings—part of Napoleon's crackdown against the ideologues whom he had once embraced. Nonetheless, Say's famous economics *Traité d'économie politique* (Treatise on Political Economy) was published in 1803 and, despite Napoleon's edict, went through four editions in Say's lifetime. Of particular interest in our discussion here is Say's successor and champion, the French economist and writer Claude Frédéric Bastiat who is, himself, an important forerunner of the Austrian School due largely to his attacks against government interventionism, which he launched as effectively as any general.

Before we leave military strategy behind us, it is worth contemplating why I treat it as perhaps the seminal thought on the means-ends framework of human strategic endeavor. I do not pretend to make warfare a metaphor for entrepreneurial competition (as Clausewitz did), nor is *tuishou* such a metaphor. Indeed, warfare and entrepreneurial discovery are antithetical. Bastiat, himself, reminds us of the inconsistencies between war and commerce: "Let us, then, cease this childish practice of comparing industrial competition to war; whatever element of plausibility this faulty analogy has comes of isolating two competing industries in order to determine the effects of their competition. As soon as one introduces into this calculation the effect produced upon the general well-being, the analogy breaks down."[2] (While Bastiat and Clausewitz were contemporaries, despite their shared teleological approach they surely shared antipathy toward each other due to their antimilitarism and Francophobia, respectively.)

Entrepreneurial competition betters the world (though, paradoxically, most often at the expense of most of the competitors); warfare destroys the world (also at the expense of most if not all the competitors). But the historical development of strategic thought we are following, specifically teleological thought, leads us to our central means-ends duality of Austrian Investing itself. We understand the universal efficacy of indirect means and, with it, the dominant role of time. Because of this universality we needn't concern ourselves with the particulars that differentiate each instance. Sadly, warfare has been all too much the story of human history. Perhaps the advent of advanced capitalist systems will diminish this; perhaps this is a naïve thought. Nonetheless our understanding of capitalist systems, of unobservable cause and effect amid the ruckus of random data, and ultimately of effective capital investment, owes much to this—and in fact requires—universal teleological thinking of means and ends, seen and foreseen.

THAT WHICH MUST BE FORESEEN

Frail and sickly for most of his life, Bastiat, who died before he reached the age of 50, may seem to be an unlikely forerunner for such an enduring economic movement as the Austrian School. Yet his life experiences provided a powerful vantage point from which to produce universal and timeless economic treatises. Born in 1801, Bastiat was orphaned at nine and raised by his paternal grandfather; by age 17, he was working in the family exporting business in Bayonne, France, where he saw clear evidence that the French government's protectionism did not bring prosperity; rather, it led to the unemployment and poverty that were all too visible in the city that drew its lifeblood from trade. Without restrictions, as Bastiat could foresee, trade would flourish among all parties, a perspective that would form the basis of his most eloquent and compelling economic arguments.

At the age of 25, Bastiat inherited the family's estate upon the death of his grandfather, which allowed him to pursue the life of a country squire and scholar. (When the Bourbons were expelled from France in 1830, Bastiat led a troop of 600 young Frenchmen to a royal fortress. No battle or glory ensued; rather, it was a quick surrender and then an invitation to come inside for dinner.[3]) A gentleman farmer, he experimented in scientific agriculture, such as crop rotation to preserve soil fertility, and hired tenants to run the farm. But Bastiat, who confessed to caring little for money, soon retreated from the daily workings of the farm to immerse himself more deeply in the world of ideas and books. Yet, living as he did on a country estate, Bastiat remained close to the land, and as such his perceptions gained clarity. What farmer sees only the apparent barrenness of a newly planted field—again Sunzi's call to see the "seed . . . even before it has grown"?[4] Would he not, like Klipp, be far more inclined to see the uncarved block, and foresee the advantages to come in the yet-unseen succession of crops? Would he not grasp and appreciate the farmer's tools as the very literal and tangible means to the desired ends of many years' harvests—the very seeds of which are the "ingredients" for next year's crop?

Bastiat: The Country Squire and Scholar

In the natural world, Bastiat also recognized an order that spoke to him of how markets and exchanges among people should be allowed to function freely, as the superior mechanism by which to pursue satisfaction of one's wants. Even apparent inequalities, the pursuit of which counterintuitively equalizes them, point to a higher order of ends pursued through intermediate means—all for the good of the beneficiary of capitalism, the consumer. As Bastiat wrote in *Economic Harmonies*, "Competition must necessarily intervene, called into being, as it is, by the very fact of these inequalities. Labor instinctively moves in the direction that promises it the best returns, and thus unfailingly brings to an end that abnormal advantage it enjoyed; so that inequality is merely a spur that, in spite of ourselves, drives us on toward equality. This is one of the finest examples of *teleology* in the social machine."[5]

Bastiat further showed his proto-Austrian nature by describing economics in distinctly praxeological terms (praxeology being the study of human action), as societies in which people "assist each other, work for one another, render reciprocal services, and place our faculties, or the results of their exercise, at the disposal of others, in consideration of a return." Individuals, like countries, are not solitary; indeed, their very survival depends upon interaction. Bastiat used such universal logic against the protectionists who "would reduce men, like snails, to a state of absolute isolation."[6]

In his early days, Bastiat expressed his profound ideas in one-on-one conversations, his favorite form of communication and persuasion. His closest friend was Felix Coudroy, a young intellectual and fellow gentleman farmer from a neighboring estate. A recent graduate of the law school in Toulouse, Coudroy was a socialist steeped in Jean-Jacques Rousseau, whose political philosophy influenced the French Revolution. Two more opposed opinions are hard to imagine; over time, though, Bastiat converted Coudroy to classicial liberalism. Bastiat chafed at arguments that power in the hands of the state was meant for the good of all, and mocked such thinking by wryly envisioning a beneficent state to dispense "bread for all mouths, work for all hands, capital for all enterprises, credit for all projects, salve for all wounds, balm for all sufferings, advice for all perplexities, solutions for all doubts, truths for all intellects, diversions for all who want them, milk for infancy, and wine for old age—which can provide for all our wants, satisfy all our curiosity, correct all our errors, repair all our faults, and exempt us henceforth from the necessity for foresight, prudence, judgment, sagacity, experience, order, economy, temperance and activity."[7] The mere notion of it collapses under the weight of its absurdity.

After years of developing his arguments, Bastiat took them to a broader audience, publishing his first article in April 1834—an entreaty to abolish all tariffs—followed by a second essay opposing taxes on wine, and a third against taxes on land (unapologetically self-servingly, no doubt) and opposing trade restrictions. When his unsolicited manuscript on French and English tariffs was published in the prestigious *Journal des Economistes*, Bastiat established himself as a strong proponent for free trade and economic freedom, and a bulwark against a rising tide of protectionism. Writing profusely, Bastiat published a collection of his articles in his first book, *Economic Sophisms*, which is still considered to be the best literary defense of free trade. It was followed by his true opus, *Economic Harmonies*, in which he argues that the interests of all members of society are harmonious if private property rights are respected. In his view, the primary role of government was to uphold rights to life, liberty, and property, and to prevent injustice.

When Bastiat was penning his economic treatises in France in defense of free trade, Karl Marx was living in London, writing his *Communist Manifesto* and *Das Kapital* and promulgating socialist theories of class struggle and exploitation of workers in a capitalist society. (Marx regarded Bastiat as "the most 'superficial' apologist of the 'vulgar economy'"[8]—surely a compliment for Bastiat, from his biggest detractor whom he held in equal contempt.) By leading the charge against Marx (which would be taken up most effectively by the Austrians, the chief enemies of the Marxists), Bastiat set forth in his *Economic Harmonies* that both capitalists (entrepreneurs) and laborers benefit from free enterprise. "This Economic Harmony, then, may be thus stated: By labor the action of man is combined with the action of nature. Utility results from that co-operation. Each man receives a share of the general utility proportioned to the value he has created—that is to say, to the services he has rendered; in other words, to the utility he has himself produced."[9] With his view that accumulation of capital enriches workers as well as the factory owners, through greater productivity, higher wages, and cheaper goods (all of which would come to pass in industrialized economies as if from Bastiat's script), Bastiat's thoughts are aligned with what would later emerge as Austrian capital theory. He also struck a blow against the socialists for their pursuit of an artificial organization, out of their belief that the natural organization of society is somewhat lacking or insufficient because of "antagonism" between capital and labor, producer and consumer. The only real antagonism as Bastiat saw it was among "two principles that can never be reconciled—Liberty and Constraint."[10] He saw as "the obvious deduction" the "harmony of interests between laborers and those who employ them."[11]

In 1848, revolution again gripped France to end the monarchy that had been reestablished post-Napoleon, and France's Second Republic was formed. Bastiat was elected to the National Assembly and became vice president of the finance committee. There, he was remembered as "a stooped, thin figure sitting on the left, among the liberals and radicals, opposite the conservatives on the right" (the origin of right and left in politics).[12] Although vehemently opposed to the socialists and communists, he was nonetheless more at home on the left than the right as he argued against government interference. (Bastiat foresaw, correctly, the end of the Second Republic due to its economic policies, believing that support of protectionism meant favoring scarcity over abundance.)

What is arguably Bastiat's best-known work was a pamphlet entitled *Ce Qu'On Voit et Ce Qu'On Ne Voit Pas*, (That Which Is Seen, and That Which Is Not Seen), written in 1850. (It was nearly not to be; the manuscript was lost during a move, and Bastiat had to rewrite it. He burned the second attempt that dissatisfied him, and finally completed a new draft just months before he died from tuberculosis at age 49.[13] Had he not recreated the essay, the world would be without not one but two classics of economic thought: Bastiat's and Henry Hazlitt's *Economics in One Lesson*, which expands upon it—my and surely many others' introduction to Bastiat and, ultimately, the Austrians.) Through a series of economic parables, using counterfactual comparisons of free trade and interventionism, Bastiat draws the reader's attention from only the seen to what is yet unseen, but which can be foreseen. As Bastiat wrote, "In the department of the economy, an act, a habit, an institution, a law, gives birth not only to an effect, but to a series of effects. Of these effects, the first only is immediate; it manifests itself simultaneously with its cause—*it is seen*. The others unfold in succession—*they are not seen*: It is well for us if they are *foreseen*."[14] The dilemma, as Bastiat correctly pointed out, arises when favorable or unfavorable ends, whose obvious means (and their natural time element) are neglected, are thus not foreseen.

This ability to look beyond the obvious of the immediate seen and to foresee its later outcomes was, in Bastiat's view, the true differentiator. "Now this difference is enormous, for it almost always happens that when the immediate consequence is favorable, the ultimate consequences are fatal, and the converse. Hence it follows that the bad economist pursues a small present good, which will be followed by a great evil to come, while the true economist pursues a great good to come, at the risk of a present small evil."[15] In his language of "series of effects" and "a small present good" that is followed by "a great evil to come," Bastiat elevates the temporal, and with it the disdain for immediacy, the atemporal. Coupled with this is the importance of deductive foresight, a "more gentle teacher" than the far rougher one of inductive experience, which "teaches effectually, but brutally." The key is to free oneself from a tyranny of first consequences, overvaluing what comes first at the expense of what inevitably comes later. As Bastiat warned, "The sweeter the fruit of habit is, the more bitter are the consequences."[16] As we will see later in the book, in this we glean the very essence of Austrian Investing.

Through his writings, Bastiat gained the wide respect of his contemporaries, becoming one of the most influential economists of the nineteenth century, as evidenced by invitations extended to him to contribute further to the *Journal des Economistes* and efforts to have him appointed to the first university chair of the political economy in France. The 1852 edition of the *Dictionnaire d'Economie Politique*, published two years after his death, was dedicated to him. (Had he lived longer, who knows how great a contribution Bastiat could have made to economic thought, including clarifying his earlier ideas.) For all his insight, though, Bastiat's skill as a writer eventually led some to not take him seriously; even some of those who were more positive toward him regarded Bastiat as more of an aggregator of previous ideas than a trailblazer. (Economist Joseph Schumpeter called him a "brilliant journalist but no theoretician."[17]) Apparently Bastiat was too understandable and concise for those who viewed pomposity and obtuseness as true brilliance. His fate reminds us that "no man is a prophet in his own country, even among the international guild of economists"[18] (which, as we will discuss, was certainly true of the Austrian School). Other notable later-day Austrian economists, however, have hailed Bastiat as one of the most important economists ever, as well as a "significant theoretician" who contributed to the theory of value.[19]

Bastiat explained and defended his style by saying "we always want to give complicated explanations to the most simple facts, and we think we are clever only by looking for difficulties where there are none"; he believed simplicity to be the "touchstone of truth."[20] Over time, however, Bastiat fell into obscurity, yet another victim of the Keynesian avalanche that would threaten to sweep away many a free-market advocate, and he all but disappeared from most economics texts, save a cursory mention. However, Bastiat had a place in the Austrian School, whose core elements of *a priorism* and praxeology he, in many ways, foresaw. (His name lived on, in particular, among the Austrians in The Circle Bastiat, established by Murray Rothbard and his closest friends in 1953 as a venue for intellectual discussion and camaraderie, which continued until 1959.) Although Bastiat may not be as appreciated as he deserves to be, it is well recognized that his work serves as an "intellectual bridge between the ideas of the pre-Austrian economists" and the Austrian tradition that began, officially, with Menger.[21]

Today, Bastiat is widely acknowledged to be a pre-Austrian; Menger, however, did not embrace him, as he did not share Bastiat's normative approach. Although that does create some tension in the Austrian economics narrative, Ludwig von Mises, himself, considered economic science to be neutral and objective, but yet he was polemical (understandable, perhaps, since he witnessed firsthand the horrors of the most extreme state interventionism in Nazism). In Menger's view, though, Bastiat was just as much an ideologue as any socialist, who started with preconceived value judgments and worked backward through economic analyses. Menger, Mises observed, "heartily disapproved of the interventionist policies that the Austrian Government—like almost all governments of the epoch—had adopted. But he did not believe that he could contribute a return to good policies in any other way than by expounding good economics in his books and articles, as well as in his university teaching."[22] Menger upheld economics as being *wertfrei*, or value-free and thus neutral and objective. Shades of this positive/normative dichotomy still exist within the Austrian School today. (It is also possible that Menger was mistaken in his judgment of Bastiat as not being *wertfrei;* indeed, should it be assumed that just because a doctor is passionate about funding cancer research he must follow subjective medical theories?)

Bastiat, in the tradition of Turgot and Say, is widely acknowledged to have contributed significantly to the methodology of the Austrian tradition, particularly with his extreme *a priorist* approach (which was most like that of Mises).[23] Thus, Bastiat helps lay the cornerstone of the Austrian *Weltanschauung*, a worldview which emphasizes the importance of the subjectivity and choices made by the "acting man"—the term that Mises would use in his *praxeology*. As Bastiat, a prototypical Austrian and "a praxeologist ahead of his time,"[24] observed: "Our theory consists merely in observing universal facts, universal opinions, calculations and ways of proceeding that universally prevail; and in classifying these and rendering them co-ordinate, with a view to their being more easily understood."[25] In his seen and unseen, Bastiat's legacy is to understand the economy as a series of intertemporal exchanges, the teleological connection of proximate means and ultimate ends, so that what we do and the tools we employ upstream (the *Ziel*, the strategic positional advantage) gives us greater efficacy later downstream (the *Mittel* to achieving a *Zweck*). Thus, our roundabout path continues, leading us now to the nexus of economic thought: nineteenth-century Vienna, and a charismatic and ambitious young economist and journalist, whose writings would make an indelible mark on this discipline and establish a school inadvertently as a namesake to his homeland.

AT THE VIENNESE CROSSROADS BETWEEN EAST AND WEST

Vienna has long been the "crossroads between east and west" (apropos, on the geographical journey of this book), as traders and crusaders passed through via the mighty Danube.[26] By the nineteenth century, among the conquerors of Napoleon, the Habsburg Dynasty basked in a golden age of its crown jewel: Vienna—the site of the world meeting to redraw borders and reconstruct Europe after the French defeat and surrender. As the third-largest city in Europe, behind London and Paris, it had become a center of liberty and with it the center of culture, music, art, politics, and intellectual pursuits. The dawn of a new era of achievement and grandeur was captured in the construction of the *Ringstrasse*, an elegant boulevard encircling the inner city district.[27]

(The city remains, in my estimation, the most eminent in the world.) One can imagine the likes of Gustav Mahler, the head of the Vienna Court Opera and one of the greatest composers who ever lived, strolling the streets of Vienna alongside equally significant scientists, philosophers, and economists—including, as we will discuss in this chapter, the founder of the Austrian School, Carl Menger. The flowering of thought in Vienna across disciplines provided the fertile ground that seeded the Austrian School at a unique time and place in history, as a renaissance in teleological thinking emerged, a means-ends framework aroused in the philosophy of Immanuel Kant. This included such diverse thinkers as German biologists, perhaps most notably Karl Ernst von Baer. But in Kant, Baer and his colleagues did not find a prescriptive approach to conduct research in natural science; rather, they grasped a clear synthesis of principles that linked teleology with mechanics.

A confluence of intellectual events—spanning Kant, Clausewitz, Baer, and, now, Menger—came together within a means-ends framework that acknowledged, as Menger wrote, "All things are subject to the law of cause and effect."[28] It would not be too far a stretch to imagine (as some notably have) that this commonality was, in part, because of the German language itself, which articulated clear distinctions between the proximate objective of *Ziel* and the ultimate end of *Zweck* (which Baer adamantly distinguished in Kant, no doubt having read Clausewitz from a few decades earlier), a distinction perhaps absent amid the "poverty" of other Western languages.[29]

Teleology's revival got its start in the natural sciences, as a group of German biologists recognized a purpose imputed in life forms, while also embracing quantitative, experimental science (the two not being mutually exclusive). This was the latest in the evolution of teleological thinking, which began with Aristotle and, by the Middle Ages, had come under the influence of Christian theology and its views of a divine plan in nature. Kant, however, ruled out such thinking. There were two forms of teleology: one theistic, with nature seen as directed by a master agent, and the other mechanistic, with a "cybernetic" (a scientific approach I will discuss in Chapter 8) functioning within individual organisms and species. While Charles Darwin, in his 1859 *On the Origin of Species*, did not specifically seek to counter teleology (in fact, in his time he was roundly criticized as a teleologist, which today has a more theistic meaning), his theory of evolution through natural selection had the effect of diminishing its influence. In fact, to Darwin the ideal of natural selection did not falsify the teleology of Aristotle and Kant, but rather supported it. Teleology introduces other forces into the natural world, in addition to the familiar physical laws.[30]

Meanwhile, Baer, who also rejected a theistic, anthropomorphic, and agent-based viewpoint in natural science, nonetheless offered a decidedly non-Darwinian view of evolution, grounded in Kant's "teleo-mechanism" framework. Baer saw teleological relationships as the basis for exploring the causal relationship between form and function within organisms and the natural world.[31] (This would also be taken up, for instance, by D'Arcy Thompson in his fascinating 1917 book *On Growth and Form*, which observed quantitatively consistent physical and mechanical rules of biological growth and evolution.)

From Kant, the German biologists acquired the importance of the original state that plays a determining role in later stages. Thus, as Kant argued, a higher form of organization cannot issue forth from a lower form; rather the higher form is encoded in the lower form. (This view is reminiscent of Stephen Wolfram's modern-day scientific approach, which assumes programmatically complex systems with "explicit evolution rules" instead of the random mutations of natural selection.[32]) Though such purposes are hidden from us, Kant nonetheless urged their assumption—certainly more conceivable within acting humans than biological systems. This thinking finds an important application in the embryological studies of Baer, who regarded the embryo as the most essential aspect of the adult animal, whereby "the animal develops in a pattern leading from the most universal and essential to the more specialized and individual characteristics."[33] In fact, universal characteristics, not the addition of new parts, lead directly to subsequent development and individuation; "in short, the future is at work shaping the present."[34] (Though we embark on another brief tangent into biology, following our discussion in Chapter 2 of conifer teleology, our roundabout discussion here is quite purposeful, as the means of demonstrating a very important end: In Kantian teleology is yet another expression of our universal stratagem of ascending stages—of acquiring later stage advantage through an earlier stage disadvantage— that transcends any one subject or school of thought. Its treatment by many disciplines underscores its importance to each one, including economics.)

THE TELEOLOGY OF BAER'S BUTTERFLY

The influence of the needs of the future on the present is no more eloquently illustrated, perhaps, than in the metamorphosis (or production) of the butterfly, which emerges later out of the caterpillar and its current structures and behaviors (most specifically, its ravenous appetite). It is once again the plodding conifer that accelerates to a sprint, our tortoise into the hare.

First, there are the fat-bodies of the caterpillar, a creature that to the untrained eye bears no resemblance to the ethereal version it will eventually become. Yet even in that lowly original form, it is uniquely endowed to become a butterfly. For instance, unlike most animals that assimilate the nutrition they need and excrete the excess, caterpillars store a portion of it in their digestive tract for later use during its chrysalis stage. When all is developed, the caterpillar loses its voracious appetite, seeks a place to spin its cocoon, and begins a metamorphic process that will transform its nervous system and produce wings, antenna, long feet, and other structures that are distinctive of the butterfly and not associated with the caterpillar.

The caterpillar retains the means in resources today, which are the ingredients that will produce the purposeful ends of structures tomorrow. In other words, the future of the butterfly influences the shape and development of the caterpillar. The fat bodies are drawn down to provide the necessary material to build out the structures that were present only rudimentarily before. As Baer observed, "How is it possible to mistake that all of these operations are ordered with respect to a future need? They are directed to that which is to come into being. Such a relationship was designated by the Latin philosophers a *causa finalis*, a cause 'which lies in an end or result'."[35]

Baer would have surely made a highly acclaimed Austrian economist, if not naturalist, biologist, et al. This remarkable teleo-mechanism of the caterpillar—like Robinson Crusoe, in his construction of a boat and net in a stage at which these tools are useless to survival and useful only in a stage to follow—is precisely the Austrian model of capital, production, and investing that will be our entire focus in Austrian Investing II (Chapter 10).

As in his embryological studies, Baer recognized these biological phenomena: that the means to what must be present later (e.g., in the adult) must first exist in the forerunner (the embryo). This pointed to the existence of a teleo-mechanical framework within biological organisms, a "harmony of nature" in which there exists mutual regulation, which could not be explained by chance (which Baer believed could lead only to destruction). This has been renamed *teleonomy*, or intermediate ends of necessity masquerading as rational agent-selected ends—again conflating *Ziel und Zweck*. (Here we see again Bastiat's unintentional "*teleology* in the social machine," as well as the theme of Norbert Wiener's later *Cybernetics*, as explored in Chapter 8.) Such harmonies might evoke a "Bach fugue or a Beethoven sonata," as they present "a grand, personal and somehow inspiring nature" as depicted by Baer.[36] Within this metaphor of the ultimate's influence on the proximate, the end that determines and directs the means, we also find the orchestration of the Austrian entrepreneur who by acquiring and assembling resources seeks to harmonize them into a desired final result of meeting the wants and desires of the consumer.

MENGER ESTABLISHES THE AUSTRIAN SCHOOL

It was never Menger's intent to cleave with the classical economists and establish a unique school of economic thought. Yet such was the result of Menger's prodigious scholarship that began, curiously, as a journalist, but became increasingly robust as a full-on economist and professor at the famed University of Vienna. Rothbard has noted that Menger didn't so much found an entirely new school of thought, as much as further develop earlier proto-Austrian (and even Aristotelian, but I have hopefully supported an argument for Laozian) thought that couldn't survive the classical school; thus is the ever-cumulative nature of human discovery.

He was born Carl Menger Edler von Wolfesgrün in 1841, the son of an old family in Galicia, part of the Austrian empire in what is now Poland. His ancestors included musicians and army officers, craftsmen, and civil servants; his maternal grandfather, a Bohemian merchant, had made a great deal of money during the Napoleonic wars, which he invested in a family estate where Menger spent much of his childhood. (Menger later dropped the nobiliary "von" from his name and shortened it considerably.) After studying economics at the Universities of Prague

and Vienna from 1859 until 1863, Menger went to work as a journalist. In 1866, he left the *Wiener Zeitung* newspaper where he worked
as a market analyst and began to prepare for his oral examinations for
a doctorate in law, and then went to work as an apprentice lawyer in
1867—that same year, he received his law degree from the University of
Krakow. Soon thereafter, Menger returned to economic journalism and
helped found the *Wiener Tagblatt*, predecessor of the *Neue Wiener Tagblatt*,
which became one of Vienna's most influential newspapers.[37]

He forever changed the world of economics with the publication of his first book in 1871, a slim and narrowly read volume called
Grundsätze der Volkswirtschaftslehre (*Principles of Economics*). The book
grew out of his years as an economic journalist in Vienna, during which
time he discovered the importance of subjective demand in price determination. Specifically, Menger, as Austrian economist Friedrich Hayek
later observed, had been struck by the "glaring contrast between the
traditional theories of price and the facts which experienced practical men considered as decisive for the determination of prices."[38] His
attempts to resolve that difference led to the publication of *Principles*,
the dissemination of which was restricted by the author's perfectionist
tendencies as he later went through countless revisions.

His writing style, reflecting his journalistic background, was not
what people expected from a German scholar. Then again, Menger
was not a German, but an Austrian, and not even an ordinary Austrian
but a resident of Vienna.[39] Unlike previous German economics books,
Menger's *Principles* did not lean toward metaphysical existentialism
with a moral or religious framework; indeed, it was the first German-
language secular economics textbook.[40]

Menger's *Principles* coincided with two other independent, yet
simultaneous, discoveries of the principle of marginal utility (simply
stated, that people use means to achieve various ends, according to
their priorities) by William Jevons and Léon Walras. The objective of
Menger's work was to present a uniform theory of price with which to
explain all price phenomena and in particular also interest, wages, and
rent.[41] As Menger wrote in the preface to *Principles*, "I have endeavored
to reduce the complex phenomena of human economic activity to the
simplest elements that can still be subjected to accurate observation, to
apply to these elements the measure corresponding to their nature, and
constantly adhering to this measure, to investigate the manner in which

the more complex economic phenomena evolve from their elements according to definite principles."[42]

Unlike Jevons and Walras, Menger favored an approach that was deductive, teleological, and, in a fundamental sense, humanistic. While Menger shared his contemporaries' preference for abstract reasoning, he was primarily interested in explaining the real-world actions of real people, not in creating artificial, stylized representations of reality. Further demonstrating his teleological thinking, Menger saw the inherent means-ends relationship in human choice. Jevons and Walras, however, rejected cause and effect, which then became the standard in economics—except among the Mengerians and the Austrian School. Instead, Jevons and Walras opted for a "simultaneous determination" approach to find an economic equilibrium.

When Menger wrote his *Principles of Economics*, what followed was no less than a groundbreaking study of economics, particularly around the determination of value, which, as he saw it, must automatically take into account the usefulness (utility) of a thing in order for it to be considered a good. As Menger observed, "Our well-being at any given time, to the extent that it depends upon the satisfaction of our needs, is assured if we have at our disposal the goods required for their direct satisfaction."[43]

Evidence of Menger's teleological thinking can be found in his early notebooks, in which he recorded his activities and thoughts at various periods of his life, including his many influences. One of his notebooks, among the materials donated by his son to Duke University, shows a table of keywords that construct a distinct means-ends (*Mittel-Zweck*) framework for organizing his thoughts around economics; for example, the table (read vertically and horizontally) shows a good (*Gut*) as a means (*Mittel*) for achieving the satisfaction (*Befriedigung*) of a desire or need (*Bedürfnis*).[44]

Menger set forth four specific criteria, which had to be present simultaneously in order for a thing to be considered a good or, as he put it, to "acquire goods-character": a human need; properties that render a thing capable of "being brought into a casual connection" to satisfy the need; human knowledge of that connection; and "command of the thing" sufficient to satisfy the need.[45] Human well-being, then, was achieved through goods at our disposal for the direct satisfaction of our needs, thus highlighting the teleological thinking that satisfaction of the need (the end) is essential to the goods-character.

ZWECK	MITTEL	VERWIRKLICHUNG
(ends or goals)	(means)	(achievement)
MENSCH	AUBENWELT	LEBENSERHALTUNG
(human being)	(environment)	(subsistence)
BEDÜRFNIS	GUT	BEFRIEDIGUNG
(desire or need)	(good)	(satisfaction)

Yet goods that could meet our needs directly—what Menger called "goods of the first order"—were not the only things that possess "goods-character." Using the example of bread, a "first-order good," there are also other goods that meet consumer needs, specifically the flour and salt to go into the bread, and fuel to heat the oven. "We find that implements and tools for the production of bread, and the skilled labor services necessary for their use, are regularly traded. All these things, or at any rate by far the greater number of them, are incapable of satisfying human needs in any direct way—for what human need could be satisfied by a specific labor service of a journeyman baker, by a baking utensil, or even by a quantity of ordinary flour? That these things are nevertheless treated as goods in human economy, just like goods of the first order, is due to the fact that they serve to produce bread and other goods of first order, and hence are indirectly, even if not directly, capable of satisfying human needs."[46]

Furthermore, as Menger demonstrated, the value of these ingredients, the *factors of production* (used to make a final good), is always derived from the value of the consumer good, and not the inverse. (One example given is a bottle of wine that is not valuable because of the land and labor invested in it. Rather, it is because consumers value the wine that the land and the labor invested in winemaking are valuable.[47])

Menger also augmented Smith's declared central driver of "universal opulence," the economic progress of civilization and the extension of prosperity throughout. Smith saw this progressing division of labor as the driver. However, it was clear to Menger that this was "but a single cause of progress in human welfare"—that is, a proximate cause—whereas the higher level, ultimate cause was "the increasing employment of goods of higher order upon the growing quantity of goods available for human consumption (goods of the first order)."[48] This simple logic will become an essential piece of Austrian Investing.

In addition to his writing, Menger extended his influence, importantly, as a teacher (whose most notable student was Eugen von Böhm-Bawerk, who in turn, taught Mises—sequential growth in this school of thought). At the University of Vienna, Menger was part of the Department of Law and Political Science (economics was part of the law curriculum in Austria), first as a part-time unsalaried lecturer (the custom was for the students to pay the instructors directly) and then, by 1873, as a full-time paid professor. In his seminars, a select group of advanced students, including those who had already received their doctorates, assembled to debate the carefully prepared papers of one of the members. The students led much of the discussion, but Menger assisted greatly with the papers, including by opening to students his vast personal library of more than 20,000 books (now at the Hitotsubashi University Library in Tokyo). His tutelage extended to organizing the papers and discussing the main points, and even teaching them elocution and breathing techniques.[49]

His brilliant mind and his pedagogical gifts contributed to Menger's stature and soon he attracted the attention of none other than the Habsburg court, and in 1876, he took his most prestigious and influential teaching assignment: as tutor for the Crown Prince, Rudolf von Habsburg, the only son of Emperor Franz Josef I of Austria and Empress Elisabeth, and heir to the throne of the Austrian-Hungarian Empire.

TUTOR TO THE PRINCE

For the first three months of 1876, Menger gave the 18-year-old Prince Rudolf a crash course in economics, using Smith's *Wealth of Nations* as his primary text (Menger believed that Smith was sufficient to teach the prince *economic policies*, and that a deeper understanding of economic theories was unnecessary).[50] After each lecture, Rudolf was required to write extensive notes, produced entirely from memory, which Menger reviewed and edited. After the formal private lectures concluded, Menger stayed on with Rudolf, traveling with him throughout Europe

**Carl Menger: Scholar, Teacher, Writer, and Founder
of the Austrian School**

for the next two years; those conversations would change the course of history.

A staunch antisocialist in his personal views, Menger sought to counter what he saw as the destructive intellectual currents through which Prussian universities were spewing poison into the world.[51] The fight, though, was a futile one, and Menger became filled "with a dark pessimism," as Mises said of the Austrian School founder; he foresaw that the policies being pursued by the European powers would lead to a "terrible war ending with gruesome revolutions, the extinction of European culture and destruction of prosperity for people of all nations."[52] This gloomy foreboding was passed on to Rudolf, eventually leading to a tragedy of not only personal but, ultimately, global proportions, known as the Mayerling Incident.

On the morning of January 30, 1889, the bodies of 30-year-old Rudolf, who was married, and his 17-year-old lover, Baroness Marie Alexandrine von Vetsera, were discovered at the Imperial hunting lodge at Mayerling, in the fabled Vienna Woods, victims of a murder-suicide. With the death of the crown prince, the direct line of Habsburg succession was broken, and so would go to Franz Joseph's brother, Karl Ludwig, who quickly renounced the throne and soon thereafter died of typhoid fever, making the heir apparent his son, Archduke Franz Ferdinand. The transition in power upset the balance within the empire, and the resulting destabilization between Austrian and Hungarian factions escalated with the assassination of Franz Ferdinand and his wife Sophie by a Serbian nationalist at Sarajevo in June 1914—becoming, in essence, the first shots fired in The Great War.

In his *Memoirs*, Mises (whose grandfather had conversed with Menger's brother, Max) offered a startling perspective on Rudolf's death: Economics, not a love affair, caused Menger's pupil to kill himself. "The crown prince took his own life because of despair over the future of his empire and that of European civilization, not because of a woman. The young girl had a death wish of her own and he took her into death with him; he did not commit suicide on her account." For Rudolf, foreseeing destruction of all he valued led to despair and depression, Mises noted. Menger, at age 48, "barely had the first half of his life behind him" and had foreseen nothing less than "the inevitability of the demise of his own Troy," a pessimism that "consumed all the sharp-sighted Austrians."[53]

So what exactly had Menger taught Rudolf? The evidence came to light many years later when Rudolf's notebooks were published, which demonstrate the crown prince's nearly total recall of the material, and, more important, Menger's biases (which had been carefully cloaked in his published works) with regard to government policies, including radically noninterventionist statements that directly opposed the policies of the Austro-Hungarian Empire under Franz Joseph. Rudolf embraced these teachings and wrote articles under an assumed name that were critical of his father's policies.[54] The author's identity and Menger's influence apparently escaped the notice of the emperor.

Meanwhile, Menger's service as royal tutor had so impressed Franz Joseph that he approved Menger's appointment as the chair of law and political economy at the University of Vienna, a prestigious position that may have indicated he was being groomed to become prime minister (although the prince's death dashed any possibility of that occurring). Nonetheless, Menger enjoyed the life of a popular and well-paid professor until, suddenly, in 1903, he retired at the age of 63 (normal retirement age for professors was 70), and retreated to his library where he wrote and saw university students frequently. Although an unspecified illness was offered as the explanation, the truth of the reason for his departure was likely the birth of an illegitimate son, Karl, born a year and a half before Menger's retirement. Menger never officially married, but had a "common-law marriage" with Karl's mother, Hermine Andermann, who inherited his library upon his death. (Speculation is that Menger, a Catholic, could not marry Hermine because she was either Jewish or divorced; all marriages in Menger's time were religious ceremonies.[55])

In his seclusion amid his books, Menger threw himself into a complete and systematic revision of *Principles*, but as his scope of study and reading material expanded to philosophy, psychology, sociology, ethnography, and other disciplines, he apparently lost his way. Unsatisfied with his revisions, he continually postponed the publication of a revised edition, while the original *Principles* went out of print. Menger never allowed it to be reprinted or translated during his lifetime, believing it to be incomplete; *Principles* was not published in English until 1950, which greatly diminished the spread of his ideas. Fortunately, the works of his followers, especially Böhm-Bawerk's *Positive Theory of Capital*, were published and translated into English in the late nineteenth century, which as we will discuss in Chapter 5 advanced Menger's theories. Otherwise, the founder of the Austrian School could have faded into obscurity. Menger's legacy, however, extended far beyond one book to an entire methodology that set apart the Austrian tradition.

METHODENSTREIT

In his preface to *Principles of Economics*, Menger saluted German scholars in economics, offering his book "as a friendly greeting from a collaborator in Austria"[56]; not everyone returned the sentiment. By rejecting the slavish reliance on data that marked the German Historicists who engaged in lavish recordkeeping and classification of economic data, Menger took an entirely different approach that embraced universal economic laws, which he deduced from the law of cause and effect using means-ends reasoning. Menger was an antipositivist, although the full implication of his position may not have been realized at the time; thereby, he established the foundational Austrian tenet that economics is not a science derived from data, but rather uses *a priorist* methodology, grounded in observation and deduction of human action (thus opening the door for Mises's praxeology). In essence, Menger's *Principles* can be seen as "an exercise in pure theory."[57]

To their critics the Austrians and Menger were antiempiricists, which made them unscientific (certainly not a criticism to an Austrian). In a lecture on Menger and Böhm-Bawerk, Rothbard stressed that this aversion to mathematics was due to no lack of understanding; both men, indeed, were trained in mathematics. "They understood it all too well, which is why they rejected it," Rothbard said, referring to the use of mathematics in economic theory (certainly not a blanket rejection of mathematics, *per se*). As a result, "Austrian books read differently, look differently, smell different than the old, classical books. One thing, there's no math in them, or very little. They're clear, they're logical, they proceed step by step. There's no sort of sudden flights of abstract fancy not grounded in actual individual action."[58] Later Mengerians, most notably Mises, would be the ones to define the epistemological foundations of Austrian economics.

Menger and his followers were not opposed to using empirical methods to understand the economy. Their objective, as Mises observed, was "to put economic theory on a sound basis and they were ready to dedicate themselves entirely to this cause." The German Historical School, led by Gustav Schmoller, however, harbored a deep distrust of theoretical analysis, and its adherents "emphatically denied that there are economic theorems of such a universal validity."[59]

Although Schmoller's embrace of positivism may not have been explicit, his attack on Menger's economics—deriving universal laws using deduction without relying on empirical evidence and scientific induction—showed his alignment with positivist thinking. By responding to standard positivism, Menger effectively destroyed Schmoller's nuanced position.

Schmoller, himself, never offered a definition of positivism. For that, along with the inherent inadequacies of induction from historic experiences, we rely on the words of Mises in *Human Action*: "Historical experience as an experience of complex phenomena does not provide us with facts in the sense in which the natural sciences employ this term to signify isolated events tested in experiments. The information conveyed by historical experience cannot be used as building material for the construction of theories and the prediction of future events. Every historical experience is open to various interpretations, and is interpreted in different ways." In Mises's view, the "postulates of positivism" are "illusory"; one cannot study the science of human action using the same approach that applies to physics and natural science. "There is no means to establish an a posteriori theory of human conduct and social events. History can neither prove nor disprove any general statement in the manner in which the natural sciences accept or reject a hypothesis on the ground of laboratory experiments. Neither experimental verification nor experimental falsification of a general proposition are possible in this field."[60]

The conflict between the Mengerians and the German Historical School, known as *Methodenstreit* (the battle of methods), intensified with the publication of Menger's second book, with the catchy title *Untersuchungen über die Methode der Socialwissenschaften und der Politischen Oekonomie Insbesondere* (*Investigations into the Method of the Social Sciences with Special Reference to Economics*). Published in 1883, *Investigations* was more or less addressed to the German economists as a kind of "methodological house-cleaning" to rid the historical school of its antitheoretical stance.[61]

Unlike the friendly greeting of *Principles* extended to the German Historical School, *Investigations* was nothing less than a weapon wielded in a war between partisans[62] in the ongoing battle over social science and Menger's defense of the importance of theory and laws that are universal, independent of time and place. As Menger wrote, "The historical understanding of concrete social phenomena, however, is by no means the only thing that we can attain by way of scientific research. Rather, the *theoretical* understanding of social phenomena is of completely equivalent value and of equal significance."[63]

Reactions were mixed, from wholehearted embrace to vehement rejection, the most strident of which came from Schmoller, who penned a scathing review in which he dismissed *Investigations* ("We have finished with this book!") and claimed that Menger was devoid of a "universal, philosophical, and historical education, as well as a naturally broad vision," which would have allowed him to appreciate the historicists' viewpoint.[64] Menger replied with his own scornful verbiage, challenging "Schmoller, the methodologist" to "strike like a lion in the sands of the Spree" (a river in Berlin, where Schmoller taught at the university), "shake his mane, brandish his paw, and yawn epistemologically; only children and fools will take his methodological gesticulations seriously henceforth."[65]

This battle over economics revived old resentments, harkening back to Austria's defeat of Prussia in 1866, in the war against France. The Austrian-Prussian divide even led to fistfights between German and Austrian students at the University of Vienna.[66] (As for the rivalry between Menger and Schmoller, there was a comedic side in Menger's odd preoccupation later in life of collecting pictures of other economists to establish who had the longest beard. Just before his 70th birthday, Menger desired to have formal portraits of every economist in the world taken and sent to him in order to determine who was the most the amply whiskered, which Menger, the likely victor, upheld as the true measure of a professor's dignity. Not surprisingly, Schmoller and fellow German Historicist Franz Brentano, apparently still smarting from the *Methodenstreit* some 30 years before, refused to participate.[67])

Menger's break from the German Historicists spawned comments about the "Menger School," and then an "Austrian" or "Viennese School," a pejorative label applied by Schmoller meant to portray Menger and his followers as isolated and obscure. The Austrian School embraced it gradually, until Menger, himself, mentioned the *Österreichische Schule* in a newspaper article in 1889,[68] a distinction for the Austrian-born economists, who as time went on would leave their homeland that never embraced them. (The irony is that Austria is decidedly non-Austrian, economically speaking. As Mises observed, "Those whom the world called 'Austrian economists' were, in the Austrian universities, somewhat reluctantly tolerated outsiders."[69]) Years later, Mises would take on the historicists in his book, *Theory and History*, countering their view that economic theorems are void because they rely on *a priori* reasoning and that only historical experience is valid. As he wrote: "Such historical experience does not give the observer facts in the sense in which the natural sciences apply this term to the results obtained in laboratory experiments." He further criticized those "who call their offices, studies, and libraries 'laboratories' for research in economics, statistics, or the social sciences" as being "hopelessly muddle-headed." Mises stated, "Historical facts need to be interpreted on the ground of previously available theorems."[70]

German Historicists, however, were in essence denying the existence of such economic theories; therefore, their views, as Mises argued, were "tantamount to the apodictic negation of economics as such."[71] Menger, in contrast, was dedicated to distilling economic theories of a universal nature, which could apply to all nations, cultures, and eras. This necessitated a means-ends framework, which Menger, in many ways, pioneered. Such thinking must have been completely unpalatable to the German Historicists, who rejected cause and effect (and, therefore, means and ends).

The debate between Schmoller's historicists and Menger's theorists had far wider consequences than the use of data and application of economic theory. The German Historical School in prewar Imperial Germany, comprised of the leading German economists, historians, and political scientists, sided with the socialists and upheld the belief that an unregulated free market would result in exploitation of workers and run counter to national interest. However, they differed with the socialists on the need for a revolutionary overthrow, and instead offered as a solution "state socialism" with social reforms such as the modern welfare state imposed by Chancellor Otto von Bismarck (known as the "Iron Chancellor") in the 1880s and 1890s. In his book of essays, *Planning for Freedom*, first published in 1952, Mises traced the lineage of "present-day interventionist progressivism" to the "supreme brain-trusters of imperial Germany," especially Schmoller, setting up a "clash of two orthodoxies; the Bismarck orthodoxy versus the Jefferson orthodoxy."[72] Others have made a stronger and more insidious connection, connecting the rise of the socialist Nazis to the seeds "sown by Bismarck and his contemporaries."[73] When admirers of the Austrian School see it as a bastion of freedom (as Ron Paul does in the Foreword to this book), they do not overstate their opinion.

ÖSTERREICHISCHE SCHULE

Menger dared to take economics down a different theoretical path, away from the empiricists and historicists, by acknowledging the preeminence of individual choice and the subjectivity of human action. The individual, particularly as consumer, is the economic agent, on whom research should be focused. (The Austrian School's common method of analysis is rooted in subjectivism, although its explicit methodology has varied somewhat from one economist to another.) As such, Menger also recognized a teleological connection between higher-order production (the means) and lower-order production (the ends of consumer needs)—in opposition to the positivists who saw no value in teleological research and clung, instead, to scientism. (We see the growing *criticality* science of today—while useful in analogy, as in Chapter 8—as even furthering, along with the vapid General Equilibrium and Modern Portfolio Theories, the neglect of the market's purposeful process.) The Austrian School was one of ontology, dealing with human action itself; their perceived world was one of apodictic, causal facts. With capital as its root and the consumer as its goal, their underlying economic realities were always genetic and teleological— with a clear identification of means and ends.

Schumpeter summed up Menger's contribution to economics in a eulogy honoring the founder of the Austrian School upon his death in 1921: Menger was "nobody's pupil and what he created stands." His discovery was not merely that people buy, sell, or produce goods or that they derive satisfaction of their needs from such goods. Menger's discovery carried a far greater weight in the simple fact that the laws of human needs, themselves, were sufficient to explain the "complex phenomena of the modern exchange economy."[74]

This singular view, putting human interaction at the pinnacle, has led to rejection and criticism, even outright attack on the Austrian School, not only among its economic peers but also politically as it denied the legitimacy and efficacy of many economic policies. Although the Austrian School was not without its opponents on the political left and right, such alienation brought its own distinction of objectivity and independent-mindedness.

Over time, many have followed Menger; gradually some, like Böhm-Bawerk and Mises, refined, modified, and made numerous substantial contributions. But Menger, unquestionably, was the beginning, the one who planted the flag for the Austrian School and its unique methodology of *a priorism*, deduction, and the importance of subjective human choice and action—all set within a teleological framework of the entrepreneur who must gather the means to achieve the ends of meeting the consumer's wants and needs.

Austrian methodology follows an intertemporal path, beyond the limits of the seen to the yet unseen and, indeed, the foreseen, the progression of the *Ziel* that becomes *Mittel* for achieving a *Zweck*. The Austrians' teleological analysis of ends and means, which began with Menger, was not merely a way to think about capital; it allowed goods and capital to be classified as higher order and lower order—itself, an intertemporal process. Upon this foundation, comprised of the building blocks of Bastiat and the pre-Austrians and formalized by Menger and those who came after him, Austrian capital theory was established, recognizing the importance of assembling capital (the factors of production) in an ever-more roundabout structure not for the sake of circuitousness, but to gain efficiency and efficacy in meeting consumer needs. This brings us to Böhm-Bawerk, the subject of Chapter 5, an early disciple of the school that Menger founded who ultimately became the one to put it on the map.

Chapter Five

Umweg

The Roundabout Path of the Unternehmer

The gospel of this book, which should be obvious by now, is the strategic positional advantage gained in the roundabout way, in the relation of indirect means and conditions to ultimate ends and consequences—that is, in intentionally (and counterintuitively) going right in order to better go left, rather than taking the direct route (the "false shortcut"[1]). We have approached the roundabout by way of synonymous concepts across the historical foundation of strategic thought, from the Daoists' *shi* to the Prussians' *Ziel, Mittel, und Zweck,* culminating now with a core tenet of the great Austrian economic tradition: *Umweg.*

Umweg, like *shi,* is a lowly and mundane term, which disguises its philosophical and practical significance. It translates literally as "detour," "indirect," or "roundabout route," and its economic meaning springs from a pillar of the Austrian School, a man who was truly a cofounder with Carl Menger: Eugen von Böhm-Bawerk. Building upon Menger's theories, Böhm-Bawerk clarified and popularized them, and then cumulatively postulated more of his own—crucial to the study of value, capital, and interest. Indeed, had it been left to Menger, sequestered in his library and consumed with constant revisions of his previous works, the Austrian tradition would have surely died on the vine. It was under Böhm-Bawerk, who was no mere disciple, that the Austrian approach acquired the rigor to be considered a school of economic thought.

Böhm-Bawerk's influence was so great, particularly in capital theory and understanding economic growth, that at the turn of the twentieth century, he was likely the best-known economist outside of the United Kingdom (so one has to wonder why today his name is barely known outside the Austrians). All of Böhm-Bawerk's weighty achievements come together in *Umweg*, which invokes the circular roadway intersections that allow traffic to merge efficiently (literally going right to ultimately go left) rather than crossing each other's paths head on. It is zigging while other zag, in order to then outzag the zaggers. So, too, is the path of this book, spanning miles and millennia, militarists and economists, conifers and entrepreneurs, circuitous yet calculated in our intended direction. By exploring universal strategic thinking, we build a structure of understanding from many sources, and thus mimic how capitalists layer their tools and intermediate stages of production. Likewise, as we will explore in the final chapters, Austrian Investing applies the same roundabout capitalistic method of looking beyond the seen immediacy of first consequences toward the unseen of ultimate consequences. It is a method of positioning upstream for full deployment downstream, of engaging "where/when it is easy," and of perceiving "the seed even before it has grown."[2]

The protagonist of the Austrian narrative is the entrepreneur, known in Böhm-Bawerk's texts as the *Unternehmer*, or "undertaker" (the literal translation from the French term coined by Say), who assembles the necessary inputs, the factors of production, into a temporal capital structure. As Böhm-Bawerk demonstrated, capital accumulation is a sequential production process accomplished through stages to produce final consumer goods more efficiently and timed for when they will be demanded—the constantly stalked strategic advantage toward the ultimate end of satisfying the consumer. To meet that objective, the *Unternehmer* must raise his sights beyond the current slice of time in the marketplace and look ahead to anticipate not only *what* goods consumers will want but importantly *when* they will want them. An intertemporal choice and tradeoff exist between present and future satisfaction, as the *Unternehmer* foregoes the "current immediate" and instead pursues a "later immediate."

The view of the capitalist/entrepreneur is unique to the Austrians, who understand the dynamics of disequilibrium in the economy, which we might think of here as opportunities to be exploited through investments in capital structure. (Mainstream economists seldom address disequilibrium because it's too messy for their mathematical models.) This structure, as first described by Menger, but not fully developed until Böhm-Bawerk, consists of capital configured cumulatively and hierarchically—from the highest order of raw materials (land, ore mined from the ground, timber from the forest) progressively altered with intermediate goods to the lower order that finally reaches the consumer. (It is an aggregate model, if you will, although the Austrians are not typically fans of the aggregate, preferring to focus on the actions of the individual.) Capital structures progress and develop as entrepreneurs weigh opportunities to make their production processes (and, therefore, their capital structures) more *Umweg*, following the roundabout path which leads to no less than the very progress of material society.

POSTULATING THE "POSITIVE"

Eugen von Böhm-Bawerk, nicknamed "Böhm," enjoyed a career that spanned academia and government, two vantage points from which he observed and postulated upon economics in action. Born in Bruno, Austria, in 1851, he was the youngest son of an aristocratic Austrian civil servant and deputy governor. Educated at the University of Vienna, where he received his doctorate of law in 1875, Böhm-Bawerk lectured at the University of Innsbruck throughout the 1880s, during which he wrote his most notable works, and then entered government, becoming Finance Minister of Austria in the 1890s. During this time (which earned him a portrait on the Austrian 100-schilling notes printed from 1984 to 2002), Böhm-Bawerk is credited with helping the country clean up its finances and stabilize its currency; he also led the reformation of the Austrian tax code.

Böhm-Bawerk made his mark with the publication of the first two volumes of his works under the title *Capital & Interest*. The first volume,

Eugen von Böhm-Bawerk, Whose Pen Was Mightier Than His Sword

History and Critique of Interest Theories, published in 1884 (when Böhm-Bawerk was only 33 years old), included an extensive discussion of interest and related theories, exposing fallacies and demonstrating that the notion of interest is not artificial or usurious, but rather is logically inherent in the market. Building upon Menger's ideas, particularly around time preference (though also highly critical of them, and giving more credit to John Rae), Böhm-Bawerk demonstrated that even when goods are equal in every other way, including quality, quantity, and form, present goods are valued more highly than future goods. The second volume and his most important work was *The Positive Theory of Capital*, published in 1889 and then immediately translated and published in English—a stunning achievement for Böhm-Bawerk and the Austrian School. (It is important to note that the word "Positive" in the book title in no way implies that Böhm-Bawerk was a positivist. The word signifies that the theory in the volume was his, whereas the intention of the first volume had been "negative"—exposing the flaws in existing theories.) A third volume, *Further Essays on Capital and Interest*, comprised of what had been appendices to the second volume, was published in 1921, after Böhm-Bawerk's death.

Retiring from government soon after the turn of the twentieth century, Böhm-Bawerk returned to academia where he taught at the University of Vienna. His lectures on capital theory and his private seminar attracted many students—among them Ludwig von Mises.

Personally, Böhm-Bawerk (who was married to the sister of his best friend, fellow Austrian economist Friedrich von Wieser, arguably third in line as a cofounder of the school), was described as the quintessential Austrian: quiet, modest, and affectionate. His diversions included music (he was a talented cellist)—fitting with his focus on the temporal—cross-country bicycling, and, during the summer, daily mountain climbs in the Dolomites.[3] Despite his robust lifestyle in the out-of-doors, Böhm-Bawerk died at the age of 62, just before the outbreak of World War I and the fall of the Austro-Hungarian Empire. Although his life was sadly cut short (many of his colleagues lived well into their eighties), Böhm-Bawerk's legacy continues to outlive him, through his notable advancements in economics, such that an understanding of his concepts of production is necessary to any discussion of capital theory today. Furthermore, he is at the very hub of the concepts converging on Austrian Investing.

PRODUKTIONSUMWEG

To explain his economic theories, Böhm-Bawerk drew from everyday experiences, from the "autistic exchange" as described in Chapter 1 to, more broadly, *methodological individualism*—a principle that stemmed from Menger's work and the belief that social and economic interactions are best studied and explained through the actions of individuals rather than groups or collectives, which can "act" only through the actions of individuals. We might also think of reducing interactions to their individual parts as a type of reductionism—albeit with an Austrian bent. Focusing on the actions of the individual is one of the core concepts of Austrian economics, as explained by Menger: "There is no economic phenomenon that does not ultimately find its origin and measure in the economically acting human and his economic deliberations."[4] The Austrians don't shy from studying complex "macro" phenomena, but the crucial point is that they seek to explain such events by tracing them back to the actions and motivations of the individuals involved.

Böhm-Bawerk's studies of the individual often used parables, which became one of his most effective pedagogical tools. They also provide a good example of the distinctively Austrian flavor of empiricism, whereby experience can yield an understanding of general principles (for example, the advantage of using tools), but not ironclad economic laws. Following Böhm-Bawerk's example, we offer illustrations that bring his concepts powerfully to life, showing *Produktionsumweg*, or "roundabout production," in action. It is important to understand that *Produktionsumweg* is not simply about having production take longer, not just indirectness for the sake of it; taking the roundabout route is not the same as merely taking more time. There is no advantage or virtue in delays, procrastination, meandering, or going out of one's way for no reason. In *Produktionsumweg*, one amasses the tools of one's trade, the intermediate goods that will add proficiency and efficiency to the pursuit, the result of which is realized in the future. As Böhm-Bawerk observed, "That roundabout methods lead to greater results than direct methods is one of the most important and fundamental propositions in the whole theory of production." (The same can be said of roundabout methods in investing.) Over time, the inputs (intermediate goods and other factors of production) are brought together so that the "desired result, the product wanted, may follow."[5]

To illustrate, we return to the parable of shipwrecked Robinson Crusoe. In their discourses, the Austrians seized upon the example of Crusoe (whose name was corrupted from the familial German "Kreutznaer") to illustrate with simplicity the evolution of a one-person economy, as Crusoe's very survival depends on him moving beyond the hand-to-mouth direct satisfaction of his needs to become ever-more roundabout.

On his remote island, which Defoe called the "Island of Despair" (the geographic location of which coincided with the island of Tobago, north of Venezuela and a short distance from Trinidad), Crusoe's first priorities are the basics of life. To obtain food, he begins with the most primitive of approaches: He goes after what he needs with his hands— or as Böhm-Bawerk called it, "*mit der nackten Faust*," literally meaning "with the bare fist."[6] (Defoe equips Crusoe with the means for hunting, growing basic crops, and raising goats; here we focus on fishing to meet his most immediate needs.) Standing in water, Crusoe tries to snatch fish as they swim by, but these slippery and fast-moving creatures are hard to catch. And so he upgrades his approach with a primitive tool (a first attempt at an intermediate good): a branch that he shapes into a spear. Although he misses frequently, he manages to catch five fish a day; but when the last bone is picked clean, he must rest up for another day of labor. Thus, Crusoe's quandary is how to catch the same amount of fish in less time and with less labor, or a greater number of fish in the same amount of time. The answer is to become more roundabout.

The problem, however, is that even with his spear, Crusoe spends so much time trying to catch five fish for the day that the only way he can invest in better tools (improved intermediate goods) is to cut back on current production. In other words, he has to "save" some of his effort instead of expending it all catching fish. This requires him to decrease his fishing time and catch perhaps only three fish a day (which means he's going to be hungry), so he can spend the remainder of his day making a simple boat out of a hollowed log and a fishing net woven from vines. The process takes weeks, all the while Crusoe foregoes full satisfaction of his current wants (a stomach full of fish) so that he can position himself for future advantage with the intermediate goods of a boat and net. Hungry, he labors upstream for more fish downstream. Putting it in economic terms, he makes use of his meager surplus time now in order to create more productive means for later.

This is *Umweg*: Crusoe ultimately catches more fish by first catching fewer fish, by focusing his efforts in the immediate toward indirect means, not ends.

Importantly, Crusoe demonstrates that savings is not mere renunciation, nor is it simply deprivation. Rather, it is highly strategic, yielding or "losing" now to realize an advantage in the future that—the saver hopes—more than justifies the setback and waiting to be paid for the fruits of one's labor and investment (if, indeed, there is ever a payoff; entrepreneurial ventures naturally do not come with any guarantees of feasibility or profitability). Here again we find the exchange across time: loss now for greater gain later. Thus, as Böhm-Bawerk recognized, savings is not negative, but rather deferred consumption, which provides the productive resources for greater consumption later.

At last the boat and net are ready. The hungry Crusoe takes to the water and in less than two hours catches five fish. Now, with his daily needs met, he can invest in other roundabout production, such as, in addition to repairing his boat and net, a rack for drying fish and evaporating seawater to collect salt to preserve them. Soon, Crusoe has an exceedingly efficient fishing operation: catching far more fish than he can consume and accumulating a stockpile of protein for his diet—and, equivalently, *a stockpile of time* for replacing and creating even more capital goods.

Now that he is more roundabout thanks to his boat and net, Crusoe can draw from his stockpile of dried and salted fish to keep up consumption while he makes a second net to replace the first when it finally wears out. Capital must be thought of as a temporal structure that is always dwindling away. Moreover, the advantages and gains that are realized today are due to capital that was invested previously. The same process, we recognize, is occurring with our conifers of Chapter 2 that seed into the rocky, inhospitable places where they initially will fall behind—growing slowly and hungry for nutrients—but from which they will realize greater growth and opportunism later, thanks to their buildup of advantageous efficiency, position, and vantage point.

But what if it had turned out differently for Robinson Crusoe—and for the conifers? Instead of taking a few weeks to make a net and simple boat, during which time he had to reduce his daily consumption by two fish (to three from his usual five), suppose the process took two months to complete? Similarly, for the conifers, what if it took longer for them to reach a faster growth stage, or if there were fewer land-clearing fires and thus less turnover in the fertile areas? What if it all took too long, because time is so costly? For Crusoe, the issue is whether the productivity gained from the net and the boat would off-set his cost in time, which he measures in terms of forfeited fish (two fish times 60 days, or 120 fish)? How much weight would he have lost from caloric deprivation? To be sure, he would use the boat and net if someone gave them to him as a free gift, but would he invest the time and effort to *make* them at a cost of 120 fish? Would the increased pro-ductivity justify that cost? In Crusoe's very real terms, would the payoff make up for the anguish—both physical and psychological—of being near starvation for two months? (Humans' constant necessity of caloric intake creates a natural impediment to the immediate privation of capi-talistic production.) Here, again, we can see economic productivity in action: *It is not just enough to be physically more productive; it has to make economic sense as well.*

Again, it is naïve to think that just because a process is more round-about it will automatically be more advantageous. To take a silly exam-ple, Crusoe could use a "process" that involved climbing a tree every time he wanted to catch another fish; this obviously would confer no advantage over the more direct approach. However, Böhm-Bawerk concluded that the only reason for *Produktionsumweg* to take longer is to acquire a future productivity advantage (made better and/or with less labor, energy, or raw materials) in creating things that someone really wants—and when they'll want them. Sometimes the round-about method exhibits its physical superiority by making more units of output with the same amount of inputs. In other cases, however, the roundabout process yields a desired output good that literally cannot be produced by any shorter, more direct process. Thus, by using what Böhm-Bawerk called "wise circuitous methods," "the superiority of the indirect way manifests itself in being the only way in which certain goods can be obtained; if I might say so, it is so much the better that it is often the only way!"[7]

As Crusoe shows us, entrepreneurs engaging in roundabout pro-duction must contemplate the basic considerations of how long it takes, what it costs, how many resources must be invested to get increased output, and how long one has to wait for a payback (all of which, as we will see, are impacted by the level of interest rates).

Crusoe's one-man economy serves to "clarify the simplest, most fundamental features, to teach the skeleton, as it were, of the whole structure of economic processes." In that, Böhm-Bawerk noted, "Robinsonades and pictures of primitive circumstances are very good when the object is to present clearly the simplest typical principles—to give a kind of skeleton of economic procedure." At some point, however, the bare bones must be made more substantial with "the living actuality of a modern economic community," and filled out with "abstract formula with explanation and illustration taken from life." Thus, the study of *Produktionsumweg* must "leave the lonely shore of our Crusoe, and come to the industrial conduct of a great nation with millions of people."[8]

In all economies, large and small, the choice in production and deployment of capital comes down to gradations between the direct way and the roundabout way. As Böhm-Bawerk wrote:

> We either put forth our labour just before the goal is reached, or we, intentionally, take a roundabout way. That is to say, we may put forth our labour in such a way that it at once completes the circle of conditions necessary for the emergence of the desired good, and thus the existence of the good *immediately* follows the expenditure of the labour; or we may associate our labour first with the more remote causes of the good, with the object of obtaining, not the desired good itself, but a proximate cause of the good; which cause, again, must be associated with other suitable materials and powers, till, finally,—perhaps through a considerable number of intermediate members,—the finished good, the instrument of human satisfaction, is obtained.[9]

A more lucid and concise account of strategic and teleological process—from the Warring States of China to the battlefields of Europe to the *Unternehmer* and the investor—has never been written.

We might think of the roundabout structure of intermediate capital goods as an "autocatalytic process." By that I mean a process in which the product of one reaction becomes the catalyst for further reactions—or, put another way, the process catalyzes itself, with growth equaling capital accumulation and reinvestment. (The term "auto" does not imply a lack of human decision at every step. Consumer choice is paramount, and entrepreneurs must act to respond to current and future consumer wants and needs.) Production thus becomes autocatalytic and self-reproductive, as the production of higher-order capital goods furthers the production of lower-order consumer goods, with capital continuously improved through innovation to create better lower-order goods. Looking at the process in these terms, we can think of technology, innovation, and production as adaptive learning, incremental steps generated by previous steps and that lead to other steps—each of which becomes, teleonomically, like von Baer's caterpillar's means to the yet undiscovered ends of the butterfly. There is an apparent programmatic purposefulness, even though each step merely compounds the prior. Technological advancements become embedded in and mixed with existing technologies to make possible other technologies or consumer goods, which perhaps were not possible (or at least not economically producible) before.

However, there are constraints, or brakes, on *Produktionsumweg*: namely, positive time preference and interest rates. Böhm-Bawerk used his "agio theory" to explain interest as flowing from the generally universal higher valuation placed on present versus future goods (e.g., most people would want a good today versus the same good tomorrow, or in a year's time). This is true of all goods in general; thus, there is a positive interest rate. This framing of the market phenomenon of interest as a result of subjective preferences was a quintessentially Austrian insight and the heart of the theory that earned Böhm-Bawerk such acclaim.

BÖHM-BAWERK, THE BOURGEOIS MARX

Thus far, we have covered a lot of Teutonic territory, which might lead some to accuse me of cultural bias. (For whatever reason, one simply cannot overstate the contributions of the German-speaking world— including the Judaic German-speakers, of course.) But here is one who stands out quite contrary to all those we have covered thus far: Karl Marx.

In *Das Kapital*, published in 1867, Marx challenged the thinking of classical economics by putting forth a labor theory of value (whereby labor played a dominant role in determining value). Marx's arguments centered on the belief that it was labor, alone, that produced value. Therefore, the value of a product, in Marx's view, should equate to the labor-hours invested in it. (We know from Menger's subjective theory of value, however, that it is the final product that determines the value of the intermediate inputs—e.g., the bottle of wine makes the grapes and the efforts of the vinedressers worthwhile.) To Marx's errant way of thinking, however, the market value of goods was due entirely to the amount of ("socially necessary") labor required for their production. At the same time, because workers were capable of producing more than they needed to survive, the capitalists could get away with selling products for the full amount (corresponding to the labor-hours congealed in the products) while giving the workers responsible wages necessary for bare subsistence. The gap, in Marx's view, between the two amounts was "surplus value," effectively what was skimmed off the workers' produce and taken by the parasitic exploiters.

When these radical theories were first promulgated, classical economists had no answer to Marx; therefore, it appeared he had proved his point that capitalism created a class struggle. Although Bastiat, as described in Chapter 4, stood up to the Marxists and the socialists, it was Böhm-Bawerk who defeated them so effectively with economic theories and critiques such that Marxism did not take root in economics to the degree that it has in other professions, such as sociology and history.[10]

Using impeccable logic, Böhm-Bawerk showed that the workers who are employed by the entrepreneur are paid immediately for the "full value" of their labor, so long as that value is correctly calculated by including the time element. After all, in most production processes the input of labor hours doesn't *immediately* yield a finished good. Even so, the worker is paid immediately (or soon enough), while the entrepreneur must wait (perhaps years) for any potential return. The act of organizing production is effectively the act of lending, as inputs are paid up front in order to command product for sale much later. If the profits exceed the costs of waiting, there is an *intertemporal arbitrage* between inputs and output to be had. Thus, the entrepreneur provides an income for the workers throughout the production process, paying them in advance of the output to which they contribute. Labor was but a part of the entrepreneur's roundabout, indirect means to his often remote (and merely potential) end of economic profit.

Böhm-Bawerk further demonstrated the point rather conclusively with the example of the owner of a house with a market value of £2,000, who paid out exactly £2,000 in wages to the workers who had built it. In this case, Böhm-Bawerk argued that "there is not a particle of profit" that could constitute exploitation; the workers are clearly paid the "full product of their labor," according to the Marxist dictum. However, Böhm-Bawerk further assumes that the owner can proceed to rent the house out to tenants for a perpetual annual yield of £100, going forward. It is clear that the owner is now earning a perpetual 5 percent return on his investment, which of course is a form of interest. Yet since, as stipulated, the workers had been paid wages exactly equal to the market value of the good that they produced, Böhm-Bawerk asked, "[W]here shall we find the worker from whom the £100 could have been taken either by fraud or force?"[11]

There is another component to the difference between the workers and the entrepreneur: that is, the notion of risk—specifically, that the workers have considerably less risk than the entrepreneur. When a worker sells his labor hours in exchange for a paycheck, the entrepreneur typically assumes the entire risk of whether the worker's output will end up being marketable; the worker is usually paid up front, with no strings attached to how profitable the entire project ends up. The entrepreneur always faces uncertainty as to the outcome of his investment and the downside risks of substantial debt or even bankruptcy, while still paying the workers before he himself is "paid" by the end consumer. Once we take the real-world element of uncertainty into account, it's not clear how we could even apply the Marxist prescription of paying workers the "full value" of their labor. If a firm goes out of business, should it have the right to claw back the wages it disbursed over the years, because in retrospect the workers involved were clearly overpaid?

Thus, Böhm-Bawerk, whom Joseph Schumpeter reverently called "the bourgeois Marx" for his grand and all-embracing theoretical system, mercilessly delivered a *coup de grace* to the Marxists and their exploitation theory. The subjective value theory overruled "the dialectical hocus-pocus" of Marx.[12] In addition, in his famous essay "Karl Marx and the Close of His System," Böhm-Bawerk hammered home the huge technical flaw in the Marxist explanation of interest. (Surely those today who harbor a discreet affinity for Marx are unaware of the logical fallacies they must implicitly embrace.)

Böhm-Bawerk also put forth an understanding of interest that countered the views of the ancients, who equated interest with something onerous, an opinion held by Aristotle who believed that money, by its very nature, was incapable of bearing fruit; the lender's gain could only come from defrauding the borrower. The early Christian church had similar ideas and sought to protect poor creditors from rich lenders.[13] However, interest as the cost of time has an entirely different meaning; it is the inherent price one must pay to access capital sooner rather than later, which in turn becomes the threshold for determining one's return and the prudence of making an investment. Thus, Böhm-Bawerk's theories on capital and interest point the way to guide capitalist decisions on just how roundabout to be.

By the time of Böhm-Bawerk's birth in the mid-nineteenth century, the utilization of the highest of order goods was being transformed by better and better intermediate tools and methods, which catalytically transformed the production (including delivery, via railroads) of all the lower-order goods that followed. Indeed, this burgeoning industrialization of the world was *Produktionsumweg* writ large, the greatest the world had ever known, and it was surely the source of both that very thesis of Böhm-Bawerk as well as the rationale for capitalization itself. As industrialization came relatively late to continental Europe, the advancement of certain raw materials such as coal, iron, and eventually steel only then began supplanting older, less productive factors of production, in particular timber (as an energy source). Just preceding the development of capitalization in the theoretical works of the Austrians—and perhaps even sparking it—was the expansion of agriculture at the expense of suddenly less economically viable forested land, and in particular the necessity of developing a method to weigh the future income realized over time from land devoted to forestry versus other alternatives. Although Böhm-Bawerk dealt with financial maturity of timber, discounted cash flows, and other elements of capitalization, there is no evidence that he ever heard of a German forester named Martin Faustmann, who some 40 years before the publication of *The Positive Theory of Capital* had produced the seminal work on forest economics and formalized the use of opportunity cost and capitalization.

FAUSTMANN'S FOREST ECONOMY

At the young age of 24, Martin Faustmann became co-editor of the scientific magazine, *Allgemeine Forst- und Jagd-Zeitung* (*General Journal of Forestry and Hunting*); at 27, in 1849, he published in that journal his groundbreaking article, "*Berechnung des Werthes welchen Waldboden sowie noch nicht haubare Holzbestände für die Waldwirthschaft besitzen*" ("Calculation of the Value which Forest Land and Immature Stands Possess for Forestry"). Faustmann was not the first to undertake such a study. Early in the nineteenth century, a small number of foresters in Germany and Austria endeavored to value the land capital, starting with Gottlob König in 1813, the first to treat present value discounting of a tangible asset—at least in forestry, though one is hard pressed to find it in other realms prior to König. This preceded David Ricardo's soil rent theory of 1817, though it followed Adam Smith's land capital theory of 1776.[14] Faustmann, however, is regarded today as having developed the definitive general and rigorous formula for valuation of forests and land rents. (Although some refer to the König-Faustmann formula, it is widely known today only under the name Faustmann.)

Faustmann sought to correctly answer a simple and pressing question: How economical is an area of forestland? Specifically, how do the expected future forestry economics of that land, viewed in the present (what Faustmann called *Bodenerwartungswerte*, which we'll refer to as the land expectation value—*LEV*), jibe with the current market value of bare land (the land replacement value, or *LRV*, of forestland in operation)? That is, is available land affordable for use in or for conversion into forestry, or is it better off used for something else? Essentially, Faustmann was trying to calculate the premium or discount of the appraised capitalized present value of forestry land, relative to the market's current appraisal of such available land in a fallow state (or, say, under agricultural use).

We can view this as a ratio of the two appraisals—what we'll coin as *Faustmann's ratio, LEV/LRV*. The message is clear: When Faustmann's ratio is greater than one (the *LEV* is greater than the *LRV*, or the whole is greater than the sum of its parts), invest in land for forestry (if nothing else you can probably then sell it off as a going forestry operation). If the ratio is less than one (the *LEV* is less than the *LRV*, or the whole is less than the sum of its parts), do not invest in that bare land, at least for forestry. Here, with Faustmann's ratio, from the deep coniferous forests of Germany and Austria, we have found a central economic concept integral to the rest of this book.

What made Faustmann's work so special was that he provided a way to quantify the long, roundabout period of production required in forestry, and the complication of expenses that aren't paid back for many years. Forestry is, by its nature, a long-term proposition; it is about eminently forward markets in the future. As we know from Chapter 2, the pattern for many tree species (especially the conifers) is slow growth at first as the tree builds resources and assembles "assets"—for instance, developing strong roots and thick bark—becoming more efficient and enjoying faster growth later on, until the tree reaches the culminating point of survival in the wild and, ironically, harvesting on the farm. Only by waiting can that accelerated growth be realized. (For instance, you get more wood by letting a single tree grow for 15 years than by chopping down three five-year-old trees over the same period; however, in the latter you get paid incrementally every five years, whereas in the former you get it all at the end.) Thus, before committing land to a forest that may take 15 years to mature enough for pulp and 25 years or longer for timber, one must appreciate that the benefits received in the future carry less value than the same benefits received in the present moment. Forestry is the textbook roundabout industry.

Faustmann devised a formula for the *LEV* whereby one can compare the long-term production of forestry with much shorter-term agricultural production, such as hay or barley. During Faustmann's day this was a particularly pressing concern since forestlands were being overtaken by more profitable agricultural production, which in addition to the difference in price also brought to bear the time horizon for production. Both hay and pine (certainly at the opposing extremes of production periods, the former with multiple harvests per year and the latter with perhaps a handful of harvests per century) could be compared as alternatives for a given area of land (assuming the suitability of the land for both) and thus require an economic basis for the conversion that was literally sweeping the land. Faustmann's formula was absolutely essential, and the formal conception of capitalization and what economists would later call "imputation" was thus born out of necessity.

Suffering through the slow-growth present is but a means to the future fast-growth end, but first the forester must overcome the external constraint on his patience: the *opportunity cost* of capital. And to German foresters' credit, this was an idea hinted at by Frédéric Bastiat but not yet discovered or formalized until Menger, and ultimately coined in 1914 by Menger's pupil, Wieser. In opportunity cost the Austrians recognized not only what one must pay, but the *foregone opportunity* of what that same amount of capital invested elsewhere (with similar risk) could have earned. An entrepreneur who, for example, invests a sum of money in land must consider not only what he will get from whatever he builds or plants on that property, but also what he could have gotten from alternatives—including leaving it in the bank. The interest rate, therefore, becomes an objective way of determining the true economic costliness of *Produktionsumweg*.

Faustmann's formula for the land expectation value (in simplified form) is:

$$LEV = \frac{B}{(1+i)^r} + \frac{B}{(1+i)^{2r}} + \frac{B}{(1+i)^{3r}} + \cdots + \frac{B}{(1+i)^\infty} = \frac{B}{(1+i)^r - 1}$$

where B is the cash value of the wood at each discrete harvest, less the present value of any thinnings and all ongoing costs along the way (which I have spared the reader for simplicity); i is the appropriate interest rate, the opportunity cost of capital; and r is the rotation period, the number of years between each harvest, when revenues are received. Here Faustmann converts an infinite flow of future land "ground rents" (*Bodenrente*), a periodic annuity from a series of forest rotations in perpetuity, into their present value, an infinite geometric series that has a conveniently simple result. Faustmann's contribution was thus a rigorous method for determining the land expectation value to a forester, which "has been the spinal cord of classical forest economics" ever since.[15] In fact, Faustmann was likely the first economist to get present value right in this way,[16] using a discounted cash flow analysis that today, of course, is used to value any stream of income (certain or not), most notably stakes in debt and equity (where it has come to be known as the "dividend discount model" of modern finance theory). The capitalized value of the land is based on the net rents (B in Faustmann's formula) that we get out of it relative to what we forego to receive those rents, the opportunity cost of our capital (the discount rate i in Faustmann's formula).

Naturally this approach is oversimplified somewhat because it does not take into account that there could be other uses for the land that have a higher value (for example, crops requiring less time to mature for harvest and more frequent cycles of rotation), and that a stand can be chopped down at any time as factors change. There is a well-studied switching option embedded in land. Faustmann cared only about the land as forestland.

The only thing unusual here is r, the rotation period. In fact, determining r was another principal takeaway from Faustmann's formula. Even assuming that tree growth is constant, if we start at zero and then increase the rotation period, it will first raise the LEV and then eventually will lower it; the maximum LEV value then corresponds to the optimal rotation period. (Note that in Faustmann's formula, the cash value of the wood sold at each harvest, B, is itself influenced by the rotation period, as trees keep growing through longer rotations.) Faustmann's formula also recognizes, of course, the importance of the interest rate—something that the layperson might think has nothing to do with managing a forest. What follows is *the axiom of the axe*: When the physical growth of the forest and the expected future price of timber are such that they yield a greater return than the market interest rate, the opportunity cost of cutting the timber and selling at the spot price is too high; the forester should stay his axe. However, when the physical growth and expected future price yield a lower return than the interest rate, then the benefit of today's revenue exceeds the opportunity cost of cutting; the forester should chop away. Clearly, then, an increase in the interest rate, with all else equal, reduces the optimal r rotation period—in other words, *increase the interest rate and you shorten the profitable period of production*. (This could be taken right out of an Austrian textbook.) The intertemporal decision of when to cut the forest was thus solved: Taking the price of timber and the interest rate as given, as well as the relation between the period of rotation and the revenues to be received from each cutting on this schedule, Faustmann showed foresters how to maximize the LEV by finding the optimal r. From there, the true economic discounted value was solved.

As an aside, Faustmann also proved that the capitalized land value is not dependent on whether the trees are planted as a single-age stand (intermittent management) or are of diverse ages (sustained management). Within a cross section of a forest one could find only a single stage in the lifespan of a tree represented and the land value (the forest value less the growing stock value) would be equivalent to a forest whose cross section included an entire lifespan. This means we can look at annual rents made up of a subset of the entire growing forest (the annual thinnings), rather than waiting each intermittent rotation period for an entire forest to be leveled. The rotation period is still just as important, as it determines how much is harvested (the magnitude of B)

and replanted each year. But now the harvesting frequency is every year (so $r = 1$). This is nontrivial, as it simplifies our land expectation value to something even more intuitive by allowing us to compare the cash value of the wood each annual harvest with the annual discount rate:

$$LEV = \frac{B}{i}$$

Despite Böhm–Bawerk's time spent surrounded by the Vienna Woods, and despite his fixation on the temporal aspect of production, for which the timber industry is perhaps the model case, he never referenced Faustmann's formula. He does, however (along with, most notably, his Swedish disciple Johan Gustav Knut Wicksell), repeat Faustmann's conclusion, *the axiom of the axe*: that timber is economically viable (and thus immature) as long as new growth in tree value as a percentage of the current land and stand value (the return on invested capital, *ROIC*) exceeds the compounding opportunity cost of owning that land and stand value (the opportunity cost of capital, i).

This brings us back to Faustmann's ratio. We can say that the annual economic return on the land (the harvest value as a percentage of the land replacement value) is

$$ROIC = \frac{B}{LRV}$$

and thus the land expectation value can be restated as

$$LEV = \frac{LRV \times ROIC}{i}$$

So now Faustmann's ratio is, in fact,

$$\frac{LEV}{LRV} = \frac{ROIC}{i}$$

As we can see, the ratio depicts not only the affordability of bare land (the land replacement value), but more specifically, the relationship between the tree value production (as a percentage of the *LRV*) and the rate at which we are discounting that production. It is, in essence, *the return derived from invested capital compared to the replacement cost of that capital*. As before, when *ROIC* exceeds the opportunity cost of capital (the interest rate i), timber should be farmed. When it does not, then interest rates do not warrant the slow tree growth; the soil is too expensive and is better used for a faster-rotation crop, such as hay (or perhaps for nothing at all). Indeed, *the axiom of the axe* has become a fundamental canon of corporate finance today.

What does this mean when growth is slow at first and fast later—as in our accelerating-tortoise and hare fable of the conifer? Is it really ideal to chop down the slow-growing (young tree) at its first hint of life, or to call the race before our tortoise finds his legs? This is the paradox of the roundabout (which we recall as Klipp's Paradox): You cannot simply measure the economics in the immediate stage, as that would make you Bastiat's "bad economist"; the immediate may show a loss that is but the means for a later exceedingly profitable stage bestowed by a longer period of production.

Faustmann's ratio, as a rule of thumb, holds for all capital, beyond only trees and dirt. Thus, we can see the common ground of Faustmann's discovery of the obvious in forestry and, right behind him, Böhm-Bawerk's theory of capital and interest: Lower interest rates—or, more precisely, lower time preference (saving now to consume later)—lead to more *Produktionsumweg*, whether in a pine stand or any other capital goods.

RINGS OF CAPITAL

The intertemporal aspect of capital shows that it is heterogeneous—a reality that the Austrian tradition embraces (whereas other economic schools of thought typically treat "capital" as an amorphous homogeneous blob, which allows them to grossly undervalue its importance and its modifications). Such heterogeneity means not all capital configurations are the same nor do they generate the same return. Moreover, the expansion of the capital structure does not entail a simultaneous and equiproportional increase in capital throughout its higher and lower orders; rather, it is a redistribution of proportionate capital among the various orders. Because they explicitly acknowledge the heterogeneity of the capital structure, Austrians are in a unique position to study the market mechanisms that keep the economy's intertemporal production plans in line with the intertemporal preferences of consumers.

Böhm-Bawerk had his favorite metaphors for capital heterogeneity. His stream, which is not "of equal breadth at all stages," with "dams at certain points, and leakages at others,"[17] evokes the favorite image of Sun Wu. Best of all, though, and conveniently following our conifer *leitmotif,* Böhm-Bawerk offered the depiction of a tree's growth, specifically a crosscut, essentially a large trunk, revealing its annual growth rings in a pattern of concentric circles ("*konzentrische Jahresringe*"). (See Figure 5.1.)

What better image is there of the intertemporal, cumulative meansends process that, as I argue throughout this book, is the very process of productive capital investment? Lose sight of this intertemporal structure—lose one's *depth of field*—and the productivity is lost. (Figure 5.1 should perhaps be affixed to everyone's Bloomberg screen.) If this book accomplishes nothing else but makes this point clearly, it will have reached its intended *Zweck.*

As the concentric rings illustrate, the production process and value emanate cumulatively from the core. The process flows outward over time, through successive rings as more factors of production are added

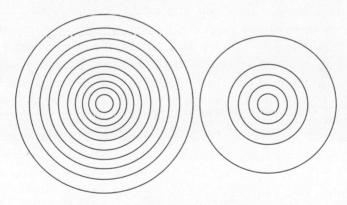

Figure 5.1   Böhm-Bawerk's *Jahresringe.*

Shown are depictions of the capital structure of two different economies, where the "life cycle" of a production process starts on the inner rings and moves outward over time. The economy on the right is less roundabout (and very likely poorer and less productive), as most value is added in lower-order goods (the outer rings), where the goods are closest to the final consumption point.

Source: Eugen von Böhm-Bawerk, The Positive Theory of Capital, *1930, G.E. Stechert & Co., NY.*

to the previous inputs, turning them into intermediate goods. The more intermediate layers there are the more roundabout production becomes. Then, at the outermost ring, a final, finished good is pushed out into the marketplace. (Unlike a tree's static rings, however, the area between each ring is constantly being expanded or contracted.)

Each of the concentric annual rings represents what might be termed a "maturity class." The outermost ring includes those parts of the capital that will become finished consumption goods within the next year (ring); the second outermost ring contains the capital that will mature into consumption goods in the second year, and so on. There are other variations within the structure depending on, for example, how developed an economy is. A hypothetical very underdeveloped economy based on only one raw material or one good, perhaps a basic manual tool for digging, would consist of one ring. At the other end of the spectrum, a highly industrialized economy would be depicted by many well-formed embedded circles, with a width that represents the magnitude of the asset classes involved; there will be more rings, reflecting more years and more circuitous processes of production. As Böhm-Bawerk explained, "Within each production area the amount of capital invested increases with every forward step to a lower maturity class."[18]

Böhm-Bawerk pointed out that capital structures are cumulative (indeed, autocatalytic); what comes before leads to and is contained in what comes later. In effect, we might think of all the previous capital and inputs congealing (or becoming encapsulated, if that's a more palatable term) in the next ring. For instance, a most elemental capital good dating back some 10,000 years is a goat, which can be consumed at once as meat or (if female) can become an intermediate "tool" which produces milk to consume. Furthermore, that milk (when recombined with a goat's stomach and rennet) can become a factor of production of cheese; the cheese can become an ingredient, perhaps to make fondue, and so forth. Each of these consumer goods, in turn, becomes a sequential intermediate good for (and, thus, is "contained" in) the next subsequent consumer good, and each adds another ring to an increasingly roundabout production process. Not butchering the goat now—sparing the golden goose, as it were—and instead waiting, hungry, for months for a great many (hopefully) exquisite goat's milk tommes is the capitalistic intertemporal tradeoff in a nutshell, the very source of humanity's emergence from its historical hand-to-mouth existence.

HENRY FORD: THE ROUNDABOUT
UNTERNEHMER

Capital drives research and development, modernization of plants and processes, creation of new products, and improved distribution systems to bring those products to consumers. And there is but one source of that capital: savings. In the nineteenth century, the savings rate in the United States, for instance, rose from 15 percent before the Civil War to 24 percent in the 1870s and 28 percent in the 1880s.[19] During this time of great industrial expansion, capital deepened as profits were invested back into businesses, such as those named Carnegie Steel and Standard Oil. Vertical integration created huge industrial firms that controlled successful stages of manufacturing (all the "rings" of production) from raw material to finished products, thus magnifying more *Produktionsumweg* advantages. Workers also benefited from the intermediate capital goods that made them ever more productive and increased their earnings power (and their ability to benefit from greater consumer goods). The proliferation of measurement devices, cutting tools, lathes, and machine tools detonated a "chain reaction of development of machine tools to make other machine tools to make tools."[20] That tools beget greater tools is the very point of capitalistic production (and, along with an understanding of monetary interventionism's bastardization of this process, of Austrian Investing itself). The autocatalytic "multiplier effect" wrought enormous productivity increases everywhere, from farms to factories; at the same time, industrial development spawned new commercial and savings banks, life insurance companies, and investment firms, and the stock market became a dominant source for capital investment.[21]

Just before the dawn of the twentieth century, inventors in Germany, journeying the road of the *Unternehmer* as laid out by their "neighbor" Böhm-Bawerk, introduced a new mode of transportation that would literally change the world, putting horse-drawn conveyances out to pasture and replacing them with vehicles propelled by gasoline-fueled engines. The automobile can be traced back to a German-born Austrian inventor, Siegfried Marcus, who around 1870 put an internal combustion engine on a handcart—the "Marcus car." The fabled German engineering continued as inventors Nikolaus Otto, Gottlieb Daimler, and Wilhelm Maybach in 1876 produced the first four-cycle engine, although official credit went to countryman Karl Benz (later of Mercedes-Benz fame) in 1879 when he was granted a patent for the internal combustion engine; in 1886 Benz patented his first automobile.

On the other side of the Atlantic, in the summer of 1876, a 13-year-old Michigan farm boy was mesmerized when he saw a contraption with a crude steam engine trundling down the road, the first vehicle he'd ever seen powered by something other than a horse. The boy was none other than Henry Ford, who would later recall, "It was that engine which took me into automotive transportation."[22] An entrepreneurial pioneer, Ford put the average American in the motorcar, and established a global enterprise with European operations especially in Germany, where Ford's fabled "mass production" was immortalized as *Fordismus*, an industrial ideal that raised efficiency and productivity. By the time Ford's autobiographical *My Life and Work* was translated into German in 1923 (*Mein Leben und Werk*) Ford was hailed as an American industrialist superstar.[23] (Ford, a pacificist who opposed war as wasteful, was also given the abhorrent honor in the early 1930s of having his portrait displayed on the wall behind Adolf Hitler's desk.) Ford was not without his faults, some of them egregious, such as his distrust of financiers, which he personified into a disgusting dislike of those of Jewish descent (sadly, he was not alone; many espoused the prejudices of the day). But here we separate the man from his mission, and recognize him as the embodiment of the roundabout entrepreneur who created a new paradigm of production, the assembly line, as the culmination of vertical integration that depicts the improved efficiency and productivity gained by spanning Böhm-Bawerk's *Jahresringe* with factories and power plants to turn coal, iron ore, and steel into automobiles.

Hailed as one of the true luminaries of the modern age (in 1999, *Fortune* named him the "Businessman of the Century"), Ford deserves yet another title, though one he never wore in life: He is the quintessential roundabout entrepreneur in the Austrian tradition. Although he probably never read Böhm-Bawerk (but who, no doubt, must have followed this American *Unternehmer*), Ford seemed to be singing out of the Austrian hymnal when he wrote in his 1926 classic, *Today and Tomorrow*, "The time element in manufacturing stretches from the moment the raw material is separated from the earth to the moment the finished product is delivered to the ultimate consumer."[24] The Austrians described what the *Unternehmer* knows in his gut. (Ford held similar

Austrian views on such things as profits as the source of productive capital that must be reinvested to the ultimate benefit of consumers, and a loathing for the actual operation of the banking and monetary system, which, he famously said, if people understood, there "would be a revolution before tomorrow morning.")

Before the entrepreneur, though, there was the farmer's son, born in 1863, at a time when his Midwestern home state was a wooded frontier covered by dense forests of oaks, ash, maples, and, of course, conifers. Ford was expected to follow in the footsteps of his father, William, but his natural fascination was for all things mechanical: As a boy, he fashioned for himself a set of tools (from a nail and a corset stay) with which to repair watches (perhaps foreshadowing the entrepreneur who would invest a tremendous amount of time and effort to assemble the tools of production in order to improve speed, efficiency, and output in his manufacturing processes). Mechanics versus farming sparked conflict between son and father, and, in 1879 at the age of 16, Henry left home and traveled to Detroit where he worked in a machine shop and then a shipbuilding factory. After returning to his father's farm in 1882 to help with the harvest, Ford became interested in agricultural equipment and was hired as a machinery demonstrator and repairman for Westinghouse, traveling from farm to farm from 1883 to 1885. In 1886, it was timber that brought Ford back to the farm—specifically, to 80 acres his father offered him in return for a promise to give up being a machinist. Ford agreed (temporarily, of course) and set himself up in the lumber business (apparently, with a favorable *Faustmann ratio*). In 1888, he married Clara Jane Bryant; the couple had one son, Edsel, named after Ford's closest childhood friend.

Despite the deal he'd made with his father, Ford never lost his interest in engines, and by 1890 was working on a double-cylinder engine. When he and Clara moved to Detroit where Ford took a job as an engineer and machinist at the Edison Illuminating Company (eventually becoming chief engineer), his obsession with the "horseless carriage" intensified; by 1892 he had built his first motor car, and by 1893 he had a model he could test on the road. By the time Ford built a second car in 1895, he already faced a competitive market, including a German Benz car on display at Macy's in New York.[25] In 1896, Ford sold his car (the "Quadricycle") and, like the roundabout entrepreneur he was at heart, invested the proceeds in R&D; indeed, over the course

**Although he was one of the greatest
entrepreneurial capitalists of all time, Henry Ford preferred
the simple pleasures of rural life.**

of his lifetime, Ford Motor Company would not have prospered had
the founder not committed to continuous long-term investment in
improvements and roundabout production.

Although his name is synonymous with automotive manufacturing and entrepreneurial success, Ford failed in his first two ventures
(backed, in part, by a local lumber baron). (Some of the greatest entrepreneurs have suffered such setbacks and some, like Ford's good friend,
Thomas Edison, went bankrupt; often these experiences pave the
roundabout routes to crazy and obsessive goals.) Finally, in 1903 Ford
Motor Company was incorporated, and its prototype Model A went
into production in a 50-by-250-foot assembly plant, using parts bought
from suppliers. Ford was also passionate about racing, believing that (fun
aside) it would generate publicity for his cars. In 1904, he set about to
break the world's record for land speed, refitting a racer with a Model B

engine and racing it across the frozen Lake St. Clair. He completed the third mile in 36 seconds, for a speed of 100 miles per hour, shattering the previous record of 77 miles per hour.[26] His racing stunts apparently worked, and also in 1904, the growing company moved into a larger factory; in 1905–1906 the company rolled out the four-cylinder Model N (selling for $600), as well as the six-cylinder Model K ($2,800). Ford's true vision, which sometimes put him at odds with his business partners, was not to make roadsters for the rich, but to produce modest, reliable, high-quality cars for working people of more modest means, such as his iconic Model T, introduced in 1908 to an enthusiastic public that, just a few years before, did not even know they craved cars. (As Ford once said, "If I had asked people what they wanted, they would have said faster horses.") With the Model T, Ford transformed his company, and brought the American public into the modern era.[27]

Led by Ford's vision, the company made the roundabout transition from assembler to manufacturer in every process along the way in order to reduce costs, gain more control over supplies, and eliminate unnecessary inventory, thus making huge gains in efficiency and innovation (Detroit was the Silicon Valley of its day). The decision was driven by economics; with mass production, Ford could make parts at a lower cost and more quickly than buying them from suppliers.[28] The flagship for his roundabout production was the River Rouge plant, which included a port and shipyard, steelmaking, a foundry, a body-making plant, a sawmill, rubber processing, a cement plant, a power plant, and an assembly plant. It was the epitome of *Produktionsumweg*, which at the outset literally consumes time and requires great capital expenditures to be, in Ford's words, "turned back into the business so that it may be still better fitted to serve, and in part passed on to the purchasers."[29] The roundabout paradox is that the process of becoming more circuitous takes a tremendous amount of time, during which there is little to show for the sacrifice (*à la* Robinson Crusoe), but at the end results in significant time savings; like the conifer it is slow at the start so that it can accelerate at the end.

After showing extraordinary patience during the building of the roundabout production process, once it was in place Ford switched gears temporally and became obsessed with timing the car-making production process to see how he could make it faster, as annual output of the Model T rose from 585,000 vehicles in 1916 to 1 million in 1921, and then doubled to 2 million just two years later. Speed and efficiency were crucial as supervisors patrolled the plant floor with stopwatches to time production. Newspapers wrote about the astonishing pace of the assembly process; one 1913 account told of a Model T put together by a team from preassembled parts in two-and-a-half minutes. Soon the company would boast a new Ford was born every 24 seconds.[30] Ford, the entrepreneurial hero of the common man, believed the production gains at River Rouge would "cut deeply and in many directions into the price of everything we make," bringing down the prices of cars and also farm equipment. "It is important that it shall be cheap," Ford said of the tractor. "Otherwise power will not go to the farmers."[31] By getting the farmer used to the comfort and power of the automobile, Ford hoped to convert them to mechanized farm equipment to ease the physical labor of farming, a drudgery he knew all too well.

Contemplating Ford's life and work, we see how the pursuit of *Produktionsumweg* is the indirect path, but one that is undertaken with single-minded purpose and tenacity. Yes, Ford had his share of trials and errors as part of the learning and discovery process, but his mission to efficiently produce cars for the masses never wavered. Although it has become fashionable in some quarters to speak of following one's bliss, hoping to stumble upon profit as if blindfolded along a daisy-strewn path (as John Kay, author of *Obliquity*—an academic's take on indirectness—might have us believe[32]), this is not how the real world works and progresses. Entrepreneurs do not dabble, willy-nilly, in pursuits of fancy, chasing butterflies or endless real optionality; theirs is a practice of assuming an uncomfortable position in the difficult sunk costs required for the tools to achieve their clear goals. Even when their roundabout processes take them back to the drawing board countless times, to reinvent the very tools they need to produce their final goods, they are decidedly and determinedly purposeful. Nor do entrepreneurs pursue rainbows down some picturesquely meandering path because of serendipity, kismet, and chance. Their indirectness is always calculated; they know where they are going (though never knowing, of course, if they will actually get there), while keeping their minds open to the evaluation and modification of goals from what is learned along the way. They move in a circuitous fashion from *Ziel* to *Ziel*, but never forget for an instant that these are the *Mittel* to a *Zweck*. This is the singular and profound teleological discovery process of markets.

For Ford, the *Ziel* of increased efficiencies and lower production costs drove toward a *Zweck* of lower prices for consumers (and, ultimately, a more productive business), believing that the ultimate beneficiary ought to be the public—a postulate that would have put him in good stead with the Austrian School. (If it were within my power to go back in time to arrange a meeting, it would surely be between Ford, Böhm-Bawerk, and Mises, whose lives overlapped.) Ford stood for the "buying public" and its right to goods and services at the lowest possible cost. He believed it was far better to "sell a large number of cars at a reasonably small margin than to sell fewer cars at a large margin of profit." With this attitude, he viewed a profit as "far more a fund to insure future progress than it is a payment for past performance."[33] Paying out profits in the form of dividends, particularly on preferred stock with burdensome payouts, put profits into a few hands rather than back into more roundabout production. As Ford said, "The owners and the workers will get their reward by the increased amount of business the lower prices bring. Industry cannot exist for a class."[34] (Insufficient capital reinvestment, as we will revisit later on, is essentially capital consumption in lieu of the roundabout.) Focusing on profits over productivity, ends over means, was, in Ford's words, "trying to drive with the cart before the horse."[35]

Ford warned against "the most common error of confusing money and business," which he blamed on the stock market for leading people to believe that "business is good if there is lively gambling upward in stocks, and bad if the gamblers happen to be forcing stock prices down." He eloquently viewed the stock market as a "side show,"[36] and little did he know how increasingly true this would be—as so much of investing today is the domain of "punters" over seekers of productive capital. To Ford, like in *taijiquan* and at the *weiqi* board, there were two distinct games going on between the stock market and true investment, the former a mere shadow of the latter. Disdainful of finance and suspicious of banks all his life (his abominable stereotypes and prejudices aside), Ford made the "shortsighted finance" of Wall Street his nemesis, viewing it as "strings on a business" in stark opposition to his roundabout redirecting of profits back into the operation and focusing instead on an immediate return. "The majority are so interested in getting the utmost out of the machine that they will give no time to improving it as it runs."[37] Ford cited the "Parable of the Talents" (interestingly, as Clausewitz did, in Chapter 3) "to whom much is given, of him shall be much required," thus exhorting entrepreneurs never to sacrifice working capital for the sake of amassing personal fortune. He exposed what he called the "fallacy which has steered our country and other countries wrong on so many matters touching industry—the fallacy that business is money, and that big business is big money."[38] Make no mistake: Ford was a true-blue capitalist, who believed in making profits, but rather than consuming the capital produced today, saw the infinitely better wisdom of reinvesting intertemporally for a position of greater strategic advantage.

As Ford Motor Company expanded, the costs were paid for by efficiencies gained through faster output at the last "ring" of production and by eliminating in previous "rings" stockpiles of iron, coal, and steel—all unnecessary inventories that Ford saw as idle waste. By the mid-1920s, he would boast, "We do not own or use a single warehouse."[39] Ford also didn't believe in having too much labor on hand, considering hiring two men for the job of one to be a crime against society, although he did have to account for high turnover because of the tedium of the assembly line work. In 1913, turnover reached an unbelievable 370 percent, and Ford hired more than 50,000 people to maintain an average labor force of about 13,600.[40]

When profits swelled, he paid well for labor, creating an uproar when he doubled the basic wage to $5.00 a day, which triggered a virtual stampede of job seekers. Paying higher wages for labor was not altruistic in Ford's eyes. Moreover, it wasn't simply that Ford was trying to pay his workers "enough to buy back the product," although he *did* preach a high-wage doctrine after the stock market crash in 1929. Rather, paying relatively high wages was, for Ford, a matter of smart business. He regarded well-paid skilled workers as important as high-grade material. By paying workers well, he effectively *lowered* his costs because higher wages reduced turnover and the need for constant training of new hires. (At the time, the newspapers saw Ford's wage increase as an extraordinary gesture of goodwill.)

With his wage policy, Ford also fired a shot across the bow of Roosevelt's New Deal, which he vehemently opposed, believing that higher wages and less restriction on business, and not higher taxes, would benefit the country. Unlike the other automakers, Ford refused to go along with Roosevelt's "Blue Eagle" campaign, an insignia for goods manufactured by companies that supported the administration's economic and wage policies. An enraged Ford blustered, "Hell, that Roosevelt buzzard! I wouldn't put that on my car!" Rather than embrace the National Recovery Administration (NRA) and the New Deal, which Ford dismissed as "these alphabet schemes," he preached that American businesses should "take hold of their industries and run them with good, sound, American business sense."[41] Ford, perhaps more than any other industrialist opponent of the New Deal, could take such a public stand with confidence: Nobody could accuse *him* of hiding behind empty rhetoric, since he had voluntarily raised his workers' wages amid the ravages of the Great Depression. It wasn't a matter of his personal greed, or indifference to the plight of his employees; Ford really *did* believe that the Roosevelt Administration was overstepping the proper bounds of the federal government.

Ford extended his production metaphors to the "economic machinery" of the country, believing it wisest to make improvements when things were going well, rather than waiting for a breakdown, and warned against seeing "depressions as unpreventable epidemics." (As we will read in Chapter 7, such words would have rung true with Mises.) As Ford observed, "The seeds of bad times are in the mistakes which we make in the good times. Yet in the good times no one wants to hear of the mistakes we may be making. The policy then is to 'get while the getting is good'."[42] The economic machine breaks, Ford believed, "because of our ignorance of all the natural laws which regulate economic health," our mistaken belief that business "can run only so long without smashing."[43] (As we will see in Chapter 8, the economic machine does have natural, internal controls that govern it, and they are undermined and short-circuited by the ignorance of interventionism.)

Warning against the evils of inflation that gives the illusion of buying power and speculation that comes from the perception of shortage, Ford sounded decidedly Austrian themes. When it came to monetary reform, Ford was all for sound money, but unfortunately, under the influence of his friend, Edison, supported a monetary system backed not with gold, but instead with American agricultural products. Known as "Ford-Edison money," the proposal was motivated by a desire to spare farmers the expense of interest payments to the bankers—a position that neglected Böhm-Bawerk's insights about the genuine fact of time preference as the "cause" of interest; while naturally favored by farmers, it failed to find widespread support and was abandoned.

Our focus on Ford, though, is not for his political or monetary ideas, but for those in which he showed genius like none other, as a roundabout entrepreneur who rightly regarded capital as the lifeblood of a progressing business and economy. His was an inherently intertemporal orientation, and his depth of field stretched beyond any one year or season (like the good farmer he was at heart). It was no coincidence, then, that the more successful Ford became the more he embraced his agrarian roots, which he had never really abandoned. He immortalized the rural ideal in his Greenfield Village near Dearborn, Michigan, where more than 80 historic structures are preserved, from the Wright Brothers' cycle shop to Edison's Menlo Park laboratory where he experimented with the electric light. (Wandering the grounds gives insight into Ford's resolve for authenticity, simplicity, and patience—one can imagine him, in his later years, reveling in threshing hay by hand; indeed, in these he gained his greatest edge.) These icons of the past, however—so revered by Ford—are not merely dusty relics. In them are preserved the seeds of the future they sowed, the very tangible reminders of the roundabout process of discovery and innovation that leads to the progress of capitalism and the advancement of civilization.

THE ROUNDABOUT OF LIFE

Much of human activity, particularly in endeavors that are more strategic (and I use the Clausewitzian *Ziel-Zweck*, "means of gaining greater superiority" definition) or higher-order versus those that are less so, benefits from roundaboutness and a decidedly indirect means-end approach. Despite the strategic advantage of being *Umweg*, it is extremely difficult to think and act in this way (as we will address in the next chapter); most people just can't do it. (If roundabout were easy, then everyone would do it, and no doubt the strategic advantage derived from it would be eliminated altogether.) Moreover, the roundabout route may very well be overlooked because all we tend to see is the final product, the ultimate end—while we are blind to what came before, the remote means to that end.

And yet, there are enough examples in life that demonstrate the advantages of roundaboutness (even outside of the obvious martial applications). Once again, like good Daoists, we turn to nature. The evolutionary mechanism of mate selection often employs a strategy whose aims are *indirect benefits* in the form of better adaptive genetic characteristics for the offspring, as opposed to direct and immediate benefits realized by the mates. This is a pretty extraordinary thing, the same intertemporal, intergenerational strategy of the conifers growing on the rocks, where what happens in this moment is but a means to a strategic advantage for the progeny. Selection for offspring fitness in this way shapes the very mechanisms that enable this roundabout process to persist.

As we look for other examples of strategic means-ends thinking, when the talk of strategy shifts from the theoretical to real-world applications it is unavoidable to consider sports. Clearly across different sports there exists a gradation between the tactical (e.g., executing one isolated play at a time) and the strategic (e.g., treating individual plays as intermediate parts of a greater play). Along this continuum, surely basketball falls as more tactical, the execution of an independent series of two- and three-point plays (spurious momentum aside). Football (American as well as European) would perhaps fall somewhere in the middle, as mostly tactical and only somewhat strategic in the Clausewitzian sense. Others stand out as more roundabout, higher-order games.

For instance, there was a lesson to be learned in the 2006 British Open of golf, which was won by Tiger Woods with what appeared at the time to be a counterintuitive and counterproductive strategy. On an extremely difficult course, Woods, one of the longest hitters on the tour at the time, retreated from his signature massive drives and instead teed off using only four and five irons meant only for medium-range play. The reason, as author Andreas Kluth relates in his book *Hannibal and Me*, is that Woods had "*inverted the mental process* of the ordinary golf player." This calls to mind the same inversion needed at the *weiqi* board in Chapter 3, as well as the maxim of Carl Gustav Jacob Jacobi, the nineteenth-century German mathematician, "*Man muss immer umkehren*," or, loosely, "Invert, always invert"—meaning solutions to difficult problems can often be found by examining them in the inverse. In his game, Woods "looked beyond the fairway to the pin—not the green, but the pin."[44] He then figured out where on the fairway his ball should land that would give him the positional advantage of the optimal spot from which to approach the pin. Thus, his early shots were mere means for his advantageous later shots, with the ultimate end of an easy putt.

Such inversions reveal, and are perhaps the only way to come to, the counterintuitive optimal approaches in such roundabout games. Like the strategy of *tuishou* from Chapter 1, there are the feints of fencing, tennis, and especially the gentleman's game of squash, where progressive drawing shots pull the opponent out of position and set up a subsequent decisive attack; it is generally understood in squash (specifically the "softball" or "international" game) that one must think (by inversion) two or more shots ahead. This is a simpler instance of an intrinsic strategy in perhaps the most roundabout game of ice hockey (the traditional sport of Ford's north woods "hockeytown" home): the patient cycling of the puck around the offensive zone—a literal roundabout—using time to tease out imbalances and a seam in the defense and find an open shot or passing lane to the goal, as opposed to charging directly through traffic. (Hockey's dominant forecheck strategy is another less obvious instance of the circumvention strategy at play.) Again, this is about planning several passes ahead, *shi* versus *li*—strategy as a sequence of stages inverted back from the goal. (Surely Wayne Gretsky was referencing Bastiat when he said, "A good hockey player plays where the puck is. A great hockey player plays where the puck is going to be.")

It was through the sport of sailboat (dinghy) racing on a small Lake Michigan bay that, as a child, I first encountered the countertuitively circuitous (and surely sports are the best way to discover it as children on our own). A persistently shifting wind favors the boat on the seemingly least direct upwind route, thus saving the most direct route for when it is most advantageous. Even on a downwind leg, the straightest line along a racecourse from buoy to buoy, although clearly the shortest route, is best avoided for a roundabout one. Heading away from the buoy (on a slight "reach") at first in order to then head directly at it with a much speedier point of sail creates a longer but surprisingly faster course.

Perhaps nowhere is this subtle intertemporalizing into *Ziel-Zweck* stages more plain than in baseball. This was particularly exemplified in the coaching philosophy of Hall of Famer Earl Weaver, one of the greatest managers in the history of baseball. Weaver—who, in late January 2013, as I was still drafting this chapter, died at the age of 82—won four American League pennants and a World Series during his 17 seasons with the Baltimore Orioles (to which my beloved Rochester Red Wings was a farm team). With the view that "baseball is plain old common sense"—so reminiscent of Klipp—Weaver's approach to the game could be best described as *Produktionsumweg*, and stressed using his player rotation to gain the greatest chance for an eventual opportunistic swing of the bat—but not every swing of the bat, nor certainly even every at-bat: *shi* versus *li*. As Weaver told his players, "Wait for the pitch you can hit out of the park. If it doesn't come take the walk down to first base so you can score if the next batter gets *his* pitch."[45] Weaver's words recall the advice of Ted Williams to wait for the "fat pitch," a famous model of Warren Buffett, but Weaver's approach is much more nuanced, employing *depth of field* rather than just patience. The key was to see beyond the immediate at-bat—never waste an out with a bunt or an attempted steal—and maximize the potency of later at-bats. (Base runners even give advantage to the batter by creating gaps.)

There are two distinct parts to implement a Weaver strategy. The first is the *Ziel* of getting on base, which then becomes the *Mittel* for the *Zweck* of scoring many runs (i.e., winning games), likely through a multiple-run homer. But if batters try, instead, to go directly for the *Zweck* of a run with every batter, every runner, and every inning, then that will be the result: one run eked out at a time—a decidedly less productive approach. By focusing on the *Ziel* of runners on base, meaning focusing on high on-base percentages, Weaver increased his chances of realizing a *Zweck* that won games. (This was and remains a highly controversial approach, now known as "big ball," from Michael Lewis's wonderful book *Moneyball*—though more aptly should be known as Weaver, *shi*, or roundabout ball.) As we might see through the Austrian lens, Weaver extended the team's period of production within each inning by building his "intermediate goods" in runners on base, and then, when all goes right, came the final "consumer good" when the *Unternehmer* finally gets paid—the base-clearing hit. Again, the inverted path traced back from ends to means reveals a circuitous route.

We instinctively understand the roundabout in much of sport—it is perhaps what makes it so interesting. (How, then, do we so often disregard it in investing?) It is a superior strategy in perhaps more than we think, pervading even the more prosaic games of chance—from the vulnerable "builders" of backgammon to the trapping bluffs of poker (where early bluff losses are a means to eventual big pots when the advantage is greatest). Finally, we can return to the supreme game of strategy and one of the very oldest in human history, *weiqi*, which reminds us that victory does not come from the direct pursuit of one's aims, with the do-or-die of a *li* strategy, in which every engagement (every tee shot, every at-bat) has its own *Zweck*. Rather it belongs to the *shi* strategist, who retreats now (going for a shorter shot to the fairway or taking the walk to first)

Böhm-Bawerk and Ford Vying Through *Produktionsumweg*

in order to gain the *Ziel* of greater positional advantage from which to achieve the ultimate *Zweck*. Within this multistage, indirect means toward remote ends, we find *wuwei*—not going directly for the goal, and in so doing reaching it all the more effectively. And what holds true at the *weiqi* board also applies to the Austrian *Unternehmer*, who engages in an intertemporal exchange for advantage later.

In the universality of strategic thought and decision making, of *shi* and *Umweg*—embraced and embodied by the Austrian who defined the roundaboutness of successful entrepreneurship and the American who put it into practice—we have completed the path through our Austro-Asian world, and brought it to the New World.

For now we stay in the realm of Böhm-Bawerk and the *Unternehmer*, for whom the opportunities and the challenges are the same: to become ever more roundabout, overcoming our innate desire for immediacy— all for the ultimate benefit of the consumer and, by extension, to all of material society. Yet, as we will soon see, pursuing that goal is completely contrary to that very humanness about us.

Chapter Six

Time Preference

Overcoming That Humanness About Us

I t is an inconvenient and unfortunate fact about Austrian Investing, the destination of this book toward which we have been making our way: It is nearly impossible to implement. A very real and deeply encoded impediment acts as a natural, built-in barrier—that humanness about us. We are not made with a predilection toward *shi*, roundaboutness, and capitalistic production and investment. We are adaptively designed to favor the tactical *li*—immediate, direct, decisive—over the strategic *shi*—intermediate, indirect, roundabout. It is no wonder, then, that having an intertemporal perspective and perception is such an underestimated and overlooked advantage, and yet it is also one of the most influential, a distinct intelligence, and key to our success.

Our perception of time is central to this book and to our ability— or far more likely inability—to implement its methodology of Austrian Investing. You see, the roundabout runs afoul of the very way we perceive the ticking of the clock, and, more specifically, all the moments in all those ticks and tocks. As we will see, our perception of time is diametrically opposed to our appreciation of and our ability to engage in the roundabout.

And yet, because the direct, the *li*, is endemic to humans, we have within our grasp the means to exploit it in others—that is, if we can overcome the seemingly insurmountable. To do so, we must make the turn toward *shi* by going against the grain of our very nature. This requires a complete inversion of a behavioral pattern known as *time inconsistency* (and generally expressed mathematically with a *hyperbolic discounting* model). This pattern, present in all of us and distorted to extreme and even dangerous levels in the cases of addictions, is to be impatient now, all the while holding fast to the self-delusion of being able to be patient later. (And, of course, when later becomes now, we are just as impatient.) We expect to act very differently through time than we actually do, predictably throwing a wrench in our best-laid plans, especially the more roundabout ones. This phenomenon plagues us, in all aspects of life; not just in financial decisions, but also things such as weight loss, learning a foreign language, catching up with old friends, and so forth. We always want to do something a bit onerous that will shower us with long-term benefits, but we never want to do it *today*. Unless we find a way to deal effectively with our skewed time expectations, everything we have discussed up to this point becomes moot—a mere intellectual flight-of-fancy with no chance of ever being implemented.

In Austrian Investing, we must plan to do and then actually do the complete opposite of these ingrained time expectations; we must, instead, become strategically patient now—but not as the practice of some virtue toward realizing a platitude-laden future. Rather, we are patient now for the sole purpose of becoming intensely and rapaciously impatient later; though difficult to perceive, this is the teleological, causal *arrow of time* in roundabout investing. This calls to mind Henry Ford who exhibited tremendous patience as he waited for months if not years all the while spending profits on a production plant and equipment to become more roundabout; then, when production started, he stood there impatiently with a stopwatch, counting the seconds until each finished car rolled off the assembly line.

This roundabout ideal is a temporal two-step, a dance of duality that defies the reality of how we really think and act over time. (Just ask any dieter, who absolutely must have a slice of *Schokoladenkuchen* now, but is completely convinced of having the ability to start and stick to a diet tomorrow.) Impatience now with the belief that we can and will be patient later is the way of all flesh.

So we must see time differently, in a whole new intertemporal dimension. The roundabout—the pain of positioning and paying now for the advantage and payoff later—only works when we remove our temporal blinders that keep us hyperfocused in the moment. Then, and only then, can we pursue those proximal aims intended to give us an intermediate advantage from which the distal ends are more easily and effectively achieved. To say this is extremely challenging is an understatement.

The reason for this difficulty can be found in our wiring, those genetic tracings of our evolutionary journey rooted in survival, when overlooking immediate needs was reckless and life-threatening. Yet, the continuation of that same journey has been made possible by gains attained sequentially along the roundabout: making simple tools; domestication of animals; growing, harvesting, and storing grains; smelting ores and metals; and, eventually, through the ongoing march of entrepreneurial progress, amassing the most intricate capital structures (building "inner rings" of capital as Eugen von Böhm-Bawerk showed in his *Jahresringe*) from which the grand scope of the industrial and digital revolutions arose. These monumental human achievements would not have been possible without the ability to forego in the immediate (*li*) for potential advancement in a forward slice of time (*shi*). To follow this path, this *Dao*, we first must become aware of our inherent *time preference* and subjugate our *myopic time inconsistency* that makes us extremely impatient (with a high time preference) now while anticipating subsequent abundant patience (with a low time preference). We must become like the Daoist manipulative sage, who first "humbles himself to be in a better position to rise" later,[1] the archer with crossbow drawn seeking the positioning, or *hsing*, from which to then overwhelm the enemy.

Grasping time preference and time inconsistency is the gateway between learning about the roundabout and actually putting it into practice; the sole purpose of this chapter is to help make this mental leap. These two interconnected and complementary concepts provide a baseline of instinctual habit and behavior, from which we must resolutely deviate. The objective is to arm ourselves with intertemporal tools that allow us to accumulate and distribute positional advantage through time, rather than concentrate it in a decisive, arbitrary present.

Here, too, is the invaluable legacy of the Austrians and most notably the great Böhm-Bawerk, whose pioneering work in time preference brought into the spotlight the cognitive, emotional, and psychological origins of this behavior. Thus, the man who gave us the roundabout also concurrently first spelled out the severe dilemma in its implementation, while also providing a roadmap of awareness to help us navigate the traps of our own perception and cognition. Following Böhm-Bawerk, we must learn to hold our desire for immediacy in abeyance and plumb our full depth of field, requiring the disposition of the roundabout Böhm-Bawerkian *Unternehmer* who needs patience in the first stages in order to become impatient in the latter—to position for eventual rapacious opportunism. (As his student Ludwig von Mises would later stress, there is no point in *perpetual* abstinence or waiting; eventually the individual must decide to consume, and in that moment the primordial fact of time preference—the desire to act in this moment—manifests itself.) In this way, what I have dubbed Austrian Investing contrasts starkly to the far more typical investing approach that only weighs current contemporaneous opportunities, one against the other, hungry for yield, blind to the changing opportunities likely to materialize around the next bend (the atemporal head-on clash, which, unlike the *shi* approach, assesses each exaggerated present moment as the same). As I intend to show in the final chapters, without the benefit of a singular intertemporal orientation, we deprive ourselves of perhaps the best capital investments.

As we remind ourselves from Chapter 1, adopting an intertemporal depth of field is *most definitely not* about merely "having patience," nor is it the clichéd "long-term view," anchored in the present moment, that is a constant refrain among many investors—most notably the time frame of "forever" advocated by value investors such as Warren Buffett. In fact, it is quite contrary to it. Long term is but a trajectory from now to the distant future that effectively, and by definition, must ignore the sequence of many ripe time slices in the middle.

Austrian Investing is about an *intertemporal exchange* as the very source of profit—now for an anticipated later. This exchange was central to the wisdom of our old grain trader Everett Klipp at the Chicago Board of Trade, where demands for immediacy in the pit bestowed an edge on those able to provide it—the basis of virtually all bonefide investment edges. For this task, we embrace the circuitousness of *wuwei*, of "doing by not doing," and "gaining by losing" (and of Klipp's "loving to lose"). All the while, we keep in mind that the patience and "false humility"[2] of *wuwei* are neither procrastination nor passive waiting. Robinson Crusoe did not forego fishing with a spear in order to lie in a hammock all day. He retreated from the water and the fulfillment of his daily needs (eschewing the smaller, sooner reward) so he could redistribute his resources of time and energy to build a boat and make a net, and thus fish all the more effectively later on. In that forward moment he could be greedy for all he could catch, the larger, later reward; but first, he was mighty hungry. And so we, too, must be willing to do the difficult and uncomfortable, to reallocate our attention span intertemporally, sharpening our perception of the forward moments from telescopic, fuzzy, and ill-formed to clear and salient.

There has been one continuous theme to this book: utilizing the present as means for opportunistic exploits in the future; in Böhm-Bawerk's words, "our economical conduct has exceedingly little reference to the present, but is, almost entirely, taken up with the future."[3] But how do we accomplish such a feat for ourselves? It starts with the basic metaknowledge of our time preference (and in later chapters we will come to understand the costs of our often misplaced biology). We acknowledge that time preference is so subjective and contextual, with variability from one individual to the next (due to factors such as age and environment) *and* within the same individual from one moment to another due to circumstances or a particular slate of choices. But mostly, we must recognize our consistent temporal bias. Although it may seem irrational, it is not; rather, it is how we got here, part of the calling card of membership in *Homo sapiens*. And so, we confront our evolutionary fears of scarcity and even of our own mortality.

Awareness of Time Brings Us Face-to-Face with Its Finite Supply

Becoming aware of and even overcoming our time preferences do not occur simply by wishing or wanting it to be so. If it were that easy then everyone would do it and, as we said about *Produktionsumweg* in Chapter 5, any advantage from it would no doubt disappear. (There would be a great many Henry Fords foregoing profits to build more tools.) The key is in the human brain and what we know about those gray-matter structures that govern our thoughts, impulses, desires, and behaviors. But before going to the scientific and empirical, we again follow the lead of the Austrians by taking a logical, deductive approach that starts with the individual.

In his astute observations of human nature, Böhm-Bawerk was the first (along with John Rae, an obscure nineteenth-century economist whom Böhm-Bawerk thanked for his contributions, which he then greatly surpassed) to connect the dots from time preference to time inconsistency (and hyperbolic discounting) as the most daunting challenges to *Produktionsumweg*. To see that Böhm-Bawerk anticipated the modern work in behavioral economics and finance, consider this passage: "Who of us, faced with disagreeable but unavoidable visits or errands or tasks that had to be attended to within a certain time, has not postponed them from the days when it would have been relatively convenient to attend to them, and then finally been forced to act in hurry and haste . . . ?"[4] To model *procrastination*—where someone really does intend to do something, just not right now—involves not merely a discount on future enjoyments, but a more subtle problem of time inconsistency, of thinking that what is too onerous in the present will somehow be easier to endure in the future. (For example, we have a high time preference now with a predilection for consumption, but we expect that in the future our time preference will somehow be lower, enabling us to forego consumption and/or save later on.) Universal to us humans is the difficulty of doing the exact opposite: inverting our natural drives and desires so to endure a negative present stage in order to enjoy a positive future stage. Yet the time inconsistency identified by Böhm-Bawerk had remained all but unknown in finance until its empirical discovery a few decades ago by behavioral psychologists (most notably studying addiction); its tremendous financial implications specifically to capital investment and valuation remained unrecognized until now. Thanks to Böhm-Bawerk we can build the awareness and self-knowledge that allow us to apply these means to our desired ends of Austrian Investing. For that, we return to a pioneer in the identification and study of what we now call time preference.

"RADICAL" BÖHM-BAWERK AND THE PSYCHOLOGY OF TIME PREFERENCE

Böhm-Bawerk viewed economics and time as inextricably linked. Like time is to music (something close to the heart of any Viennese), it is the very canvas of capital and economics; it can be stretched, compressed, and distorted, with dramatic implications.

These implications were the whole point of his groundbreaking views of the intertemporal trade-off between present and future, the first to move beyond capital productivity and interest theory alone and, as noted earlier, bring in cognitive aspects. Where he became truly radical, however, was in the emotional factors, particularly by introducing the concept of willpower (clearly an emotional force) and the effort required to delay gratification. By acknowledging the psychological and emotional aspects of time preference, Böhm-Bawerk made a distinct departure from any depiction of intertemporal choice solely with regard to the cognitive, and in so doing made strides in understanding how all these triggers influenced perception and behavior.[5]

Although the present moment is all that we can experience, our future is certainly no less material. As Böhm-Bawerk observed, "What is going to happen to us in a week or in a year is no less something touching *us*, than what happens to us today. It is therefore equally entitled to be considered in our own economy, for the object of that economy is to provide for *our well-being*."[6] Böhm-Bawerk's prescription for the organization and management of our resources is the "equal treatment of present and future as an ideal"[7]—in other words, temporal depth. We engage in more than just the current moment, the realm of our immediate self; Böhm-Bawerk evokes all of our many forward moments that "touch" all of our many forward selves. All are equally our selves, all have "equality of rights"—though "[w]hether this equality of rights as a matter of principle is matched by a full equality of rights as a matter of practice is another question." (Here Böhm-Bawerk anticipates the "future self" psychological-disconnect literature that started in the 1970s.) We are estranged from our forward selves, because we lack "the gift of literally *feeling in advance* the emotions we shall experience in the future."[8] Our chauvinism for the present self—the one certainly closest in temporal proximity and the most tangible to our experience—is such that we often neglect our forward selves. As Böhm-Bawerk cautioned, "How often does a man, 'from weakness,' let himself be hurried into taking some step, or making some promise, which he knows at the moment he will rue before twenty-four hours are over!" The cause of such hasty actions, he added, is not a lack of knowledge, but rather a "defect of will."[9] This is Böhm-Bawerk the proselytizer of the emotional will required for *Produktionsumweg*, for tolerating a present "loss" in order to achieve a future advantage.

So, given the future's importance to our well-being, how can the present hold us in such a vice grip? It is understandable in the case of the person in want—from Chapter 5, Böhm-Bawerk's poor peasant or starving artisan. If one's future existence is in question there can be *only* the present to consider, as surviving the present is a necessary condition to making it to any future. The same might be said for anyone who most acutely feels his mortality, such as people engaged in "very perilous callings."[10]

What about everyone else, though, who presumably can and certainly should be more thoughtful of the future than the current moment? It is a problem that has plagued people across cultures and centuries. As Böhm-Bawerk observed, "How many an Indian tribe, with careless greed, has sold the land of its fathers, the source of its maintenance, to the pale faces for a couple of casks of 'firewater'!" The same behavior is observable, he added, in "the working man who drinks on Sunday the week's wages he gets on Saturday, and starves along with his wife and child the next six days."[11] Because of pleasure in and the availability of the moment, opportunity and well-being are easily compromised for the future.

The "present," of course, carries quite the emotional charge—the desire to "live in the moment." There is a whole system of thought, prevalent in eastern and western meditation, to expand one's awareness of the present; and, of course, there is merit in stopping to smell the proverbial roses. Our *carpe diem* attitude, however, should be to seize *every* day, each individual slice of time, but never one at the expense of all the others to come. (The German-born physicist Albert Einstein once wisely consoled a grieving friend to hold past and future moments as equals to the present.) Our live-for-today culture has been invaded, like a deadly virus, by an insidious attitude that teaches this moment is all that matters just because it is all we see and experience—right now. The symptoms of this affliction can be found in the chronically low savings rate in our culture (ranging from financial to even fresh water, soil, and, of course, forests) and, analogously and most incredibly, governmental fiscal deficits that deviously and increasingly rob future generations—our helpless intergenerational forward selves. Thus, to think and act intertemporally, we must go against what our culture teaches us. Would we not want to live our lives as a complete series of moments to the best and fullest way possible?

It takes more than flipping a temporal switch to adopt a more time-consistent orientation, just as any positive or therapeutic behavior change—dieting, smoking cessation, or overcoming an addiction—takes effort and commitment. Because we cannot feel our future feelings we focus, often obsessively, on the present. As Böhm-Bawerk wrote, "Whether it be that our power of representation and abstraction is not strong enough, or whether it be that we will not take the necessary trouble, the consideration we give our future and, particularly, our far-away future wants, is more or less imperfect."[12] A decided "incompleteness of the imaginations"[13] keeps us from projecting accurately, even perceiving at all what lies ahead.

The prospective is not the only span of time slices altered by perception; its mirror image, the retrospective, has its own brand of myopia, called *static gestalt characteristics*: We tend to remember things based on singular moments—how they come to a close (in addition to the peak intensity moment), their most temporally adjacent moment that marks the end of the past and the beginning of the future. Researchers have explained this phenomenon with a metaphor inspired by writer Milan Kundera, that "memory does not take film, it takes photographs."[14] We can see this as a "focusing illusion," whereby, as Daniel Kahneman wrote, our mistake is one of "attention to selected moments and neglect of what happens at other times."[15]

We just don't process and perceive time very well, neither forward nor backward. Our mental time travel, forward and back, is imperfect. (Interestingly, amnesiacs and schizophrenics, who experience memory losses and deficiencies, struggle with planning for and imagining the future.) All of us, to some degree, experience, perceive, and recall time very differently than the linear movement of the clock, and downright erroneously. We weight the future and the past subjectively and disproportionately, such that, like the warnings on the rear view mirror, they seem fuzzier and further away in proximity to the present.[16]

Fortunately, despite the difficulties, humans *are* capable of making certain intertemporal compromises (overcoming our time inconsistent hardwiring); if we were not, our species would still be living in caves using the most basic of tools. Humans are not alone in this capacity, which we share with many animals, birds, and even plants (in particular the oldest species on earth, the conifers). The more developed the species, the deeper its depth of field, taking a teleological series of intermediate, interconnected steps as a necessary expedient for later competitive advantage. Similarly, older people are better at overcoming the impulsivity we associate with youth. Ironically, it is the young adult, in the deep end of the temporal pool, who lives like there is no tomorrow, while older folk who have far fewer actuarial years ahead are better able to make intertemporal choices that prepare for a future (perhaps that may very well exceed their own lifespan—thus thinking and acting for the benefit of intergenerational fitness and advantage).

It is a universal trait within living systems to make intertemporal trade-offs as if on the basis of some cost/benefit analysis (though skewed), with the willingness to pay a cost early on provided there is a sufficiently larger benefit to be realized later. In contrast, the river, as an example of a nonliving, complex system, can do naught but follow the direct course. It cannot bend right with the intention to bend left, for example, running uphill now in order to descend down an even steeper hillside later on.[17] (Although the surge of pent-up water is a favorite Daoist image of *shi*, we cannot take on the mindless meandering of the river.) This temporal teleology is, indeed, a mark of life itself. We must actualize this capacity to make decisions and take actions whose consequences unfold intertemporally, with a separation between cause and effect, means and ends, *Ziel und Zweck*.[18] But as we will see, there are tragic and revealing circumstances when the structures that allow for intertemporal thinking and action—curbing our high time preference for "now" and favoring a low time preference for "later"—become lost or damaged. In the worst of scenarios the person is left to drift constantly in the present with nary a thought or ability to grasp or plan for the future.

THE CURIOUS CASE OF PHINEAS GAGE

In the voluminous libraries dedicated to neurology there is no more oft-told tale than the curious case of Phineas Gage. In the summer of 1848, this 25-year-old railroad foreman in Vermont suffered a gruesome brain injury that left him irreversibly altered in temperament. Here we find a poster child of sorts for time preference in the most extreme, while, at the same time, gaining a unique and early look into the neurology behind human behavior and the brain structures that are the command center of our tolerance for roundaboutness.

In the mid-nineteenth century, the Industrial Revolution was in full swing in the United States, creating the autocatalytic demand for raw materials to fuel economic expansion and the railroads to transport them. The Rutland & Burlington was the dairy line, carrying creamery products from the Green Mountains of Vermont to market (it was known for bringing butter to Boston, packed in ice in refrigerated cars). As the line expanded with new tracks, crews for the Rutland & Burlington ran into outcroppings of hard rock along the Black River. Rather than take the literal roundabout route, the railroad decided to blast its way to a direct shot from one point to another—illustrating yet again that the direct route, while quicker, is more difficult and, in very many cases, inferior to the circuitous. The foreman for this job was a man described as efficient and capable, valued by the company and well-liked and respected by his work crew: Phineas Gage.

We can picture this hardworking fellow, accomplished in the precise art and science of putting powder and fuses into the holes drilled into the rocks—highly responsible, level-headed, and with a steady hand. From this we can infer the behaviors that would go with such a description: moderate in eating and drinking, with no extreme vices (those who knew him would later report he was more apt to speak like a choirboy than a railroad ruffian), and was likely even in the habit of saving a portion of his pay. In other words, we can picture Gage as a typical man of his day, with a garden-variety or even rather low time preference (despite working with explosives) that would have some emphasis on present consumption (he was 25, after all), but could very well have also included a forward-leaning perspective through upcoming slices of time—perhaps he planned to marry, start a family, and build or buy a home.

Alas, that stretch of railway that was to be made straight rather than roundabout would have dire consequences for Gage, completely subverting his ability to ever again be forward-focused and leaving him to flounder in an impetuous life filled only with now. It happened one day when, after loading a charge and fuse, he became distracted. Before another man on his crew had time to pour sand into the hole drilled in the rock, Gage began tamping it with an iron bar. The charge ignited and blew upward into his face, propelling the bar—weighing some 13 pounds, measuring over 3 feet in length and over an inch in diameter—through his head. The bar entered his left cheek, passed through the front of his brain and exited through the top of his head, before landing more than a hundred feet away, covered in blood and brains. Amazingly, Gage was still alive.

Later, the story was written up in the New England newspapers as a horrific accident and a miracle of survival. As a medical case, it was discussed under the headline "Passage of an Iron Rod through the Head" in the *Boston Medical & Surgical Journal*. These accounts tell of Gage's treatment by the town physician who was amazed that his patient was conscious and able to converse naturally, while the doctor could observe the "pulsations of his brain" through the wound in his skull. (The doctor never considered his patient as anything other than completely rational.) Although Gage lost vision in his left eye, he could see perfectly out his right, and had no impairment of hearing, touch, speech, or language. But as his recovery ensued, the people who knew the man were soon to conclude that this was not the same Gage.[19]

He was described as "fitful and irreverent," indulging at times in "the grossest profanity," and became highly impatient, unable to exercise any restraint or heed any advice when it conflicted with his desires in the moment.[20] Some reports describe Gage as vulgar and bawdy, indulging in excesses in drinking and sexual behavior, lying, and thieving. Yet that was not the only dramatic change in Gage after the accident. He was completely unable to plan for his future or to carry out any planned activity. His teleological functioning was severely impaired.

After the railroad refused to take him back because of his aberrant behavior, Gage drifted from job to job, working on horse farms and at one point becoming a circus attraction who showed off his wounds and the iron bar that caused them. By the age of 38, his health deteriorating,

Gage developed severe seizures and went to live with his mother and sister. The convulsions worsened to the point of being continuous, which ultimately caused his death.

A tragic tale, yes, but that is not what draws our attention here, nor, quite frankly, is it why Gage has earned notoriety in the neurological world beyond having survived an iron bar passing through his brain. Rather, this rare case provided the first clinical proof positive that specific parts of the human brain were dedicated to temporal reasoning, with structures that allow for the ability to curb impulses and make intertemporal choices and future-based decisions. Here was the irrefutable clinical evidence, in Gage's almost Jekyll-to-Hyde personality transformation, of how time preference is part of our biology.

THE *SHI* AND *LI* BRAIN

It should come as no surprise to the parent of any toddler or preschool child that with maturity the human brain develops the capacity to wait for longer periods of time. (I await my children's passage as the moment that reason and thus bribery becomes an effective parental tool.) Such development manifests in the ability, emotionally and cognitively, to defer satiation of wants and needs, so that the temptation of a smaller sooner reward does not overwhelm one's longer-term best interest for achieving a larger or better later one. Self-control and willpower combine as the necessary ingredients that allow for delayed gratification— in effect, the emotional and psychological underpinnings of becoming roundabout. And we had help from Phineas Gage in understanding where exactly such capacities reside.

From a neurological standpoint, this maturation is found in the development of the hippocampus, which is essential to the transferral from short-term to long-term memory (an intertemporal retrospective), and the frontal lobe, a region of the cerebral cortex loaded with dopamine-sensitive neurons, which play a major part in reward, attention, motivation, and planning. (Interestingly, serotonin is known to support functioning in the frontal lobe and other forebrain structures associated with decisions and choices involving time and future consequences. In clinical experiments, scientists administered tryptophan-depleting drug mixtures to volunteers to test the role of serotonin on future-based decision making. The conclusion: Serotonin plays a vital and impactful, but not exclusive, role in time discounting and intertemporal choice.[21])

In terms of brain structure, development of the frontal lobe and hippocampus, which begins around age four, allows for impulse control to override the basal structure (including the amygdala or "lizard brain"), which researchers have connected to instinctual behaviors. Stated another way, the developed brain with a fully functional frontal lobe is a "cool system"—the cognitive "know" system that is emotionally neutral, contemplative, and capable of generating purposeful strategic action; the "seat of self-regulation and self-control"—or, as we might say, the roundabout, *shi* system. In contrast, the "hot system"—the emotional "go" system—is the center of fear and passion, immediacy, impulsiveness, and reflexive behavior, truly the locus of *li* that undermines self-control. In a healthy brain, the interaction of these *shi* and *li* systems enables people to prevent powerful stimuli from triggering impulses, and thereby allows them to exert their willpower and self-control. It is the means by which they break free of the so-called "pleasure principle"—driven by impulses and ignoring reason.[22] In the dynamic between cool and hot is the means to access willpower and self-control to pursue deliberate ends.

A classic and amply cited illustration is the 1972 "marshmallow test" by psychologist Walter Mischel of Stanford University, who studied 32 preschoolers (16 boys and 16 girls with a median age of four-and-a-half years). Children were given a choice of a treat—marshmallow, Oreo cookie, or pretzel stick—and told they could eat one immediately, or wait 15 minutes and receive two. Left alone in a room without any distractions, the children, who were observed through one-way mirrors, exhibited attempts to exert self-control—closing their eyes, playing with their hair, and so forth. Some of the children were able to wait long enough to get a second treat, while some ate the treat immediately. And, interestingly, mistrust—the fear of never even getting a marshmallow at all—was a major consideration in their unwillingness to wait, rather than just impatience. Most unsurprisingly, age was a major determinant in the ability to defer gratification. (I remember with a combination of fondness and fear my kindergarten teacher who tried to drill self-control into her young students. Mimicking her, I used to roam the house repeating, "Self-discipline! Self-discipline!"—much to the amusement of my parents, who must have been dismayed at my apparent abandonment of this mantra in my teenage years.)

The significance of this study, replicated many times since and which has become a classic in the gratification paradigm, was that it turned out to be highly diagnostic of self-control and self-regulation, and even predictive of behavior into adulthood. Children who successfully delayed gratification were later shown to perform better on SAT tests and exhibited higher personal and interpersonal competencies (though, sadly, likely didn't have promising futures as hedge fund managers or Wall Street traders). Although marshmallows may seem like an odd proxy for roundabout capitalistic production and investment, the same basic elements apply: One must look beyond the seen immediate moment to the unseen next moments, and thus curb the immediate impulses (and skepticisms) and instead jockey for larger later advantages.

THE SUBJECTIVITY OF TIME

Within our human tendency to overemphasize the present and underemphasize forward slices of time, there is a great deal of subjectivity. As Böhm-Bawerk noted, people may discount an interval of time by 100 percent, by 50 percent, or by only 1 percent, and some may go to the other extreme of grossly overvaluing future utility. This subjective variation, from person to person or within a single individual based on particular circumstances, shows that such discounting is not, in the words of Böhm-Bawerk, "graduated harmoniously"[23] by a constant amount over a particular length of time. We cannot say, as Faustmann and others later posited, that if one discounts by 5 percent what is expected to be received in a year, then an additional 5 percent discount must be applied to a subsequent year in order to discount a total of two years, and so forth. "On the contrary," Böhm-Bawerk observed, "the original subjective undervaluations are, in the highest degree, unequal and irregular." There can be "strong differences" between present and future enjoyment, while there is only a "very small difference, or no difference at all" in the evaluations of one enjoyment that is "pretty far away" and another that is "farther away."[24] Nonetheless, "[t]hese imagined future emotions are comparable. Indeed, they are comparable not only with present emotions experienced at the moment, but also with each other; and that comparability, furthermore, obtains irrespective of whether they belong to the same or different periods of time."[25] (Subtle observations such as these show that Böhm-Bawerk went beyond mere time preference and recognized time inconsistency.) Like the Austrian economists who followed him, Böhm-Bawerk deduced praxeological phenomena—of time inconsistency and hyperbolic discounting—through a general understanding of the human condition, rather than though clinical data. What Böhm-Bawerk gave us in his observations is a phenomenon, a propensity that we all share, whereby we assign greater value to what is most salient, available, and tangible to us (typically, the present moment) compared to what is beyond the grasp of our imaginations or that we, for whatever reason, doubt will even materialize, and how these recognizable human traits lead to familiar (and regrettable) actions such as procrastination and addiction. This field of study is captured by the modern concept of hyperbolic discounting, though in an austere mathematical formulation as opposed to Böhm-Bawerk's intuitive verbal exposition.

The general tendency toward time inconsistency was later concisely illustrated in an example that we'll call "Thaler's apples" (named for the University of Chicago economist Richard Thaler who hypothesized it), which presents the following choices:[26]

A1. One apple today
A2. Two apples tomorrow
B1. One apple in one year
B2. Two apples in one year plus one day

The typical impatient human would likely opt for one apple today (A1) over two apples tomorrow (A2). As the old adage goes, we prefer the "bird in the hand" instead of multiple birds in the bush. Acting like preschool children, we seize even the smallest enjoyment in the current moment, regarding it as outweighing, as Bohm-Bawerk observed, "the greatest and most lasting advantage."[27] On the basis of time preference alone, and the general present-bias, this makes sense—we want the smaller sooner rather than wait for the larger later. (It appears we change from preschoolers less than we think.)

Where the time inconsistency revealed itself was in the projection a year hence. In his experiment, Thaler found that no one would settle for only one apple in a year (B1) when waiting an extra day would yield two apples (B2). As we know, the tendency is to prefer a more valuable later outcome as the temporal distance is extended. Hence the reversal in time preference: As the clock ticks, at some point the preferred B2 gradually becomes the spurned A2 and we inexplicably change our minds.

Although we can surely sympathize and see the rationale, such determinations are, nonetheless, highly inconsistent ("irrational"). If we would not want to wait one more day now (preferring the immediate apple rather than two in a day) why would we be any different in the future (willing to wait a year and a day for double the reward)? The problem is *not* in a particular value judgment, but rather in a person who apparently fails to realize that his future self will not be able to carry out the choice that his present self announces. What does it mean to say that in one year, he would prefer to wait an additional day to get two apples, when his current behavior shows the opposite to be the case? In his observations around time inconsistency, Böhm-Bawerk seemed to presage this oddity in us that would only later be verified in the lab. Our focus away from the abstract, like the modern "availability heuristic," toward those memories and associations that are most available in our minds is thus a focus on the immediate.

Böhm-Bawerk's description of this subjectivity in our time preference was and still is very much at odds with the way we ought to discount the future—the normative, robotic, case. In 1937, the Nobel and MIT economist Paul Samuelson (whose famous textbook, in its 1989 edition, confidently and inconceivably stated: "Contrary to what many skeptics had earlier believed, the Soviet economy is proof that . . . a socialist command economy can function and even thrive"[28]—proof positive of flawed mathematical economics proofs) introduced the very exponential discounting used by Faustmann in 1849 (called exponential because of the multiplicative compounding of the discount factor $1+i$ with each successive year). Here, from an esteemed English-speaking economist (rather than a lowly German forester), was a rigorous model of intertemporal choice. It featured the familiar compound interest mathematics, an agreeable thing to do. And best of all, it treated acting man as *consistent*, and condensed his messy temporal preferences down to that single parameter i (from Faustmann). Despite Samuelson's reservations about its suitability, it really caught on in economics—to the point where today's behavioral psychologists and economists write papers showing the experimental violations of the now-standard Discounted Utility model of mainstream economics.[29]

Herein was the problem: Despite its formal elegance and convenience in "solving" for equilibria, Samuelson's model of a uniform discount on future utility didn't accurately describe the behavior of people in the real world. As discussed, we are decidedly *inconsistent* in our time preferences—that is, our preference for delay reverses as the delay period changes; and we are certainly not well-described by a single (or perhaps by any) static parameter.

Faustmann was right: His formula (developed for forestry, as the reader recalls) does provide an objective and normative way of approaching the compounding of opportunity costs and the pricing of capital. However, in the real world, we overlay our own subjective discounting apparatus on this simple compounding. Comparing this to Faustmann exposes the bias.

We can alter Faustmann's formula to allow the rate of time preference, i, to vary and in fact decline with delay. Our new *time inconsistent* Faustmann's formula for the land expectation value is thus:

$$LEV = \frac{B}{(1+i_1)} + \frac{B}{(1+i_1)(1+i_2)} + \frac{B}{(1+i_1)(1+i_2)(1+i_3)} + ...$$

where each i_n is declining as n increases (that is, $i_1 > i_2 > i_3 \ldots$). What this means, of course, is that the discounted (or capitalized) value of each successive B, or each successive marshmallow or apple, falls very quickly for short-delay intervals (near-term harvests) and then still falls but at a slower rate for long-delay intervals (harvests further out in the future). With Faustmann's original exponential discounting, the discounted B's all fall at a constant rate with each successive delay. This again, in a nutshell, describes our time inconsistency—descriptively equivalent to the hyperbolic discounting model. (A *subadditive* discounting model has also been shown to provide similar descriptions of lower discounting over longer delays, though it fails to capture the preference reversals.)

The difference between this and Faustmann's original, Jedi-like method of discounting is overwhelming: When earlier yearly discount rates in the Faustmann equation (say i_1 and i_2) are high and patience is particularly low, there will be no tolerance for the early slow growth of the conifer; the later fast growth will not be reached, when yearly discount rates are expected to be much lower and patience is expected to be high. The *axiom of the axe* will very likely cut the enterprise short, even assuming tremendous profitability. The i's are high when they are needed to be low and they are low when they are needed to be high. Despite the objective formula, realizing the economics of the exceedingly roundabout coniferous tree goes against our biology. Following any such roundabout paths, where the difficult initial stages are there to accommodate the ease of the later stages, one needs patience in the initial stages and anticipated impatience in the latter stages, not the inverse. The difficulty of this inversion becomes even more pronounced in individuals whose fixation on the immediate at the expense of the intermediate is further heightened. Bombarded by technology, they exist in a faux present in which everything is accelerated, creating a "present shock,"[30] as termed by Douglas Rushkoff, which references the view of Alvin Toffler's 1970 *Future Shock* that we struggle with processing change itself, made worse by today's ever faster (from an ever-autocatalytic) pace. (As modern as these concepts may seem, they are anchored firmly in Böhm-Bawerkian thought.)

As we might expect, research shows that children and young adults with attention deficit hyperactivity disorder (ADHD) exhibit more pronounced hyperbolic discounting and a stronger preference for immediate rewards than those who do not have the disorder. If we extrapolate these findings, how might they apply to adults who do not have attention deficit disorder (ADD), but experience "pseudo-ADD" because of the pressure of multitasking? Is modernity with its ubiquitous productivity-enhancing technology tools turning us into a society of *hyper*-hyperbolic discounters? These questions are worth considering given the findings of Edward Hallowell, a psychiatrist who, in his superb book *CrazyBusy*, discussed the plight of adults who did not have ADD, but for whom a "severe case of modern life" gave them ADD-like symptoms (what he calls "F-state" for "frantic, frenzied, forgetful, flummoxed, frustrated, and fragmented"). Although there are variations in severity, the empirical propensity of heightened hyperbolic discounting among those with these conditions reinforces the importance of awareness and metaknowledge to rein in impulses and prevent actions in the moment from jeopardizing the future.[31] (It also reinforces my long-held suspicion that PDAs—particularly those with stock tickers—are akin to spikes through the head.) Hallowell's findings would seem to make self-regulation as enabled by the cool *shi* system all the more important; without it people cannot pursue distal goals instead of succumbing to the temptation of "proximal stimuli."[32] Unless the *shi* system functions, intertemporal choice is ineffective—even to the extreme in Phineas Gage's case of being completely eliminated. Research is increasingly showing that a restorative for what I'm calling the *shi* system is time spent in the woods, particularly in children, for whom exposure to nature seems to mitigate the impact of ADHD (or, as Richard Louv calls it, "Nature Deficit Disorder").[33] By the same token, why wouldn't leisurely, contemplative exposure to a coniferous forest with its edifying successions over time help to stretch out our time perception?

Understanding this inconsistency—arbitrary, subjective, and oh so human—allows us to gauge perceptions, reactions, and decisions across time, gaining insight into others' intertemporal behaviors (which will no doubt display a well-defined present-bias) and, of course, our own. We see, as Böhm-Bawerk noted, "through the under-valuation of the future utility, men will refrain from providing for the future so amply as they would otherwise have done. In other words, this underestimate acts to the prejudice of saving and accumulation of wealth."[34] In upcoming chapters, as we move out of the world of observing particular human behavior and, soon, into some of the most intensely emotional frays imaginable—capitalistic investing—such understanding becomes our edge. And decidedly, one can only have an edge if one truly comprehends it. What we have here is a clear, systematic source of investment mispricing, ripe for *intertemporal arbitrage* (a term synonymous with Austrian Investing itself). But this bias of intertemporal inconsistency is not, and for the most part cannot, be arbitraged away, because of the simple reason that the arbitrageurs are the ones most inflicted by the bias.

THE TRADE-OFF OF AN ADDICT

Health is an area in which there is an obvious and logical time separation, particularly around choice. The most dramatic example of health-decision trade-offs is addiction. The pleasure of the substance or behavior in the moment is so strong that it overwhelms any notion of future consequence, no matter how dire—as if the person is looking through binoculars backward, the future seems even more distant and less relevant to the present. Such an attitude calls to mind the old Perry Como song, "Forget Domani," with its hyperbolic discounter's refrain, "Let's forget about tomorrow, for tomorrow never comes." The future as we perceive it—or as we perceive our forward selves—never arrives. The ease with which we expect to manage known adverse consequences is an illusion. We may tell ourselves we can change in the future, but for now the addict intends to do what he always does.[35]

Addiction can of course put health, livelihood, relationships, and even one's life in peril. Therapeutic "12-step" programs can assist in breaking the hold of an addictive substance or behavior, by supporting the recovering person's willpower and future-based decisions to experience deprivation in the moment (e.g., not drinking, not gambling, etc.) in order to experience more and improving health in forward slices of time. (The image of a heroin addict as Bastiat's bad economist who pursues a small present "good" but which will be followed by "the great evil to come"[36] is too poignant to pass up.) Interestingly, for the person with an alcohol addiction, pharmacology has been able to collapse the time between the small present good and the later great evil with oral medications (Antabuse, et al.) that produce immediate unpleasant reactions (headaches, nausea, vomiting) if someone drinks while taking it. This brings the forward back to the present to where we can best process it and feel it. Fortunately (for the persistence of the Austrian Investing edge), no such pill is yet available to economists or investors. But the trick of time compression has also been used to motivate other behaviors impacted by myopic time inconsistency and the chronic tendency among people not to maximize utility over intervals of time. Merrill Lynch's "Face Retirement" feature is an online tool that ages pictures of consumers, thus enabling them to "see" how they will appear in the future. What might be dismissed as a clever marketing gimmick is actually based on a Stanford University experiment that showed such age-enhanced pictures helped people to save more.[37] In effect, they gained more salience for their forward selves by looking eye-to-eye at them.

The Merrill Lynch tool might even be seen as playing off the theme of Aesop's fable of the "Ant and the Grasshopper," which extols the virtue of planning for the future. During the warm summer months, the grasshopper, unconscious of the lean winter months to come, spends all his time and energy singing in the sun. The industrious ant, meanwhile, with a better grasp of what is to come, works all summer to "save" for the future—storing up food to eat in the winter. When the weather turns bitter cold, the ant is prepared while the grasshopper is sorely in need. Or consider a staple of bedtime fairytales, that of the "Three Little Pigs": one who quickly builds a house of straw in order to maximize his time for pleasure and relaxation now; another who spends just a bit more time to make a house of sticks, but quickly joins the straw-builder in play; and the third who foregoes all recreation now and constructs a sturdy house of bricks. When the big, bad wolf huffs and puffs, straw and sticks cannot stand; fortunately for these two high-time preference pigs, their industrious (and no doubt Austrian-read) friend safely ensconced in brick does not bar the door.

My favorite such cultural reference to seeing beyond the present self is the short 1945 children's book *The Carrot Seed* by Ruth Krauss. "A little boy planted a carrot seed," and then had to withstand a barrage of skepticism from his family, who "kept saying it wouldn't come up," as he worked and waited to eventually attain his giant carrot.[38] (I made this book a surreptitious introductory text for my children on roundabout production and its naysayers.)

If such cautionary tales of intertemporal-swapping insects, pigs, and gardening babes are lost on us, there are other cultural threads to follow—the Protestant work ethic and the godliness of industriousness, which is found in many denominations (as well as some other faith traditions). Like their Puritan forebears, the Protestants saw work not just as a means to earn a wage, but as "an absolute *end in itself*—a 'calling'."[39] Working, saving, moderating pleasure today, and preparing for tomorrow (secularly and spiritually) encourage a low time preference, enhance a depth of field perspective (indeed, all the way to kingdom come).

When our forward perception sharpens, we can, in effect, invert the hyperbolic curve—thus becoming *more patient* in the present so that we allow ourselves the advantage to act *opportunistically impatient* in a coming slice of time. By establishing a forward-leaning means-ends framework we put the teleology of time on our side, which enables us to pursue greater exploits in the future. Importantly—and this is where *Umweg* and time preference work together—inverting our present versus future patience allows a similar inversion discussed in Chapter 5, where we start with the end and then progress backward to its means in the present (like Tiger Woods keeping his eye on the pin, not the fairway, in the 2006 British Open). In other words, when we know what the *Zweck* is, we can then establish the appropriate incremental *Ziele* that become the *Mittel* for reaching it.

NO ZEAL FOR *ZIEL* ON WALL STREET

Without a depth of field perspective, we become victimized by time. Immediacy is a tyrant, ratcheting up stress and exacerbating feelings of being time-bankrupt. And there are immense external magnifiers on our time inconsistency. When time is scarce, indeed down to the last grains in the hourglass, as the grim reaper waits, desperation sets in. There is no future, no forward moments, there is only now, now, now. In this world, there is no time or desire to pursue *Ziel*, to employ purposeful patience toward the attainment of an intermediate objective that affords a far greater strategic advantage for later on. There is only an unrelenting *Zweck*, the do-or-die of an action in the moment. This prevalent thinking of impatience now and the expectation of patience later was the opposite of Henry Ford's roundaboutness (thus affirming his exemplary status among *Unternehmer*), such as leaving successful partnerships and foregoing immediate profits in order to engage in the time-consuming endeavor of building production processes so that he could impatiently make and sell cars later.

Although Böhm-Bawerk referred to soldiers, we might think of today's CEOs, CFOs, and, most notably, investment managers and traders as having similarly risky occupations, because they must rivet their attention to the present moment or else face potential professional death.

This is Wall Street, where every trader has a short shelf life and lives in yearly (and even far less) increments. Earn your keep (literally) or you have no future. It is Böhm-Bawerk's "thought of death forced on them by peculiar circumstances,"[40] like soldiers in battle or the terminally ill. A Wall Street trader who fails to focus rabidly on making money frequently has marked himself for extinction. Therefore, there is no roundabout, no intertemporal arbitrage of today's opportunity for the superior one that will unfold in a forward slice of time. No matter how large the "later" might be, the "sooner" is all there is. In fact, time inconsistency is the source of much conventional wisdom on Wall Street, from momentum investing to the merits of monetary policy.

Wall Street's endemic problem is one of lost opportunity; you *must* go for it now, or you won't have a chance tomorrow. (Like wary preschoolers, traders see no sense in going for a larger, later marshmallow that they'll likely never even get.) The biggest sin is not losing money, but failing to make enough money each period to keep your treasured seat at the table. With the constant pressure of knowing that they could be replaced at any moment, Wall Street traders can act no differently—their entire focus must be on now.

The by-products of such present-bias have been some of the biggest failures in risk management, including the collapse of hedge fund Long Term Capital Management (LTCM) in 1998 and, ten years later, the implosion of the investment bank Lehman Brothers. This time preference-driven explanation for such failures is a very counterintuitive view. The most obvious answer to the wild gambler problems of Wall Street is the "free option" that traders possess (whereby they make enormous bonuses when their bets are winners, while not participating in the losses when their bets are losers); but the fact that these calamities and others have involved enormous personal economic loss among those who ultimately caused (or oversaw) them should give us pause in assigning blame to the free option.

While the criticism should be laid on the structure of the system, it is not how most think.

I have tried to gain intuition for what drives Wall Street's gambling madness by constructing a simple cartoon experiment (or computer simulation). In this study, robot traders with free option bonus payouts and what we'll call "knockouts"—or the requirement to exceed a specified profit level every year or else lose their jobs (i.e., get "knocked out," a very realistic scenario)—are given a menu of choices of simple investment strategies to employ: strategies that risk frequent small losses for infrequent huge gains (Marco from Chapter 1); the reverse—strategies that risk infrequent huge losses for frequent small gains (the definitive Wall Street and even hedge fund model); and strategies somewhere in between. (All these strategies—or return distributions—were given identical geometric means, so that, regardless of which strategy a trader selected, his expected strategy return is the same.) The surprising and unambiguous results: Traders with knockouts favored the huge infrequent risks—thus providing very likely career survival—whereas traders without the knockouts avoided them. Moreover, lessening or removing the free option (meaning requiring the trader to have "skin in the game," or share the losses) had no effect on strategy preference. (Preferences were based on maximizing a trader's expected personal career payout; the statistical significance in this switch between strategy preferences was above 99 percent, with no sensitivity to the magnitudes of each strategy's "skewness" nor of profit and loss participations.)

In this simple *gedanken* experiment, with full foresight of the return distributions employed, the traders take the direct approach of optimizing their chances of success each and every successive period—the overriding aim is to avoid being knocked out and thus to stay in the (very lucrative) game. The present is under a microscope (as Klipp showed, excessive carrying costs act like magnifying lenses on the immediate). To add insult to injury, in the real world this tendency is further self-reinforced as the decisive present period makes a trader's time discounting *über*-hyperbolic (literally as if they have iron bars in their frontal lobes). Furthermore, Wall Street careers have a peculiar tendency to survive extreme "take-down-the-system" losses (consider the LTCM folks), whereas small losses or inadequate gains typically cause careers to fade away. On Wall Street, roundabout investing—acquiring later stage advantage through an earlier stage disadvantage—is irrational, and acting as if there is no future is perfectly rational.

So the best solution to "too big to fail" trading risks is relieving the risk takers of their impossible intertemporal predicament. Aside from instituting for-life contracts for traders, this means more oversight from the owners of the capital—perhaps firms that engage in gambling should go back to being privately held—or else that capital should stay out of the gambling business in the first place. (Of course this responsibility is made entirely unnecessary by government bailouts of Wall Street's big gambling losses.) Our time perspective is the *sine qua non* of capital investing and risk taking; it is what matters, what determines our very opportunity set. And it is insidious, malleable, and manipulated by circumstance.

It gets worse, so much worse. Böhm-Bawerk's calls for lower time preference as a prescription to the advantage of roundaboutness are not without their own serious pitfalls. As we will see from Mises in Chapter 8, our perception of time, distorted as it is by our cognitive and emotional equipment, is highly vulnerable to other, more insidious (though seemingly benign) and far more destructive monetary distortions. This is the provenance of the acutely distorted world we live in today—the avoidance of which is a requisite component of Austrian Investing.

ADAPTING TO THE INTERTEMPORAL

One of the hallmarks in the evolution of humans is our brain, in particular, the signature large frontal lobes that allow us to shape our environment and our tools, through the use of reason, with awareness and cognition of the future. Such development moved us out of the cradle of civilization in sub-Saharan Africa, and enabled us to disperse along all points of the compass, following herds and also adapting to new climates and terrains. Tolerance for (natural) climate change and even preference for certain regions were essential to early humans as they settled far and wide. Contact with the often extreme change of seasons gave early humans their first approach to time and roundaboutness (perhaps even giving a head start to those tribes who followed their prey into the less hospitable areas). Some 500,000 years ago, the first humans in China used and controlled fire, which required supplies of fuel to be collected and stored to keep the flames alive. With the development of language, thought expanded from a preoccupation with the present to the representation and abstraction of the future.[41] As evidenced in the fossil record, human migration necessitated adaptations to time; in simplest terms, it was no longer possible to reach for perpetually ripening fruit off the nearest tree or to count on plentiful herds of animals. As humans became aware of the future, they had to learn to work with and prepare for it: drying fruits in the sun, packing meat in ice in the winter, moving livestock seasonally between mountain- and pasture-grazing (*transhumance*), and curdling milk to store as cheese—all illustrating a decreasing time preference and developing roundaboutness. Where supplies of food waxed and waned with the seasons, early humans had to learn to forego current rewards and seek future advantages for survival. Our evolutionary struggle has intrinsically been one of overcoming our inherent faulty temporal wiring, and inverting our congenital overvaluation of the present. The roundabout strategy (the *shi* strategy) has been the very strategy of our species' overwhelming (though uneven) success.

Even today as the evolutionary march continues, with technology seeping into every corner of the seven continents, we still struggle with the most fundamental challenge: our perception of time. In that, we have not moved far beyond the desperation of our ancestors who had far more risk in making this quantum leap of faith: removing the blinders of now and, thus, grasping a deeper, fuller field of time. Perhaps this will always be a frontier to conquer as we continuously fight against that humanness about us, struggling to act in our own best interest and that of those who come after us—indeed, civilization itself.

The fact remains that most people are unable to consistently take the roundabout route because of the mental trip wires that exist in all of us, insidious nooses that drag us back to the current moment and the satisfaction of current desires, the pursuit of pleasure and success now. Therein lies a systematic, universal source of edge to the Austrian Investing approach—perhaps the main takeaway of this chapter. But, as Klipp always said, "This is easy for me to say, very difficult or even impossible for you to do." To exploit this edge is to escape our temporal shackles, requiring nothing less than deliberate and continuous mindfulness and self-discipline. With the metaknowledge of the workings of our own minds we can better attempt to consciously invert our time inconsistency, becoming patient now in order to be strategically impatient later. This critical step is the only way to link the knowledge accumulated thus far along *The Dao of Capital* with its application and implementation. Much of the investment success I've had has resulted unequivocally from a constant practice and plodding, with the early, indispensable prodding of Klipp, to deal with time inconsistency— developing an ability to keep the whole sequence of the slices of time as fully part of the game, and not just maximizing an arbitrary slice at each beginning. With awareness and then some degree of mastery (it is a lifelong journey) we can thus move to the next phase in the Austrian tradition—where the market is a process and we, freed of our inborn temporal biases, can recognize and take our place within it.

Chapter Seven

"The Market Is a Process"

For more than a century the Austrian School has been dismissed as antiquated and unscientific because of its fundamental methodology. Mainstream economics—epitomized first in the early twentieth-century career of John Maynard Keynes (whose famous book *The General Theory* was literally named as an allusion to the revolution of Einsteinian relativity theory) and ultimately in the mid-twentieth-century career of Paul Samuelson (the first American to win the economics Nobel, in 1970)—moved emphatically beyond the Austrians' *aprioristic* approach. Its new direction was toward a distinct alignment with other sciences—the "physics envy," as it has been called, of quantitative and empirical techniques. But while the physicists make steady advances in their field, the "expert" fine-tuning of the mathematical economists has plunged the world back into years of repeated financial crisis and labor market stagnation—the very problems they told us they had solved after studying the Great Depression. Consumers and producers, with their subjective expectations and preferences, do not conform well to mathematical models. It is the very nature of economics as a social science that requires the logical, deductive, *a priori* approach of praxeology, the term Mises used for the scientific study of human action. Mises inherited the theories of Carl Menger and Eugen von Böhm-Bawerk involving value, capital, and time. As an independent-thinking disciple, Mises refined them and added important new theories of his own, particularly with regard to money and credit, and, ultimately, what we today know as Austrian Business Cycle Theory (ABCT), which explained the booms and busts that heaved the landscape of his times into peaks and valleys, destructive forces that continue to this day. Through his work, Mises showcased the adaptability of the Austrian School, while never straying from its methodology (indeed, he was the strictest of adherents to the deductive method of verbal logic). Moreover, Mises demonstrated the ability of the tradition to evolve, all of which opens the door for new interpretations and applications, including those presented here as Austrian Investing.

A man of his times, Mises was a witness to history literally on the front lines: as an artillery officer in the Great War; a resident of Vienna and a university lecturer as the Austro-Hungarian Empire crumbled; a scholar who developed theories of money and banking during the monetary heydays of the 1920s; and a Jew and a staunch critic of national socialism during the rise of the Nazis from whom he had to escape as he fled Europe. Then, in *Human Action: A Treatise on Economics* (published in 1949), Mises gave the post-war world the unshakeable bedrock of the praxeological nature of economics, explainable only in the context of the subjective actions and behaviors of humans. Mises, the scholar and teacher, took pains that others might understand (though, sadly, much of the world refused to listen).

This brings us to a day in 1954, when Mises, then in his 70s, addressed a lecture hall full of graduate students (among them Israel Kirzner, who would later become a venerated economist in the Austrian tradition), who no doubt heard his Austrian accent first and then his impactful words: "*Za market ist a process.*"[1] In those five deceptively simple words, Mises, perhaps the greatest economist of all time, broadened the thinking among his students; the market could not be viewed as or contained by a mere static thing or physical location, but rather as the actions of countless people (just as Klipp showed me that what was happening in the trading pit was only a manifestation of the great process of price discovery). The market can only be understood as being a process—teleological, a series of causes and effects toward the purposeful goals of its participants. Environments and perceptions change—sometimes naturally and sometimes through artificial interventions and distortions.

As much as Mises understood the market, he also knew its failings when undermined, which he captured in ABCT, the roadmap of the market as a discovery process in distorted terrain. Through it all, the processual market reacts and adapts with the push and pull, the *tuishou*, of equilibrating forces.

Nearly as important as Mises's opening line in the lecture hall that day was where he said it: New York University, the new locus of the Austrian tradition (proudly, my graduate *alma mater*). Here was the bastion of (classical) liberalism and the Austrian School, essentially reduced to one man—Mises, who kept the torch burning and refused to let it be extinguished by the hot breath of interventionism and the illiberal (in the classical sense) politics and policies so prevalent in the world. The strict, unbending principles of this refugee scholar exacted a heavy price from Mises—who was treated poorly by the profession when he came to America in 1940—yet the world is so much the better for his sacrifice and refusal to take a more compromising tone that undoubtedly would have made him more employable. As Ron Paul observed, Mises "never yielded to any temptation to soften his stand to be more acceptable to the conventional economic community, which proved him to be a man of strong will and character."[2]

He stood by his principles, which never bestowed wealth, but so much more, including the priceless honor of being, in the words of economist Jörg Guido Hülsmann in his extensive biography of Mises, "the last knight of liberalism."[3]

THE MAN WHO PREDICTED THE GREAT DEPRESSION

Ludwig Heinrich Edler von Mises was born in 1881 in the city of Lemberg, in the northeastern reaches of the Habsburg Empire, in what today is Lviv in the Ukraine. (Ironically, the birthplace of one of the most stalwart defenders of the free market would subsequently become part of the Soviet Union.) His father was a construction engineer for the Austrian railroads, which earned him the honorary "von" title, which was inherited by Mises who continued its use. The family moved to Vienna when Mises's father received a prestigious position in public administration; there, under the influence of their mother, Lu (as he was affectionately called) and his brother, Richard, received an excellent education.[4] But the differences between the brothers were apparent early on: Mises gravitating toward social sciences and Richard toward natural sciences; the divide between deduction and praxeology in the former and empiricism and historicism in the latter became more distinct over the years and was never bridged.

Mises was educated at the *Akademische Gymnasium*, where he read the classics in Latin and Greek; a verse from Virgil became his mantra: "*Tu ne cede sed contra audentior ito.* Do not give in to evil, but proceed ever more boldly against it."[5] He later enrolled in the University of Vienna and studied law and government science, and as a first-year student engaged in a research study of the Galician peasants in the eighteenth century and their attempts to win greater rights. Mises later remarked that his "constant and burning interest in history" in those early years led him "to recognize the inadequacy of German historicism."[6]

In October 1902, three months after passing his university examinations, Mises reported for obligatory military service with the Imperial and Royal Division Artillery Regiment. Stationed near Vienna, he served one year and returned to his studies in September 1903. As a reserve officer with the rank of lieutenant (he was later promoted to captain), he was mobilized two more times, in 1908 and 1912. In 1914, he would don the uniform of the Austrian army again.

Mises began his professional life as a paid intern in a civil service position, which ill-suited him because of his distaste for bureaucracy, and decided to practice law, instead. It was the scholarly life, though, that appealed most to him, first as a student and later as a teacher. Although Menger was still teaching during Mises's early years at university, Mises did not attend those lectures. However, in late 1903, Mises read Menger's *Principles of Economics* for the first time; as he recalled in his *Memoirs*, "It was through this book that I became an economist."[7] The one who had the most direct influence on Mises intellectually was Böhm-Bawerk, whose seminars he began attending at the University of Vienna in the summer of 1905, thus completing the Austrian School succession from Menger to Böhm-Bawerk to Mises.

In his first book, *Theorie des Geldes und der Umlaufsmittel* (*Theory of Money and Credit*), published in 1912, Mises explained how the banking system was endowed with the singular ability to expand credit and with it the money supply, and how this was magnified by government intervention. Left alone, interest rates would be able to dynamically adjust such that only the amount of credit would be used as is voluntarily supplied, in the form of actual savings, and demanded by entrepreneurs. But when credit is force-fed beyond that (I'll call it "credit gavage"), grotesque things start to happen.

Mises submitted *Theories des Geldes* to the university when he applied to become a private lecturer, for which he was accepted in the spring of 1913. He began teaching seminars that summer, but soon all would change when the Great War flared across Europe and Mises again reported for duty. Just as the war began, Mises's mentor Böhm-Bawerk died. With Menger in seclusion, constantly revising his works, and the more visible and prolific Böhm-Bawerk dead before his time, the weight of the Austrian tradition rested on the shoulders of a man headed to the battlefront.

By the end of 1917, Mises had been promoted to the rank of captain and was stationed in Vienna in the economics division of the Department of War. In 1918, Mises was back at the university as a lecturer, where most of his students in a course on banking theory were women; there were few male students because of the war. (Throughout his teaching career, Mises championed both female and male students.) While at the university, he met the famed Max Weber, the German philosopher who authored *The Protestant Ethic and the Spirit of Capitalism*. Commenting on Weber's death in 1920, Mises called it "a great disaster for Germany," adding that had Weber lived longer, "the German people of today would be able to look to this example of an 'Aryan' who would not be broken by National Socialism."[8]

Mises, who said he "encountered nearly all the Marxian theorists in western and central Europe during the course of my life," spoke favorably of only one: Otto Bauer who "had he not been a Marxist . . . could have become a statesman." Following the Great War and the Allied food blockade, when Bauer tried to turn Austria toward Bolshevism, it was Mises who intervened during the winter of 1918–1919, convincing Bauer "that the collapse of a Bolshevist experiment in Austria would be inevitable in a very short time, perhaps within days. The supply of food in Austria was dependent on imports made possible only by the relief assistance of former enemies."[9]

In his private seminars at the University of Vienna that winter, as the empire disintegrated and Austria transitioned from a monarchy to a republic, Mises led discussions on market phenomena and the subjective theory of value. His was the voice of the classical-liberal at a time when socialism was spreading rampantly across Europe. "Thus," as Hülsmann wrote, "Mises was known as *der Liberale*—in today's English we would say he was Mr. Libertarian, the living embodiment of classical-liberal ideas."[10] (And so we complete our arc in *The Dao of Capital* from Laozi, the first libertarian, to Mises, whom many regard as the greatest of them all.)

As an intellectual freedom fighter who waged a war of words, Mises wrote extensively on the dangers of socialism, penning a classic in 1922, *Socialism: An Economic and Sociological Analysis*. As Mises later observed, "Men must choose between the market economy and socialism. The state can preserve the market economy in protecting life, health, and private property against violent or fraudulent aggression; or it can itself control the conduct of all production activities. Some agency must determine what should be produced. If it is not the consumers by means of demand and supply on the market, it must be the government by compulsion."[11] As vigilant as a sentry, Mises continuously warned about the dangers of inflation; like the "good economist" that Bastiat had championed, Mises foresaw great evils to come with dire consequences. His was an insistent voice shouting against inflation-inducing monetary policy over the din of the government printing presses (quite literally, in one story told about him). The 1920s were marked by the brave new era of the Federal Reserve system, promoting inflationary credit expansion and with it permanent prosperity. (Economists today still do not agree that this period was driven by monetary phenomena, and in this controversy we can see the limitations of recognizing the distortions in data alone. Fortunately now, as we'll discuss later in the book, we have found a way to detect that distortion.)

In mid-1929, amid his warnings of the collapse to come from credit expansion, Mises was offered a lucrative job at the Viennese bank, Kreditanstalt. Mises gave a straightforward and prophetic rationale for turning it down. As he told his future wife, Margit, "a great crash" was coming and he did not want his name "in any way connected with it."[12]

As for the lost professional opportunity, Mises told Margit that he was more interested in writing about money than earning it. Mises did manage to protect his money—and, more important, his reputation—by avoiding the biggest crash of his day (which is more than we can say for

Keynes, who though considered more savvy was apparently blindsided by the crash). Mises himself never attempted to take the Austrian tradition to its logical investment conclusions; he once remarked to Margit that though he studied money, as a couple they would never have much of it. (Extending Austrian economics to investing is precisely what I aim to accomplish in this book.) Mises was correct in his projection: not only did a crash come, but Kreditanstalt failed, which triggered a wave of financial panic across central Europe. Thus, Mises was a harbinger of dire times ahead and the man who predicted the Great Depression.

FLEEING THE NAZIS

In January 1933, Hitler became chancellor of Germany. Two months later, despite a government prohibition of parades and assemblies, the Austrian Nazis rioted in the streets of Vienna. It was a great relief when, in March 1934, Mises was invited by the Graduate Institute of International Studies in Geneva, Switzerland, to become a visiting professor of economic relations. His move, though, was viewed as a temporary one, and he returned whenever he could to see Margit. (He waited to propose to her until after his mother's death in 1937; apparently Frau Mises did not approve of Margit, a widowed actress.) In 1934, his book, *Theorie des Geldes*, was finally published in English as *Theory of Money and Credit*, but it was too late. An understanding of it a decade earlier could have spared the world so much pain (although that does require the huge assumption that people would have paid attention). Some much deserved respect followed, although it was unfortunate that it took a disaster for people to take heed of the only predictive scholarly explanation of what was happening. Even today, much of the mainstream fails to see the root cause of market distortions, which as we will see in Chapter 8 are simply and gratuitously passed off *ex post* as "bubbles."

Soon after the release of *Theory of Money and Credit*, Mises was easily eclipsed by Keynes, when this dapper, fresh, and sophisticated English gentleman's book, *The General Theory of Employment, Interest, and Money*, was published in 1936. So what if Keynes lost his shirt in the stock market crash? Apparently more important was that his book appeared scientific and sophisticated, thanks to the inclusion of fancy math and even Greek letters, all of which conveyed rigor and modernity. And he seemed a man of action (whether constructive or destructive was perhaps secondary). The good Lord Keynes fearlessly fought the battle against unemployment with proposals of artificially stimulating demand—thus pretending that consumer preferences are different than they actually are—draining the government's coffers, and running the monetary printing press. It was a Keynesian avalanche, and Mises was swept aside—not refuted by Keynes and his ilk, but ignored. (When Keynes first read Mises's book in German, he dismissed it as unoriginal. This was understandable, since—as he himself explained—Keynes's German was good enough only to recognize what he already knew.)

In March 1938, Mises was back in Vienna for a conference (and he and Margit continued preparations for their long-awaited wedding); he could no doubt sense the mounting tensions in his home country, as the Germans appeared ready to invade. Knowing he was high on the Nazi enemy list—not only because he was Jewish, but also because he stood in staunch opposition to the Nazi *Gleichschaltung*, the totalitarian control and forcible coordination of the economy and every other part of society—Mises retreated again from Vienna, this time for good. His and Margit's von Trappian escape came just hours before the S.S. arrived to arrest Nazi adversaries and seize their property. Mises's apartment was broken into and ransacked; the Gestapo took 21 boxes full of his possessions and sealed the apartment, and returned again in the fall to take whatever was left, including books, personal correspondence, paintings, silver, and documents. After World War II, Mises's files were among the documents found on a train in Bohemia and secretly sent to Moscow (where they were obviously further disregarded). In 1991, they were rediscovered. The whereabouts of his precious Viennese library, however, is not known.[13]

After war broke out in September 1939, Mises began contemplating departure from Europe. Just as Austrian composer Gustav Mahler considered himself "thrice homeless" ("As a native of Bohemia in Austria, as an Austrian among Germans, and as a Jew throughout the world"), so too was Mises: as a Jew among Austrians, as an Austrian among Germans, and as an Austrian economist among the Historicists. Mises's fate resonates in Mahler's words, "Everywhere an intruder, never welcomed."[14]

As Mises and his wife left Geneva en route to the tiny Mediterranean town of Cerberes, France, on the Spanish border, their escape was full of close calls and near misses. The bus ride was perilous, as Margit recalled in her memoirs: "To get there without encountering the Germans, the driver had to change his route frequently, after seeking information from French peasants and soldiers . . . The German troops had advanced very far, and they were everywhere. More than once our driver had to backtrack to escape them."[15] Finally, in July 1940, they left onboard the ship *Europe* for a new home. Had Mises been stopped and arrested at any point along his escape route from Europe, his life would have been in grave peril, and the Austrian School would likely have never gained a foothold on the shores of the United States.

HUMAN ACTION

Life was hard for Mises in the United States, exiled from his beloved Austria. (By the end of World War II, all traces of Austrian Economics had been purged from Vienna. The Nazis tore down the statue of Menger at the University of Vienna; it was restored to the *Arkadenhof*, or courtyard, at the university in the 1950s.[16]) Mises went to work for the National Bureau of Economic Research (NBER), thanks to a grant from the Rockefeller Foundation to put him on the payroll at about one-third of what he had been making in Geneva. Although grateful for the opportunity to work, Mises and his wife had difficulty making ends meet. Mises was also discouraged by the ideology sweeping his new home, which had stood up against communism and National Socialism, but in the aftermath of the New Deal was leaning increasingly toward state interventionism in all corners of the economy. With his career stymied and having no way to influence the thinking of the day because U.S. publishers were interested only in the mainstream, Mises fell into despair. In 1943, after being told his contract with the NBER would not be extended, Mises went to work for the National Association of Manufacturers, as a consultant and a member of its Economic Policy Advisory Group. Then, in 1944, it was arranged for Mises to become a visiting professor at New York University, where he would give an economics seminar (though his salary would be paid from private funds). He was a "visiting professor" at NYU for more than 20 years. Although he never had the title of full professor at any university at which he taught, in his seminars (first in Vienna and later in New York) and through his writings Mises made an impact on a generation of rising intellectual leaders, such as his students Austrian-born Friedrich Hayek (who would later win the Nobel in economics) and, later, Murray Rothbard, an American in the Austrian school. However, without a full-time position at a prestigious university, Mises was unable to develop students and future professors who could have further advanced the Austrian tradition.[17] (Throughout his life, Mises remained committed to advancing scholarship in Austrian economics. His personal book collection of more than 5,000 volumes, which he amassed after moving to the United States, was acquired by Michigan's Hillsdale College; the Ludwig von Mises Room at the college's library also contains copies of personal correspondence, articles, and letters that the Nazis confiscated from Mises's apartment in Vienna and were later found in Russia, as well as his original desk and chair—incredibly made available to students to sit and study in the master's perch.)

Even without a university platform, Mises catapulted into the economics spotlight with the publication in 1949 of *Human Action*. (The original book was published in German in 1940 as *Nationalökonomie: Theorie des Handelns und Wirtschaftens*.) Rothbard rightly called *Human Action* Mises's "greatest achievement" and lauded it as "one of the finest products of the human mind in our century. It is economics made whole."[18] Mises's first American friend Henry Hazlitt (as we recall, the author of my cherished *Economics in One Lesson*) wrote in *Newsweek* that *Human Action* was "destined to become a landmark in the progress of economies." He called it "a work of great originality written in a great tradition," and praised it for extending "beyond any previous work the logical unity and precision of modern economic analysis."[19]

What critics of the Austrians fail to appreciate is the importance of the idea, as highlighted in the title of Mises's book, that economics is undeniably the study of human action, which is highly subjective and cannot be reduced to data points and mathematical models. To illustrate the point for his students, Mises would use the example of rush-hour behavior among commuters at New York's Grand Central Station. Those who studied human action would start from the premise that there is a purpose behind our behavior, which in this instance was to commute from home to work via the train in the morning and then the return trip in the evening. However, the opposite approach by the "truly scientific" behaviorist, who uses only empiricism, would merely see people rushing around randomly, without any particular aim, at certain times of the day. By this example, Mises showed which of the two approaches to human behavior would be most meaningful—clearly the deductive.[20]

In his *apriorism*, Mises took a very Kantian approach, while others were more Aristotelian, which serves to illustrate some of the diversity of opinion among the Austrians. Slight disagreements aside among the approaches of Menger, Böhm-Bawerk, Mises, and even Rothbard, the crux of the Austrian methodology is what they agree upon, and it is uniquely Austrian and essential to this book. (At times, the Austrians' methodological arguments over the flavor of *apriorism* resemble a debate over how many angels can dance on the head of a pin, which we'll save for the philosophers.) What remains most important, as discussed in Chapter 4, is that economics cannot be considered *positivist* (empirical) because there are no constants in human action, the way there are in the natural sciences (such as the charge on an electron, and so forth). It's useless to say the economist should look at history and let the facts "speak for themselves," because we need an antecedent theory to know which facts we should even consider, and to even know how to classify a "fact" in the first place—to call something "an exchange" relies on the observer's understanding of the concept of exchange beforehand. In Mises's view, much of the work of professional economists was not the development or "testing" of theory, but rather the chronicling of historical events. As Mises put it, "Economic history, descriptive economics, and economic statistics are, of course, history."[21]

At the heart of the Austrian methodology is healthy skepticism of data and, in particular, how economics (and, equivalently, investing) uses data to back-fit a story around spurious relationships found in the data (we call this data mining). Admittedly, we do take a peek at the data (as we will later in this book), but we do not rely upon statistical and historical information to form our understanding. In fact, I might go so far as to call myself an antiempiricist, because empiricism often creates illusions and obfuscates the true underlying mechanisms at work. As Mises explained, "Mechanical equations can be used to solve practical problems through the introduction of empirically acquired constants and data; but equations of mathematical catallactics cannot in the same way be of service to practical problems in the area of human action where constant relations do not exist."[22]

A fervent follower of praxeology, Mises used deductive *gedanken* experiments (applying introspection to the study of human action) to posit highly subjective decisions and behaviors of what he called the "acting man." Based on their actions, these "actors" communicate their preferences in the marketplace (and to entrepreneurs who observe them). As Mises demonstrated, prices are guided by human action—largely through the lens of their impact on profits and losses—as the market adjusts and corrects itself in the face of the turbulence of an imperfect world.[23] When the market is left in its natural state (as we'll discuss later in this chapter and in Chapter 8), entrepreneurs make intertemporal decisions (not infallibly, to be sure, but without outside interference that causes a communication disconnect) about whether to build ever-more roundabout capital structures to meet forward demand, or whether meeting consumers' immediate needs takes precedence.

Yet, despite skepticism of inductivist methods, observation does play a role in praxeology; as Mises said, "Only experience makes it possible for us to know the particular conditions of action. Only experience can teach us that there are lions and microbes. And if we pursue definite plans, only experience can teach us how we must act vis-à-vis the external world in concrete situations."[24] In Mises's view, the economist didn't rely on empirical tests to choose among various candidates for an economic law; such laws were determined through logical deduction. However, the economist needed to rely on observation (and his own sense of judgment) to know when to *apply* a particular economic law or principle. For instance, we can state that doubling the quantity of money, other things equal, will increase prices, and we don't need to look at history to "test" that law. Yet to *use* this law or principle to help guide people in the real world requires an understanding of what the money is in a particular community, how much it has increased, whether there are other factors that could exacerbate or mitigate the effect, and so on.

The 1970s were a time of renaissance for the Austrian School, thanks to the spirit and determination of Mises. During this time, Mises's innumerable contributions to economics became more recognized, including several studies on the business cycle, which he coauthored with

Friedrich Hayek. The Mises-Hayek studies warned of the dangers of credit expansion and predicted the coming currency crisis. This work was cited by the Nobel committee in 1974—the year after Mises's death—when Hayek was awarded a Nobel Prize for economics. (Of all the reasons to look askance on the Nobel committee's actions with regard to those to whom it gives its prize in economics, the obvious slight to Mises stands out as the most blatant of all. While the award to Hayek was certainly good for him and for the Austrian School, the fact remains that without Mises the Austrian School would have died with Menger and Böhm-Bawerk; there certainly would have been no Nobel-worthy work from Hayek.)

It is to Mises that the Austrian Tradition owes an inestimable debt, not only for hard work with little recognition (and scant remuneration), but also for his resolve to be the lone voice against huge and insidious evils that confronted the world in waves, from hyperinflation and irresponsible monetary and fiscal policies to Bolshevism and national socialism. (This rich legacy lives on, thanks in large part to the efforts of his wife, Margit, who supported the founding of the Ludwig von Mises Institute in 1982 and chaired its board until she died in 1993.) Mises remained steadfast, a light of reason, because he never forgot his roots with Menger and Böhm-Bawerk and stayed true to a tradition, which remains highly relevant today.

UNTERNEHMER IN THE LAND OF THE NIBELUNGEN

The Austrians are known for grounding all of their analysis—even when looking at "macro" issues such as recessions and inflation—within a microeconomic approach, based on the actions of individual consumers and entrepreneurs. We will follow suit here with an economic parable to illustrate how "the market is a process," not static action, where neither time nor opportunity is homogeneous. We will bring in some key Austrian concepts that are central to our story, especially the entrepreneurial discovery of "false prices." We will also discuss a new concept that I've dubbed the *Misesian Stationarity index* (or *MS index* for short), which, though not a measure developed by Mises himself, is a natural extension of the Mengerian/Böhm-Bawerkian understanding

"From the point of view of eternity and the infinite universe man is an infinitesimal speck. But for man human action and its vicissitudes are the real thing. Action is the essence of his nature and existence, his means of preserving his life and raising himself above the level of animals and plants."

Ludwig von Mises, in Human Action, *1998, The Ludgwig von Mises Institute.*

of the temporal structure of capital, roundabout production, and time preference—as well as the Misesian understanding of economic distortions that arise from monetary interventionism. Thus prepared, we proceed to the mythical Land of the Nibelungen. (My apologies to any Wagnerians.)

The Land of the Nibelungen, or Nibelungenland, is a quintessentially beautiful place of soaring mountains, lush forests, picturesque farms, and high-elevation pastureland to which the goatherds drive their animals in the annual summer *Alpaufzug* in order to graze in the sweet grass and take in the fresh breezes. In Nibelungenland there are but three landowners, Siegfried, Johann, and Günther, who gaze out their back doors each morning and survey their fiefdoms (all of which have pretty much identical land). As pasture for their Alpine goats, the land is used in a direct, relatively short production process (as we recall from Böhm-Bawerk) of about a month or so, which equates to the time it takes the grass and flora to grow before the pasture is ready again to be devoured by the ravenous goats. From this short production process flows the staple Nibelungen food product: goat's milk. Of course, grass and *Alpenblumen* are not the only things that will grow on the land; the soil, sunlight, and available water make it suitable for forestry, although timber is a much more roundabout, time-consuming process than simply keeping pastures. Rather than the quick turnaround measured in weeks, the timber "crop" might take forty years to mature sufficiently for harvest. Timber is tempting because of good demand for wood as fuel and lumber for construction, and yet the landowners can typically count on brisk demand for goat's milk, as well.

Standing at his back door one morning, listening to the melodic tinkling of the goats' bells as they head to the high pasture and the staccato pounding of hammers from new construction in the village, Siegfried gets an idea: to devote *some* of his land to pasture and the rest to timber. When Johann and Günther hear of Siegfried's plan, they say to themselves, "*Warum nicht?*" Indeed, why not: The demand for milk and lumber is such that all three devote some land to pasture and the rest to timber.

At this point in the story, Siegfried, Günther, and Johann manage to devote just the right amount of land to pasture for milk production and to forestry for growing timber stands to generate cash flow that equals the market rate of interest on their invested capital (land). We could initially imagine the three Nibelung entrepreneurs are experiencing Mises's *evenly rotating economy* (the ERE from Chapter 1), in which there are no pure profits; rather, everyone earns the same rate of return from investing in marginal land that they could get if they bought a bond. The Faustmann ratio (from Chapter 5) for each is thus equal to 1, which means the rate of return on the land investment is equal to the market rate of interest (which represents their opportunity cost of capital). There is no reason to change anything; everyone is and remains in equilibrium; the entrepreneur serves no purpose and can be ignored. (This is largely the domain of mainstream economics.)

Back when they were boys, Siegfried was always the one to watch, because he seemed to have a knack for everything, from raising goats to slaying dragons to getting the girl. (He even ended up marrying Günther's sister and, to make matters worse, won the affections of his wife.) There is just something about that Siegfried (named for "joyous in victory") that puts him a step above the rest. Eventually, even though his land is physically identical to that owned by the other two men, and his production costs are exactly the same as well, Siegfried finds an edge. He discovers that serenading his pastures with his *Alpenhorn*—or, more precisely, his magic *Wunderhorn*—miraculously makes the grasses grow fuller and faster, and he begins to do the same with his tree seedlings, with the same results. Günther naturally tries a similar trick, but he just doesn't share Siegfried's musicianship. In fact, Günther's plants actually seem to suffer when he garishly plucks his *Zither*. Johann—who is truly just the typical, "average Johann"—thinks it's all a bunch of nonsense since everybody knows grass and trees can't hear music!

So in the real world, the ERE is too demanding a benchmark because things simply don't work in that way. It is more realistic to suppose that some people are better at certain things, such as anticipating what consumers will want in the future, and more efficient in producing goods to satisfy consumer wants (both of which seem to be Siegfried's strong suits). Therefore, some entrepreneurs will earn profits and others will suffer losses. If measured by the Faustmann ratio, the results would vary considerably; the more successful would have a ratio above 1, while the laggards are below 1. But what if everyone is lumped together? The result would be a *stationary economy*, in which there are no aggregate profits or losses. The *aggregate* Faustmann ratio—the sum of all the individual numerators, or the total market capitalization, divided by the sum of all the denominators, or the total replacement cost or "net worth"—is equal to 1. In Nibelungenland, that means Siegfried's profits are counterbalanced by Günther's losses, while Johann just earns the average rate of return equal to the market interest rate.

Keep in mind, though, that the stationary economy in Nibelungenland is not an ERE, because things change. Siegfried (the Henry Ford of Nibelungenland) decides that, since he calculates that he is earning a 15 percent return on his existing land (which is above the current interest rate, which we'll say is 8 percent), rather than merely pocketing his profits as payment for his past success (he lives well enough now as it is), he will instead reinvest those profits right back into ever-more land; his operations are thus growing. Günther, having been bested by Siegfried once again, decides he better scale back his timber operation because he's earning only 1 percent on his marginal land. He sells some of his land to Siegfried. This reallocation continues until, on the margin, Siegfried no longer earns more than the cost of capital, and Günther earns at least the cost of capital. (It's possible that Günther ends up with no land, but we don't know this in general; it would depend upon specific numbers.) However, as Günther sells off his land we can assume his marginal return grows steadily higher, because he gets rid of the least-productive parcels first. Although, as stated earlier, we assume for simplicity's sake that the three men own identical land, it still makes sense to think that selling off some of it would raise Günther's return, because he has to hire workers and invest in other inputs for goat herding and forestry. By reducing the scale of his operations, Günther can let go the most inefficient workers and/or equipment, and retain the most productive combinations. (In the real world in which land quality and suitability varies, the assumption is even more correct; it would only make sense to sell off the least-fertile land first.) And we can fairly assume that if Günther couldn't increase his marginal returns by scaling back his operations, he would simply get out of farming altogether. In keeping with our story, though, we presume Günther can tweak his operation in response to his losses, rather than selling out to Siegfried completely.

Siegfried, on the other hand, would actually experience diminishing marginal productivity as he bought more land from Günther. (If this didn't happen, Siegfried would go on a buying spree until he owned everything in Nibelungenland.) One obvious cause for the decline in return, perhaps to below the cost of capital, is that he has exhausted the demand for even his premium products (the *Alpenhorn*-serenaded goat's milk and timber products), and his increased supply has put pressure on prices. Indeed, Siegfried's growth has made life better for both him and his customers. And, of course, if Siegfried were to try to add to his operations without limit, the cost of borrowing capital would, itself, eventually begin rising, which would keep his expansion in check.

As we can see, Siegfried is the golden boy whose personal market is favorably in disequilibrium and nonstationarity, because the return on his investment is higher than his cost of capital. Thus, Siegfried is "progressing"; capital accumulation is occurring in his business—as he starts more seedlings, pushing his revenues further into the future, making him increasingly roundabout in his production. (Günther, however, is "regressing," because he is shrinking his capital.) Siegfried is living proof of a Misesian maxim of an entrepreneur's intolerance for false prices. As Mises wrote in *Human Action*, "The essential fact is that it is the competition of profit-seeking entrepreneurs that does not tolerate the preservation of *false* prices of the factors of production."[25] Furthermore, these entrepreneurial activities bring about the correction of false prices, while whittling away at both profits and losses. Keep in mind that entrepreneurs make mistakes all the time, but when there is stationarity overall (absent any change in saving and investment preferences) losses from some are canceled out by profits from others, in the aggregate. We see this dynamic in Siegfried and Günther, both of whom play an essential part in the market process, through which each attempts to better his position, and in so doing ends up weeding out all false prices and removing opportunities for both profits and losses. There is aggregate stability but not cross-sectional stability in the stationary economy (that is, there is entrepreneurial dispersion). Some businesses are "progressing," some are staying the same, and others are "regressing." In other words, there are Siegfrieds and there are Günthers—and even average Johanns in between.

Taking a deeper look, we would expect that if Siegfried, Johann, and Günther sold their operations outright to capitalists (say, having decided to retire to Boca), in both an ERE and a stationary economy the total appropriately appraised sale price would exactly equal the amount of land times the market price (plus any accumulated capital, such as trees). Thus, we would expect the numerator of the aggregate Faustmann ratio (the total land expectation value, or LEV) would equal the denominator, which is the total land replacement value (LRV); the whole would equal the sum of its parts. Specifically, ownership of the land operations—entitling owners to the present-discounted value of future net rents from what the land produces (pasture or timber), the LEV in the numerator—would have the exact same value as the replacement land market price. (In short, what the land earns equals what it costs to replace.) In an ERE, this balance would be achieved by each individual firm experiencing perfect equilibrium between the return and the replacement costs. In a stationary economy, as stated, this balance is only achieved in the aggregate. Because their returns vary, Siegfried's operation that earns more than the cost of capital will sell for more than the value of his assets; Johann, whose return equals the cost of capital, will realize no premium on his operation, and Günther's operation, with a return below the cost of capital, will sell for less than the value of his assets.

It is precisely this mismatch—between the market's present value of the free cash flows from his going enterprise versus the market's value of the invested capital under his control—that compels Günther, with a Faustmann ratio of less than 1, to sell off land, while Siegfried, with a Faustmann ratio above 1, buys land. No matter that Günther might want to imitate Siegfried, his returns tell a different story; Günther is simply better off selling marginal land at the market price and investing the proceeds at the market rate of interest, and sticking to his pastureland. Siegfried, meanwhile, armed with his *Wunderhorn*, has greater profit potential from the additional land; even if he has to borrow from the bank to buy the extra land, his return is well above the market rate of interest. This balancing of resources, from least profitable to most, continues until each man finds that the present value of his future (net) cash flows is exactly equal to the value of his land—though new changes may disrupt the process before this stasis point is ever reached in the real world. (It's also true that in the real world, the spot prices of lumber and goat's milk would probably change, but such details are omitted to illustrate the concept.) In the Land of the Niebelungen, an ongoing balancing and steering process—directed unwittingly by the players in the game—moves the economy toward stationarity (and if there were no further changes in the data, even to an ERE) as false prices are eliminated. This is precisely what Mises meant when he said, "The market is a process."

The cartoonish Nibelung economy aptly illustrates Mises's concept of stationarity. When the ratio across the economy of the total present value of cash flows from the land (LEV) to the total replacement cost of that land (LRV) departs from 1, it signals a departure from stationarity. Thus I call this aggregate ratio of the LEV to the LRV the MS index, in deference to Mises, the originator of the crucial concepts involved; as such, the MS index will be a central measure and tool used in Austrian Investing in Chapters 9 and 10.

It should be noted that the MS index is similar to the well-known Tobin's Q ratio (and in fact my calculated values of the MS index used in Chapter 9 are essentially the same as the Equity Q ratio), as discussed by Nobel laureate James Tobin in 1969. Strictly speaking, Tobin's Equity Q calculation nets assets against corporate debt in the denominator; this is equivalent to our treatment of the Faustmann ratio, because debt and interest expenses can be subtracted from the LRV and LEV, respectively, without any impact or change in meaning. (Faustmann assumed no debt in his forestry operation, but accounting for it is trivial.) However, I will reserve the honor of its "discovery" to Mises, not Tobin, because Tobin's work on the Q ratio came much later and also because Tobin patently misunderstood its meaning and the consequences of using it as a monetary policy gauge of effectiveness. (The significance of the index lies entirely in the concepts—not the accounting or empiricism—behind it.) Not only did Tobin arrive at his measure via a different path from the one taken in this book, but his policy recommendations—what Tobin *did* with his analysis—were also quite different. Tobin recognized, as we have here, that loose monetary policy could cause the valuation of assets to exceed their replacement value, which would cause the Q ratio to exceed 1. Yet, Tobin, operating within the simpler Keynesian view of the capital stock of the economy, thought this would be a good thing, drawing forth (as one would expect) real physical investment in new capital goods and making the economy more productive. (As if to help me underscore this very point, just as I was finalizing this manuscript, Paul Krugman in his *New York Times* blog admitted that the economy presented some "real puzzles." Krugman wondered, "Why, with profits so high, don't businesses invest more?" and he explicitly brought up Tobin's Q. Making it all the more fitting for my point here, Krugman dismissed these "real-side" puzzles as having nothing whatsoever to do with the Fed's monetary policies, and saw no "signature" of an asset bubble.[26])

So heretofore, the MS index is what matters most, not only among the entrepreneurs in the Nibelungenland but also among the rest of us, in the real world of capitalistic investing.

GENUINE CHANGE IS AFOOT IN NIBELUNGENLAND—A MARKET-INDUCED DROP IN INTEREST RATES

Meanwhile, back in the Land of the Nibelungen, Siegfried is making money and buying land, Günther is selling land, and Johann is making the equivalent of his cost of capital. Then, like a shift in the wind, Siegfried notices changes as he walks around the village. People are scaling back their purchases of consumer goods such as goat's milk and saving more, perhaps with the intention of buying lumber (or even more goat's milk) in the future. In other words, consumers' time preferences have fallen: Savings are increasing and, as a result, interest rates are declining.

Standing at his back door on a clear Alpine day, Siegfried contemplates what this means for his land holdings, thus demonstrating Kirzner's "alertness" found among entrepreneurs who are constantly on the lookout for potential profit opportunities. Such alertness exists along the entire spectrum of entrepreneurial activity, from mere arbitrage created by price discrepancies to the development of new products and/or the discovery of new and improved production processes.[27] Siegfried engages in a kind of appraisal process known as *Verstehen*, or understanding, which is critical to the decision to become more roundabout; this is about the subjective anticipation of what consumers want, not a mechanical process of expected value and weighted explicit probabilities.[28] In Siegfried's case, he approximates the Faustmann ratio for his operation and that of his competitors, and even appraises the ratios for businesses that do not even yet exist; his analysis leads him to a decision, and he acts upon it. Hence, Siegfried is a "real entrepreneur," as Mises would have described him, a speculator who is "eager to utilize his opinion about the future structure of the market for business operations promising profits." Although the future remains uncertain, the entrepreneur relies on "specific anticipative understanding," which "can be neither taught nor learned"; he does not focus on what was or is, but acts upon what he expects the future to be. In Mises's view, "The impulse of his actions is that he appraises the factors of production and the future prices of the commodities which can be produced out of them in a different way from other people."[29]

What occurs in Nibelungenland illustrates the continuous discovery process of endless change, endless disequilibria, endless testing and correcting. What results are also endlessly changing prices and new production (and new liquidations, as in the case of Günther). As each responds to Faustmann ratios in this way, in aggregate the system responds to its MS index and thus progresses, returns to stationary, regresses, and so on. The market facilitates the vital control and communication within the system—a grand homeostatic process. Unfortunately, misunderstanding this process has lead—and perhaps never more so than today—to interventions which undermine and distort that natural process.

In this Nibelungen scenario, in which interest rates naturally respond, without intervention, to changes in time preference, Siegfried knows that lower interest rates mean that the present value of the expected cash flows from forestry rise because their more-distant profits are discounted to a lesser degree. (He might possibly also consider that consumers who are saving now could be expected to buy more things like lumber in the future.) What he knows intuitively (smart guy, that Siegfried) is that his Faustmann ratio is greater than 1—at least for now—as consumer spending is being diverted from now until later, while future expenditures are now discounted by a lower interest rate. Bottom line: the aggregate value of owning his land operations has increased. Siegfried knows exactly what to do: divert more land out of pasture and into the roundabout production of timber. (Keep in mind that, in a forest, the growing stock of trees is capital goods, not land, in an economic classification. Given a plot of suitable land, a forest can be "built" by humans, but it takes time. Thus, the amount of trees of a certain age available at a given time is not a fact of nature's endowment; it is a product of human intervention, just as surely as a tractor.) To the extent that bringing new land under cultivation requires the investment of real resources—using labor and tools to clear the land, till the soil, dig irrigation trenches, install irrigation, and so forth—the transformed product is new "capital," too, even though it might initially sound odd to describe a parcel of land as "capital."

As Siegfried and his workers labor on his landholdings, the accumulation of "capital" becomes visible as more trees are planted, leading to a perpetually larger quantity of maturing timber in any future year. (In the real world, another route by which the economy would become more roundabout would be to pull previously submarginal land into cultivation.) Most important, though, the MS index remains a robust indicator of the relationship between the aggregate return on invested capital and the associated opportunity costs, just as it did with individual Faustmann ratios. This, in a nutshell, is what's so special about the MS index.

In this section, we have been walking through the implications of a sudden and unexpected change in consumer time preference. Their sudden desire to save more will help some producers and hurt others. Milk prices fall because consumers are cutting back their purchases in order to save more. In the short run, the return on land devoted to pasture falls. On the other hand, return on more roundabout timberland rises. Siegfried makes a profit on his timber holdings, but, alas, poor Günther is once again left behind as he suffers a further decline in the profitability of his pastures. In the aggregate, though, Siegfried's gains outweigh Günther's losses because in this scenario there is genuine saving and investment. It is a classic example of what Mises called a *progressing* (no longer stationary) economy, as defined by a period of capital accumulation.

Now, we could imagine some other changes in Nibelungenland in response to the lower consumer time preference. One of our three *Unternehmer* might decide to invest in cheese production, a roundabout process of intermediate length, longer than selling goat's milk every day, but much shorter than growing trees for lumber. And, thanks to lower interest rates, it is now more profitable.

In our progressing economy, the MS index, as stated, would rise, but the effect would be fleeting. The numerator goes up because aggregate profits from timber producers would be greater than aggregate losses from milk producers (Mises and subsequent Austrians have argued that genuine savings from consumers are the source of the aggregate net profit). However, the denominator would go up quickly, too, because the new savings would be immediately channeled into financing *net* capital acquisitions, such as land and equipment for timber or cheese production.

Therefore, there is no reason to expect a genuine, savings-driven drop in interest rates (which causes a brief, intermittent move out of stationarity) to trigger a systematic change in the MS index. The increase in aggregate profits (measured in monetary terms) that causes the numerator to increase would be counterbalanced very quickly by an increase in the market value of the actual assets owned collectively. The same underlying cause—namely, a drop in time preference and, hence, increased savings by consumers—would drive increases in *both* the numerator and denominator. As we can see, the numerator would never get ahead of the denominator (or vice versa) for very long, because even roundabout production would entail immediate transactions to acquire more factors of production. (To expect otherwise is to expect "greedy entrepreneurs" to fully recognize higher profits in their operations—through a higher LEV—yet refrain from exploiting them.)

In Nibelungenland, there is a hum of activity among the timber operations, dairies and creameries, toolmakers, and all the rest. These normal market forces push the MS index immediately back to 1. As Siegfried and his peers go about their business, there is no need to take a particular stand on the "rationality" of investors or the lack thereof; they may suffer from waves of "animal spirits" (à la Keynes) or have "irrational exuberance" (à la Robert Shiller). The point is that if these traits will bid up *stock prices*, why wouldn't they also bid up *capital goods prices*? If investors are bullish and want to buy shares in a trucking company, why wouldn't people also be enticed to buy trucks? In this sense, we can view any history of a diverging MS index as quasi-proof of *distortion away from stationarity*, which as we will see creates quite a bit of havoc in Nibelungenland.

DISTORTION COMES TO NIBELUNGENLAND— THE CENTRAL BANK LOWERS RATES

One sunny Nibelungenland day, as Siegfried heads out to his lands to serenade his tree seedlings and his prime pasture, he bids a hearty "*Grüß Gott*" to his neighbor, Fritz, the banker.

As Fritz returns the greeting, he whispers a bit of news which he managed to find out before it became public from his chums at the central bank: Interest rates are headed lower. Siegfried scratches his head; it doesn't seem to him that people are spending any less and thus saving more, which would cause interest rates to drop. He gives little additional thought to it as he continues on his way, because his operations are already profitable without a change in the cost of capital (thanks, as always, to his *Wunderhorn* playing). But he isn't surprised when, a few days later, he runs into Günther and Johann, now bubbling with excitement over their newfound profitability. Indeed, with a lower cost of capital, everyone now appears to be making more money.

This time, however, it is not a genuine, savings-induced drop in interest rates. Rather, the stationary economy of Nibelungenland is rocked by the central bankers who decide to pump in more money and push down interest rates. (Strictly speaking, the Misesian theory of the business cycle need not involve a central bank, because credit expansion occurs whenever a commercial bank lends out [some of] one customer's deposits to a new borrower. However, in modern times such credit expansion by commercial banks typically occurs under the auspices of the central bank.)

Now, as households are saving less and consuming more, lumber and milk prices are going up, and all the while interest rates fall, Günther and Johann sense (finally) a chance to be profitable like Siegfried. At face value, the artificial change in interest rates and the artificial rise in consumer prices have helped *all* landowners, all of whom think they are earning profits.

The Nibelungenland Börse (the stock market) stages a dramatic rally, because the market value of firms—the price of title to existing capital—is being bid up, and people are revising upward their expectations of future net rents. (Another reason the market value goes up is that future net rents are discounted at a lower rate.) Because interest rates have been artificially lowered, the jump in the numerator is greater in this scenario than when rates respond to genuine savings. In the former scenario, as we recall, households reduced expenditures on milk. The gains of entrepreneurs like Siegfried (who had foreseen the profitability of timber) were partially offset by the losses of those entrepreneurs like Günther who had devoted most of their land to pasture; there wasn't a *general* boom. But in the euphoria induced by the central bank pumping in liquidity, *every* sector seems to enjoy prosperity—at least temporarily. In the artificial interest rate scenario, one firm's gain need not be offset by another firm's loss, and so aggregate profits increase much more—pushing up the numerator of the MS index by far more than in the earlier scenario of lower rates due to genuine saving. Everyone is a "Siegfried" now—well-dressed, smiling, the toast of the town (or so they think). Meanwhile, the forces that previously pushed up the denominator in the genuine-savings scenario are muted in the central bank-induced drama. Despite Siegfried-like profits suddenly made available to average Johanns, there is a crunch on how much new capital accumulation can occur, because there isn't any real saving. The central bank can print money, but it can't print land! Everything is encouraged to grow simultaneously—just as we saw in Chapter 2 in the fire-suppressed forest and as we will revisit again in Chapter 8. The Land of the Nibelungen, just like the real world under such intervention, is a frightfully distorted place. It is physically impossible to devote more land to timber production because all the pastureland currently in use appears to be quite profitable and, indeed, deserving of expansion, as well.

Worse yet, artificially low interest rates don't just maintain the status quo; they spur *greater* milk consumption. The Nibelungen, motivated by cheap credit, are living it up, drunk on more milk consumption. In order to keep up with the demand, some of the land devoted to timber must be diverted into pastureland. So rather than replanting trees on freshly harvested forestland, some landowners decide to transition back to pastureland in order to boost milk production. No one wants to wait; rather than accumulate assets to amass their own roundabout capital structures, people bid up prices of existing operations, whether stands of timber or goat farms and pastures. Fritz's proprietary trading desk has already been at work—front-running everyone else—gobbling up these assets whose returns now trump the lower interest rates.

Although the availability of some submarginal land may act as a safety valve, allowing the expansion of both timber and pasture (thereby lowering the aggregate return on invested capital), in general the artificially low interest rates will open up the possibility of *shortening* the overall structure of production—the very opposite of the natural response when interest rates fall due to greater savings. Mises called this phenomena *capital consumption*.

In the real world, Mises thought capital consumption occurred as a mistake driven by the perverse effects of inflation upon accounting. For example, if a business owner establishes a "sinking fund" out of incoming revenues, in order to replace his depreciating equipment, then unanticipated bursts of inflation could distort his plans. He would see "good times" in his business—customers spending liberally on his products—and would, in his mind, put aside enough to replace his equipment as it wore out, while spending the rest that he considered to be pure profit. In reality, though, it was only the result of inflation. Later, when he needed to replace his equipment, he would be shocked to discover he hadn't put aside enough; he had unwittingly "consumed" part of his business's equipment.

As we can see, inflationary credit expansion by the banks can unfortunately lead to a *reduction* of the overall capital structure (a regressing economy). Although the market value of a given capital good might rise to reflect the higher estimates of future rents, it should be clear that the aggregate increase in the denominator LRV will be at a lesser pace in this scenario (as capital stock is growing slowly or even shrinking) compared to when genuine savings allows for the production of additional capital goods.

Keep in mind that when Mises spoke of the perverse effects of inflation, he referred to artificial expansion of bank credit, and hence the total quantity of money in the economy. He did not mean the rise of a price index of some basket of consumer goods, which is what most economists and analysts think of today with the word "inflation." Although monetary or credit inflation will cause price inflation (other things being equal), this is not an essential element of the Austrian theory. Credit expansion, with its artificially low interest rates, distorts the capital structure, fostering an unsustainable boom followed inevitably by a crash—whether or not the public perceives an "inflation problem." Mises captured the false, unsustainable boom of a central bank-induced drop in interest rates in *Human Action*: "But now the drop in interest rates falsifies the businessman's calculation. Although the amount of capital goods available did not increase, the calculation employs figures which would be utilizable only if such an increase had taken place. The result of such calculations is therefore misleading. They make some projects appear profitable and realizable which a correct calculation, based on an interest rate not manipulated by credit expansion, would have shown as unrealizable. Entrepreneurs embark upon execution of such projects. Business activities are stimulated. A boom begins."[30]

To be clear, it is the abnegation of interest rates as an information and control parameter in the economy that creates the distortion, not just inflation *per se*. That is, if money was instead simply created by the central bank and wired to Congress to be spent, clearly it would be inflationary and counterproductive but it needn't create the distortions of boom and bust.

In Nibelungenland, the false prosperity has spread faster than hay fever in the summertime. Induced by cheap and available credit, consumers are buying out the shops. New businesses open up in the village, and people spend even more, maxing out their credit cards. The average Johann is remodeling his house, along with expanding his business, and even Günther is looking at getting a vacation place. Indeed, Mises could have been looking at the Land of the Nibelungenland when he wrote in *Human Action*, "They feel lucky and become openhanded in spending and enjoying life. They embellish their homes, they build new mansions, and patronize the entertainment business."[31]

TIME INCONSISTENCY AND THE TERM STRUCTURE

The canonical exposition of Mises's theory shows clearly how monetary distortions lead to the business cycle that is so evident in Nibelungenland: Credit expansion (i.e., monetary inflation coming from the banks) pushes interest rates down artificially, thereby causing an unsustainable boom period of false prosperity. Because the price-discovery and price-signaling system is distorted, entrepreneurs try to invest more while consumers save less, and, even worse, investments are channeled into the wrong lines. These "real" imbalances eventually result in a general crash, which takes many resources (including labor) out of use temporarily as the economy adjusts to the harsh reality.

In applying Misesian theory to the actual financial world, however, we will make two moves in the interest of realism: First, we will acknowledge that there are multiple interest rates rather than "the" interest rate as is often discussed in Austrian literature. Second, we will assume many investors in the financial sector are better described by the time-inconsistent hyperbolic discounting model (as discussed in Chapter 6), rather than the conventional approach of exponential discounting. (Mises and his followers don't use such terminology either way, but they don't stress the implications of time inconsistency, which can't be explained in a standard exponential discounting framework. Ironically, as we have discussed, Böhm-Bawerk anticipated much of this "modern" work, even though subsequent Austrians didn't develop it further.) Even with these tweaks to the conventional Austrian thinking, we retain the spirit of Misesian business cycle theory, and we are in a position to better explain the empirical observations of our most recent recession (and all the others).

Economists of all stripes agree that when the central bank inflates the money stock by buying treasuries (called "open market operations"), it has much more power to push down the front of the yield curve rather than the back. Intuitively, this is because the creation of more money will push up long-term price inflation, requiring higher long-term nominal yields (and, hence, the axiom that *in the long run*, the Fed can't change the "real" rate of interest, only the general rate of price inflation and, thus, the *nominal* rate of interest). Even today's "quantitative easing" programs have limited potency, because the more the Fed gobbles up long-term treasuries, the more money it "prints" and the higher price inflation investors come to expect, all of which makes attempts to knock down yields ultimately self-defeating, especially longer maturities.

Since artificially lower interest rates by the central bank are typically focused on the front of the yield curve, after a drop in rates the greatest spread, or greatest arbitrage opportunity, is in short-range investments and/or production. This also creates immediate profit opportunities in currently productive capital, which results in title to existing capital (a.k.a., the stock market) to be aggressively bid up until those returns on invested capital—more specifically, the yields on that title to capital— no longer exceed the new lower cost of capital. The most destructive of all, though, is when new owners of this capital have no desire to replace it as it depreciates, preferring instead to gain an extra current return and thus buy more title to existing capital. They do not become more roundabout, because they refrain from investing in capital that will not show returns for a period of time (or a period when the interest rate has not been lowered as much as shorter-term rates). Thus there is a hyperfocus on—and even addiction to—the yields of stocks and other risky and high-duration securities (a "maturity-mismatch"); there is an irrepressible allure to the steep yield curve. What was supposed to create patient, roundabout investors instead creates the opposite: punters in highly speculative "carry trades."

These tendencies are simply exacerbated if, as I've described, the majority of investors have sharply falling discount rates with delay— what mainstream economists now will often refer to as "hyperbolic discounting" (from Chapter 6). Even if all rates are lowered equally (the default assumption if one only speaks of changes in "the" interest rate), if investors have hyperbolic discounting, then the across-the-board drop in interest rates would nonetheless cause the biggest surge in the perceived value of projects that would yield their results in the near future.

What hyperbolic discounting implies is that we do not process a discount rate over an interval in some *gestalt* (or coherent whole) fashion, as one would implicitly assume under exponential discounting. Rather, discounting is highly sequential and intertemporal: Our willingness to endure a wait from now until next week requires our willingness to wait from now until tomorrow, from tomorrow until the day after, and so forth. And (as per the definition of hyperbolic discounting) we perceive enduring the first day as really hard, and each successive day we perceive will be a little easier. But we must make it past the earlier days in order to get to the later days (thus it is sequential).

What this means is, if we are unsatisfied with the wait early on (from now until tomorrow), we won't make it to the wait much later (from six days from now until seven days from now)—despite how satisfied we may be were we to wait over the entire period (from now until a week from now). If we are given fewer "marshmallows" for waiting early on (recalling the preschooler experiment), then we won't likely make it to see perhaps exceedingly more marshmallows by waiting even longer.

Deprived of marshmallows, investors' desire for the immediate reward of an even smaller, sooner marshmallow, over perhaps a larger one much later, is further magnified. With standard exponential discounting, a uniform drop in interest rates across various maturities would normally cause the *longest* projects to respond the most in present-value, but hyperbolic discounting concentrates the impact of a rate cut in the near term. The immediate "carry trades" over the immediate, higher discounting (that is, more impatient) period are thus made even more enticing. To say this doesn't necessarily mean that investors will invest in "short" projects in a Böhm-Bawerkian sense; it is immaterial whether this involves production that is already under way, having gone through a long period of capital accumulation, or a short period of production. The *quickness for realizing profits* is what matters and so people will tend to invest in projects where they can turn their investments around quickly. Thus, a combination of low short-term rates and hyperbolic time preferences will induce investors to buy title to already existing capital structures, rather than trying to construct them from scratch and suffering the delay in waiting for their completion.

The effect can snowball, too, as myopic investors seek to draw profits from their acquisitions. Rather than reinvesting in newly acquired and expanded operations, they will pay out higher dividends and buy back stock (and even borrow to do this, such as is happening today), or even just "sit in cash." (Each time another investor alters his strategy toward "dividend investing," and another firm adjusts to attract this investor, another bit of future progress is sapped from the economy.) Entrepreneurs and investors are, thus, consuming capital in the same analogous way they consume capital in Mises's inflationary view. Interestingly, this increased temporal myopia under *artificially* lowered rates is the very opposite effect of *naturally* (savings-driven) lower rates. Genuine, savings-driven declines in the interest rate lead to capital accumulation, more roundabout production, and a progressing economy; artificially lower rates, driven by credit inflation, ultimately lead to naught but capital consumption and a regressing economy.

When credit inflation first comes on the scene, there is a brief adjustment process where funds are channeled into investments that were previously less profitable than they now appear, and this wave of new investment pushes down yields (or the rate of "interest" income on capital investments) to the new, lower rate. *This* is the aspect of the boom on which many Austrians focus, almost exclusively. Yet I think the more insidious malinvestments occur *after* this initial burst, when the low rates have been arbitraged throughout the system. Amplified by the fact that people discount the immediate future at a steeper rate than more distant periods, we arrive at the perverse result that managers squeeze as much out of their firms as they can in the present—their immediacy is magnified—while neglecting the capital expenditures necessary to keep the firm growing (and even maintain it). The standard Austrian analysis is thus correct when it says that artificially low interest rates lead to malinvestments in projects that are too "roundabout" relative to the amount of genuine saving. But I am stressing another aspect of the boom—one also discussed by Mises—in which the capital stock is actually degraded; it becomes less roundabout. It is this second phenomenon that can explain much of the stylized facts of historical and our current recession.

This aspect can also explain, in solid Austrian analysis, the profound paradox of the MS index when it is elevated. Note that the Keynesians, with their concept of a "liquidity trap," grope around the same issues, but—as usual—they completely misdiagnose the real problem. Today's Keynesians recognize that odd things happen when interest rates are pushed down to zero; because cash and government bonds become virtually interchangeable, the Fed suddenly loses "traction" and can no longer stimulate investment. Yet because of their misdiagnosis of the problem, the Keynesian "solution" is all the worse—they recommend either government deficit spending or "unconventional" monetary policy that will convince the public that higher price inflation is down the road. Naturally, such alleged remedies will only exacerbate the misallocation of resources that the Austrians have correctly identified.

In light of the distortions generated during the unsustainable boom—and the misery that would necessarily follow in the ensuing bust—it is no wonder that Mises considered economics to be "deadly serious." To him it was no mere intellectual exercise; rather "the very future of mankind—of civilization" rested upon an understanding of these economic principles.[32]

THE DAY OF RECKONING COMES TO NIBELUNGENLAND

For a while in Nibelungenland, businesses do appear to be earning more than their cost of capital (or at least their profitability would be higher). Share prices are bid up, but the market value of their assets net of liabilities lags. Thus the MS index rises in this scenario (whereas in the natural interest rate environment, the rise was short-lived, even imperceptible); equilibrating forces that would knock it back to 1 are far weaker (to nonexistent). Miraculously, the whole remains greater than the sum of its parts. Furthermore, there is genuine misallocation of real, physical resources. Land is simultaneously tugged between pasture and timber, as both appear to be highly profitable. Entrepreneurs make irrevocable investments, such as constructing creameries and buying equipment for cheese production. When the day of reckoning does come and the crash occurs, such capital investments will be recognized as wasteful.

What was believed to have been a wave of prosperity is finally revealed to have only been distortion induced by credit expansion. The axiom of the axe is enforced. Shops close. The pounding of hammers at new construction sites ceases. Goat herds are sold off (or culled). Pasture land grows wild and unused. The shiny equipment of the creameries gathers dust. And even stands of trees are clear cut (perhaps for pulp) and the ground is not replanted.

Siegfried gets hurt somewhat by the drop in prices and a bit of his land goes fallow for lack of demand, but he remains profitable—just as he was before rates were artificially lowered. (He manages to stay above the fray; because of this, we will meet up with our hero again in Chapter 10.) He was not significantly affected by the lower cost of capital; his operations were profitable without the change in interest rates. Yet his heart is heavy when he sees the impact on his beloved village—the "for sale" sign in front of Johann's house with the new addition on the back and the "foreclosure" notice on Günther's front door. When Siegfried goes out each day to play his *Wunderhorn* his music is mournful, a dirge for the lost dreams of the Nibelungen.

THE AUSTRIAN VIEW

In the Austrian view, the familiar business cycle that periodically plagues modern market economies is the result of government intervention in money and banking; as Mises told us, once a boom sets in, a bust is inevitable—the only question is *when*. Rather than employ the typical

Keynesian solution of goosing spending to get out of a recession, the Austrians would rather avoid the preceding boom altogether. The longer the boom lasts, egged on by accommodative central bank policy—and the more distorted the capital structure becomes—the worse the ensuing crash.

By now, it should be clear why the crucial concept used in our parable and completely applicable in the real world is called the MS index, named as it is for Mises who identified the distortive forces at work in the business cycle. Mises's perspective, and that of the other Austrians, proves to be the superior one. First, we can see why monetary policy can yield a ratio that is persistently higher than 1, even though in the beginning it seems paradoxical and nonsensical. Second, we understand why the types of capital investments spurred by artificially low interest rates are undesirable. Yet with the richer Austrian concept of the round-about structure of production, we know that the *types* of investment ultimately matter even more.

Mises Points Out the Inevitable Disaster When Distortion Persists

THE MARKET PROCESS PREVAILS

When Ludwig von Mises stood at the front of that lecture hall in 1954 to proclaim "the market is a process," he labored under no delusion that we lived in a natural system, free of the distortion of intervention. In 1954, the Federal Reserve was in its 41st year, and attempting at the time to "manage" the economy after a mild recession while curbing inflation (a brief, but more severe recession would follow in 1958). Mises, the father of Austrian business cycle theory, knew all too well the disastrous effects of inflation and expansion, which prove far worse than deflation and contraction. As he wrote in *Human Action*, "Expansion squanders scarce factors of production by malinvestment and overconsumption. If it once comes to an end, a tedious process of recovery is needed in order to wipe out the impoverishment it has left behind. But contraction produces neither malinvestment nor overconsumption." Although there is a decline in business activities during a contraction, there is also less consumption of both consumer goods and factors of production. When a contraction ends, there is no need for painful healing as there is during the euphoria of an artificially induced expansion, when capital is consumed.[33]

Destructive capital consumption is more than just excessive spending; it is a deadly virus that deprives both current and future generations of the resources needed to carry on and even to advance civilization, itself. Constructive capital accumulation is an intertemporal legacy that sparks gratitude for what came before and also obligation for what will come after—indeed, a process unto itself. As Mises wrote, "We are the lucky heirs of our father and forefathers whose saving has accumulated the capital goods with the aid of which we are working today. We favorite children of the age of electricity still derive advantage from the original saving of the primitive fishermen who, in producing the first nets and canoes, devoted a part of their working time to provision for a remoter future. If the sons of these legendary fishermen had worn out these intermediary products—nets and canoes—without replacing them by new ones, they would have consumed capital and the process of saving and capital accumulation would have had to start afresh."[34]

Distortion persists and capital is consumed to the detriment of roundabout capitalistic production. And yet, the process that is the market continues. As we will see in Chapter 8, natural systems—from forests to markets—continuously seek balance. Although there may be obstacles and delays due to intervention, the drive to reestablish this balance cannot be thwarted. Adjustments may be painful; ridding the system of excesses can leave behind the scorched earth of destruction. Yet, these natural systems will always find a way.

Chapter Eight

Homeostasis

Seeking Balance in the Midst of Distortion

A homeostatic system, by its very nature, is always in flux, self-correcting when it strays too far in one direction or another. Never static, it is animated by a process of continuous discovery, balancing and rebalancing based on the information available through self-monitoring. Although the word *homeostasis* was not specifically used by the founding fathers of the Austrian tradition, its meaning is deeply embedded in this school of thought as is its observations about the functioning of the economy as it is pushed and pulled by entrepreneurial forces into and out of stationarity. Just as the Austrians anticipated many of the recent "discoveries" of behavioral scientists (in particular the work on hyperbolic discounting), we will see that the Austrian tradition describes the market process in ways very compatible with modern cybernetics—the study of communication and control within a system.

In its natural state, a system—from a forest to a market—achieves balance through internal governance and guidance, which depend upon the system's own ability to internally communicate and react to changing conditions due to the interactions of a variety of players, whether buyers and sellers in a marketplace, trees and herbivorous predators (especially fire) in the forest, or entrepreneurs deciding when and how to become ever more roundabout to meet the ultimate demands of consumers. Within the system, errors will occur and resources will need to be reshuffled; as such, there will be isolated, individual failures, whether we are dealing with forests or factories, banks or bakeries. The process will take care of itself as long as there is integrity within the feedback loop and accurate (nonmanipulated) information is allowed to flow, resulting in a suitable mix and magnitude of growth, given the available resources—whether savings for investment, or sunlight and soil for trees. However, attempts to intervene and manage such systems typically end in a paradox whereby the very opposite of an intended result is achieved; instead of order and balance there is distortion that leads, ultimately, to destruction.

Without a functioning feedback loop, the system goes haywire like a faulty thermostat that allows the interior of a house to become as hot as a furnace or as cold as a freezer. When the feedback loop is short-circuited by distortion and manipulation, rather than the system being one that cancels out its errors, it is transformed into one that even magnifies them, such that the errors of inappropriate, unhealthy growth take over the system. When this occurs the system breaks down. There is disconnection in entrepreneurial decisions of whether to invest in more roundabout production based on anticipated demand from consumers (which will probably not materialize), or whether to exploit current higher demand; trees attempt to thrive beyond the capacity of the forest ecosystem to produce and sustain healthy growth. Yet, inevitably, even if the system has been forcibly pushed far out of balance and its governing forces debilitated, homeostasis will eventually reemerge as the communication and governing forces are freed once again.

At this point we should pause to clarify one aspect of our discussion that might trouble some readers: How can we speak of a system's internal "communication," when there may be no conscious mind at work? And how can we define "thriving" or "failures" within a system, in a nonarbitrary way? In the case of a thermostat, these terms might be innocuous enough—since we can take the goals of the human designers as given—but what about an ecosystem? Such talk might even seem inapplicable to the market economy itself, which is *not* consciously planned by any single mind or group of experts, as the Austrians themselves stress.

To defuse possible misunderstanding, let me be clear that in this discussion I am drawing on the concepts and terminology of the cybernetics literature (which we will explore later in the chapter). The pioneers of cybernetics described self-regulating feedback mechanisms as *teleological*, a term suggesting that they have a goal or purpose. Now it's true that later critics suggested an alternate term, *teleonomic*, (as mentioned with von Baer in Chapter 4) to characterize systems that merely exhibit *apparent* purpose. (For example, the standard view of modern biologists is that evolution is a teleonomic process, because although life forms demonstrate great internal order and self-regulation, they were presumably not consciously designed.) However, such distinctions are unnecessary for our purposes, because I am focusing on the *intentional*, teleological behavior of market participants—what Ludwig von Mises called "human action." When it comes to the interactions of these intentional individuals in the broader marketplace, even Austrian economists can and do quibble over the extent to which the resulting outcome is due to "rationality" versus "spontaneous order." Yet what is *not* controversial is the notion that capitalism—with private property and free markets—serves as an exceptional institution to mobilize the localized information that is dispersed among many different individuals, each with admittedly subjective goals. The market's ability to do so, relying on systemwide equilibration forces—feedback mechanisms—is my focus in this chapter. And, when we discuss financial crashes and depressions later, the reader will have little difficulty understanding what constitutes a "good" versus "bad" outcome.

THE TELEOLOGY OF THE MARKET

We have already explored in the last chapter the economic parable of the Land of the Nibelungen, in the context of the market process and some stylized facts about booms and busts. In the current chapter, we discuss the same topic but from the perspective of homeostasis. In booms, assets are overaccumulated and bid up in value to untenable levels, until homeostasis prevails—a teleological, goal-seeking mechanism (Kant's very "teleo-mechanism" of regulation) that ultimately guides the system back to the balance of stationarity, and reality. Perhaps it is difficult to visualize an impersonal horde of ravenous speculators as part of the rebalancing process, yet that is precisely what is occurring. The market does not just bob around, rudderless. It is the flock of birds that appears to swoop and dive aimlessly, while hidden within its cascading members are the navigators themselves. Although there are random entrepreneurial errors that take place, as we saw in Chapter 7, the entrepreneurial process is teleological because volitional beings bring about a series of causes and effects in reaction to changes within the system. The system itself moves or "strives" toward stationarity—balance. With this understanding of the markets, we can see the advantage of also taking a teleological approach to investing—as Siegfried, our entrepreneurial hero, does and as we do with Austrian Investing—with a means-end strategy that is predicated on the knowledge of capitalistic investing as an intertemporal process.

To observe and appreciate the homeostatic nature of the market (the market that, as Mises reminded us, *is a process*) we must shift our perception and stop thinking of systems as being driven only as a hapless victim of random shocks (such as lightning strikes that start fires), and instead embrace the reality of the system as adapting to those shocks in an ongoing discovery process.

Clearly, though, there is a dichotomy: on one hand how things should function in their natural state and, on the other, how and why they fall into dysfunction (where the fault is almost always outside manipulation, not the system itself). Yet that is not what most people see. They cannot see the forest because they are trying to save each individual and immediate tree, and in so doing lose all depth of field and of focus on the generations of trees and the intertemporal search for their mix and magnitude of growth within the forest to come. All too often, particularly today, the focus is only on the shocks and fires with a desire to control and prevent. The desire is to interfere and, perhaps innocently, override the system's natural governors that maintain balance; in so doing, things are made so much worse. We have thus succumbed to a blind faith in bureaucratic authority over natural processes.

And yet, we do well to heed the words of Austrian economist and Mises protégé Friedrich Hayek who observed, "Before we can even ask how things might go wrong, we must first explain how they could ever go right."[1] Homeostasis is the process of how things "go right." Within the roundabout of capital accumulation in a progressing economy (the figurative directional "going right" that is, indeed, how things "go right" in a healthy manner) homeostasis recalls *shi*—the propensity of all systems to restore balance through self-righting movements that in a natural world are no more disruptive than ripples on a pond.

We think of the Daoist concept of reversion, of things becoming their opposite—soft in order to be hard, weak before strong, retreating before advancing—and Klipp's Paradox of losing in order to win. An intertemporal balance can be achieved, however, only when communication and controls are allowed to function naturally.

THE YELLOWSTONE EFFECT

The study of homeostasis and its pursuit in natural systems brings us back, once again, to what has become our primary pedagogical tool, nature's classroom—the forest. We start by reminding ourselves of the particular dynamic within the scenarios explored in Chapter 2: the head-to-head competition that occurs when conifers that are slower growing at first try to thrive amid the faster-growing and sunlight-stealing angiosperms. In a natural forest (without the practice of forest management), the endless tug-of-war battle of succession for available resources is a part of an elaborate homeostatic process, whereby the angiosperms dominate for a while in prime fertile areas where they can outperform (at least at first) the competition, while the conifers take root in the out-of-the-way places, rocky and inhospitable, where few can survive. Once areas of the angiosperm-dominated forest become overgrown, they become prone to small wildfires; when fire breaks out, the land is cleared and the way is opened for the patient conifers—nature's great fire opportunists—to reseed. This is the continuous, intertemporal turnover of the forest's succession. Not only are wind-borne seeds brought to the fire-cleared land, but the resin-coated serotinous cones of many conifer species have been opened by the flames and intense heat of the fire. The system has natural regulators that control unsuitable growth and help to keep it balanced with the available resources, the "savings" of the forest.

As we recall, this is particularly important when the forest experiences "recruitment bottlenecks," such as among conifers that are mal-seeded among the faster-growing angiosperm competitors. The young conifers fail to reach a threshold of development sufficient to accelerate to maturity—our tortoises never make it to become hares—and instead become sick and spindly, literally consuming each other as they grasp a meager share of the resources and remain extremely fire-prone. When flames sweep through these stunted trees are wiped out, and resources are naturally redistributed to healthier growth. The fire, therefore, is not merely destructive, but must be viewed as a catharsis, a cleansing process—an agent of *creative destruction*, to borrow a term from the Austrians—and part of the cybernetic control and communication within the system to return the forest to homeostatic balance. As Murray Rothbard would say, the fire "*is* the 'recovery' process," and, "far from being an evil scourge, is the *necessary* and beneficial return" of the forest to "optimum efficiency."[2]

Forest fire turns especially deadly, however, when smaller blazes are suppressed, creating the illusion of fire protection. Admittedly, fire is a complex subject in forestry; on one hand, it would seem to make intuitive sense that forest preservation would mean limiting, controlling, or outright prevention of fires that kill trees. At the risk of oversimplification, however, such thinking has proved to be a *li* strategy focused on the direct means of today's trees and keeping the forest status quo at all costs. The roundabout *shi* strategy is the willingness to pursue—or, more specifically in this case, allow—an intermediate objective of naturally occurring fires that do destroy trees (and some healthy specimens right along with the unhealthy ones) now, in order for a succession of forest growth to emerge intertemporally. Between conifers and angiosperms in particular, the ecosystem must always discover the right balance, which changes and adapts to climate and other environmental shifts.

Fire is a natural dynamic force of change like any other predator whose presence is crucial to maintaining the health of other species (just as rabbits would overrun and destroy the meadow and ultimately starve themselves were it not for the foxes that hunt them). When a population within an ecosystem exceeds the amount of resources present (too many rabbits in the meadow) it must be controlled by predator-consumers (the foxes, which do not have to try very hard to capture their next meal). And when the system reaches balance (just the right number of rabbits), the predator-consumers are also managed; they go hungry or move elsewhere. In the case of the overgrown forest, control most often comes from the most ravenous and indiscriminant of all herbivorous predators—fire, thus becoming the consumer that most often accomplishes the control function.[3] Smaller, low-intensity fires manage the forest with great expediency, reducing density by clearing underbrush—including the stunted and spindly conifers that cannot compete with larger angiosperms—while leaving the canopy growth untouched.

Paradoxical, yes, but forestry practices of old that have regained respect of late underscore the importance of letting small fires burn in order to manage the forest, and to prevent the bigger ones that inevitably and cruelly result from attempts to stop fire. Suppression now undeniably leads to greater destruction later on—once again our "bad economists" (who continually crop up in this book, clearly one of its main points). Nowhere in the history of forestry was that evil more savagely felt than in Yellowstone National Park in 1988, when nearly 800,000 acres—well over one-third of the park—burned and/or suffered fire damage. It was a catastrophe of unprecedented proportion in the history of the National Park Service, and its root cause was fire suppression.

The spread of fire-suppression mentality can be linked to the establishment of forest management in the United States, such that by the early 1900s forests became viewed as resources that needed to be protected—in other words, burning was no longer allowed. The danger in this approach became tragically apparent in Yellowstone, which was recognized by the late 1980s as being overdue for fire; yet smaller blazes were not allowed to burn because of what were perceived to be risks that were too high given the dry conditions. And so smaller fires were put out, but in the end could not be controlled and converged into the largest conflagration in the history of Yellowstone. Not only did the fire wipe out more than 30 times the acreage of any previously recorded fire, it also destroyed summer and winter grazing grounds for elk and bison herds, further altering the ecosystem. Because of fire suppression, the trees had no opportunity or reason to ever replace each other, and the forest thus grew feeble and prone to destruction. A lattice of unwarranted and anemic growth (what was ill-seeded from the start and never had a chance of reaching maturity) became a grid that linked and transmitted the costs of the forest's distortion to a much wider area than would have been affected by a series of natural, smaller fires over the years. It was the Yellowstone effect.[4]

LESSONS FROM THE DISTORTED FOREST

The disastrous Yellowstone fire of 1988 leads to the conclusion that 100 years of fire suppression—a zero-tolerance approach to stamp out even naturally occurring, low-intensity blazes—had made the forest dangerously prone to catastrophe. It becomes clear, then, that low-intensity blazes marshal the resources and oversee an orderly succession in the homeostatic forest, as evident in patterns of heterogeneity—conifers here and angiosperms there. The back and forth of a forest system seeking equilibrium avoids the dangerous overgrowth caused by everything trying to thrive all at once—extracting resources for survival now, foregoing the roundabout strategy. In nature, as in the economy, there must be a free transfer of resources between higher-order and lower-order production. When human intervention interferes with nature's cycles, the system's natural homeostatic, negative-feedback forces are weakened (negative feedback being the system communicating to its internal governors how far from balance it is, and the governors then bringing it back). From a forestry point of view, the lessons have been learned. In 1995, the Federal Wildland Fire Management policy recognized wildfire as a crucial natural process and called for it to be reintroduced into the ecosystem.

As I observed in a 2011 piece in the *Wall Street Journal*, central bankers, too, could learn a thing or two from their forestry brethren. The federal government has another "fire suppression policy" that started, coincidentally, just a few years before the Yellowstone blaze, with the 1984 Continental Illinois "too big to fail" bank bailout. This was followed by Alan Greenspan's pronouncement immediately after the 1987 stock market crash that the Federal Reserve stood by with liquidity to support the economy and the financial system. In its actions in the 1980s, the Federal Reserve telegraphed to the world that it would no longer tolerate fires of any size—which heralded the birth of the "Greenspan put."[5]

In the financial forests of our own making, suppression is particularly problematic—and even deadly. Excess and malinvestment thrive for a time, only to be destroyed by ravages caused by their own vulnerability. Yet, as we will see, even such high-intensity "fires" (of the forest and financial varieties) will free up and redistribute resources; in the case of the market, it releases capital to areas previously avoided due to the myopic distortions of monetary intervention. (The Austrian School naturally understood this well, as we explored with the Austrian Business Cycle Theory as explained in Chapter 7.) Central bankers and interventionists need to stop approaching the system as one driven by random shocks, because this mind-set leads them to manipulate and attempt to control the system—a cycle that destroys far more in the long run than it saves temporarily. The longer their erroneous thinking persists, the more out of balance things become, until there is a tinderbox of malinvestment, ready to ignite in a massive, uncontrollable inferno. Density (overgrowth) and uniformity (too much of one thing—namely immediate-returning or high-yielding capital, as opposed to the more roundabout variety—growing in the economy and "fertilized" by distortion) are the evidence of malinvestment in the economy, exceeding the amount of available resources. Investment cannot exceed savings any more than seeding in the forest can exceed land, nutrients, water, and sunlight—but under these interventions, the system acts as if that's what is happening. This is what makes the boom so delusive and ultimately illusory.

Here, we encounter the profound paradox that government interventions systematically achieve the very opposite of their intended goals. So governments, unlike entrepreneurs, try as they might and despite perhaps good intentions (I'll give the Paul Krugmans of the world the benefit of the doubt), simply cannot achieve their intended outcomes by interfering with the operation of the system. (They cannot act teleologically, as it were.) Governments and central banks undermine the natural homeostatic process by short-circuiting the governors and adaptive teleological processes in the system.

Suppression of the market's natural homeostatic tendencies—such as proclaiming things to be "too big to fail" or by cutting interest rates when the stock market takes a dive—only make things worse by artificially propping up assets that should be allowed to fail, and free up resources for another, perhaps more productive attempt. (A perfect example is the Troubled Asset Relief Program of 2008, or TARP, a completely unnecessary action by the U.S. government to buy equity stakes in and underwater assets from financial institutions as a response to the crisis that, like a wildfire, was trying to correct the artificial distortions in the system; rather than precluding a catastrophic event, TARP precluded rational market adjustments.) Suppression makes the cure that much worse than the initial ill, until exponentially more damage is done, calling to mind the wry observation of Mises: "If a man has been hurt by being run over by an automobile, it is no remedy to let the car go back over him in the [opposite] direction."[6]

Blaming wild market volatility on the "animal spirits" of the herd mentality takes the focus off where it belongs: on the actions of the government. Instead of functioning as instruments of information, signaling to entrepreneurs how and when best to serve consumers, interest rates are perpetually manipulated by central bank actions to the point of meaninglessness. Artificial changes in interest rates become a deceptive feint by which entrepreneurs succumb to malinvestment, because they believe there are more resources (i.e., savings) in the system than there really are. Monetary policy insidiously plays with our time preferences and our very ability to engage in economic calculation. The greater the distortion, the greater destruction needed to correct it.

The financial crisis of 2008 could have been the wake-up call that, like the Yellowstone fires of 1988, alerted so-called "managers" to the dangers of trying to override the natural governors of the system. Instead, the Federal Reserve, with its head "ranger" Ben Bernanke, has deluded itself into thinking it has tamped down every little smolder from becoming a destructive blaze, but instead all it has done is poured the unnatural fertilizer of liquidity onto a morass of overgrown malinvestment—making it even more highly flammable. One day— likely sooner than later, as argued in the next chapter—it will burn, and when that happens, the Fed will be sorely lacking in buckets and shovels and must succumb to the flames.

The Fed's Attempt at "Fire Suppression" Leads Inevitably to Bigger and More Deadly "Forest Fires"

MARKET CYBERNETICS

The devastation of a Yellowstone forest fire or the financial crisis of 2008—and all the big blazes yet to be—do not need to occur. Without the distortion of intervention, the system can govern itself. In the Austrian view, healthy growth of an economy occurs through heterogeneous capital structures that are allowed to morph and adapt through the intertemporal coordination of production in sync with consumer time preference. Within the process, entrepreneurs rely upon price signals to guide their decision making in order that resources might be deployed in the most appropriate ways.[7] Respecting the process allows homeostasis to be pursued through a connection that detects, communicates, and responds to the available resources in the system; to better understand this connection, we explore a branch of the interdisciplinary control systems theory of engineering, known as *cybernetics*.

The word cybernetics comes from the Greek *kybernētēs* meaning pilot or governor, and *kybernan* to steer or govern. Cybernetics focuses on the role of servomechanisms (or "servos" as they are called) that regulate systems through the detection of errors and the responsive use of feedback (specifically, negative feedback that tells a system when it is out of balance, and by how much, in order to correct). For our purposes here, we might think of cybernetics as how servos regulate systems (from machines to bodies) through such mechanisms as the steam engine governor, a thermostat, and the functions that control body temperature or blood glucose level (the failure of the feedback process in maintenance of healthy blood glucose levels leads to diabetes).

Norbert Wiener (coincidentally, his last name means Viennese, although he was born in Missouri) was a mathematician and originator of the field of cybernetics, who saw homeostasis as a process in which "some sort of feedback is not only exemplified in physiological phenomena but is absolutely essential for the continuation" of that system.[8] Feedback is crucial, and must be continuously given by and within the system in order to make the necessary, typically small corrections to keep on course. Sometimes that correction happens quite literally, as in the example given by Wiener of the car being driven on an icy road. The driver makes a series of small movements with the wheel, which are not enough to induce a major skid, but provide feedback "to our kinesthetic sense whether the car is in danger of skidding, and we regulate our method of steering accordingly."[9]

The concept of "control by information feedback" makes intuitive sense; in order to operate in an environment, one must have input *from it* and thus make continuous adjustments to compensate for certain conditions or changes in conditions. Each movement is a return to balance in the moment, never expected to be permanent, but to last until the next shift or turn of the wheel is required. We might also think of balance sought in the homeostatic process in terms of the "basin of attraction," a scientific concept best illustrated by the traditional *shi* image of the boulder that is pushed up the steep grade of a hill, only to fall back down to the bottom of the valley. Similarly, when a system is perturbed, forces push it back to the balance of the basin. This is precisely what happens on an infinitesimal scale as a natural market is perturbed by changing time preferences and innovations.

Drawing an example from nature and his own observations of it, Wiener compared the back-and-forth wrestling between counterbalancing forces in a system to a fight between the mongoose and cobra (which calls to mind the battle of the magpie and the serpent that legendarily inspired the creation of *taijiquan*—though now the tables have tragically turned on the snake). Although there is no evidence that the mongoose is faster or more accurate in its motions, it almost always delivers a lethal bite to the cobra. The mongoose has his teleological, multistage strategy to thank (basically that of the squash or hockey player from Chapter 5). He begins with a feint, provoking the snake to strike, which the animal manages to dodge and then follow up with another feint, a "rhythmical pattern of activity" that develops progressively. The mongoose's moves come earlier and earlier, until finally coinciding when the snake is extended and the attack is clinched with a deadly bite to the cobra's brain.[10] Within the mongoose's triumphant roundabout strategy lies the cybernetic strategy of steermanship: Don't overcontrol, don't overgrip, but rather let the system make its mistakes, and then opportunistically bring it back—*wei wuwei*.

Within the economy, as Hayek stated, the "mutual adjustments" of individual participants occur through negative feedback.[11] Government and central bank interventions can at best *postpone* the negative feedback mechanisms; they can't repeal them. Too often, however, people regard the market as a *positive* feedback system, which self-reinforces the continuation of a force (as in momentum) in the same direction. However, a positive feedback system is actually contrary to the way markets naturally work. In fact, they become positive feedback systems (temporarily) only when they are distorted; the tendency to see only positive feedback processes and thus assume imitation-like strategies (of momentum, carry, etc.)—a simple extrapolation of the seen—is an obvious consequence of our natural shallow depth of field further compressed by the spell of artificially low rates. It may not be apparent, but a crash is ultimately a negative feedback system in action—despite the proximate positive feedback route at work on a more immediate scale; once we recognize the dominant negative feedback nature of the markets, the routes start to make sense as but a teleological means to an end.

Within the cybernetic feedback loop, the detection of "entropy" (the amount of disorganization that exists) forces the system to maintain its structure, in order to avoid a breakdown from disorder. Thus, in a natural economy, rising interest rates are a brake on roundaboutness (and, bizarrely, as per the "capital consumption" discussed in Chapter 7, so too are artificially lowered rates); when rates are higher, it becomes more costly to accumulate a deeper and longer capital structure. If interest rates reflect our true time preferences and the resulting activity in the economy, this isn't a problem. The correct or "natural" market interest rates will, by definition, adjust to allow entrepreneurs to "get through the wait" of longer production only when savers really are extending their durations (as savers will offer their savings at marginally lower rates for longer periods). But when this communication is broken, and rates are pushed down (independently of economic reality) in parallel shifts (and even worse in steepening shifts), one of the consequences of lower rates is to make us exceedingly unsatisfied with waiting right now (as the lower rate is below what we intrinsically require for waiting—particularly in the immediate). Thus we are "trapped" into grabbing the immediate marshmallows, regardless of and ignoring relatively more abundant marshmallows off in the future. Thus the apparent paradox—owing to our myopic time inconsistency from Chapter 6—that even a parallel shift of the entire yield curve downward can give more of an artificial stimulus to existing assets with a quick turnaround (such as a quick momentum trade, or a quick dividend), even though normal accounting would make us think the long-term projects would see the biggest jump in demand. Disorder reigns.

HOW THINGS "GO RIGHT"

With the Austrian School we see how the natural market would function *sans* intervention, with its propensity to seek stationarity, allowing us to appreciate that the "busts" are a correction to counterbalance the "booms," such as in the way a pressure valve finally regulates a system gone awry, as a distorted system is finally overwhelmed by the governors of savings, investment, and credit. Here, we might think of the Daoist image of the surge of pent-up water, only this time it has been held back by the artificial barrier of a levee, which is breached when it can no longer control what is meant, by nature, to flow freely and seek balance.

Hayek makes this connection and cements it strongly within Austrian theory, by recognizing the cybernetic quality of economics, as information is detected and acted upon. (Without that dispersed knowledge, entrepreneurs have no way of knowing what the optimal deployment of resources would be.) "Thus the whole economic order rested on the fact that by using prices as a guide, or as signals, we were led to serve the demands and enlist the powers and capacities of people of whom we know nothing," Hayek wrote. The insight needed to construct the highly configured means of production sufficient to support a growing world population comes in the form of prices. "Basically, the insight that prices were signals bringing about the unforeseen coordination of the efforts of thousands of individuals was in a sense the modern cybernetics theory, and it became the leading idea behind my work."[12]

Hayek gave initial credit to Adam Smith, who "had basically grasped the point that the success of our economic system was the outcome of an undesigned process coordinating the activities of a myriad of individuals."[13] Where Smith and others left off, Hayek picked up as his responsibility to continue: trying to inform others of the wealth of information to be found in the signals within the well-functioning system that informs, albeit imperfectly. Competition is not only a discovery procedure, as Hayek termed it, but also a selection process, whereby entrepreneurs try out new strategies and profits and losses work as a cybernetic negative feedback mechanism,[14] selecting the strategies that work and eliminating those that do not work. The Hayekian market can thus be seen as a process of phylogenetic evolution of entrepreneurial ideas or *evolution in the market*.

We can aptly apply Mises's notion of the market's *state of rest*—my way of thinking about the mini-routs back in the trading pit—to this Hayekian cybernetic construct. Recall from Chapter 1 the *Preiskampf* ("price duel") of perpetual self-correcting balancing acts that always fail, yet are "always disquieted by a striving after a definite state of rest."[15] Each successive state of rest is the result of a self-correcting readjustment in light of new information or circumstances, and in a constant environment would culminate in the ever-elusive final state of rest; such is the entrepreneurial charge to unwittingly steer the system toward stationarity.

SPONTANEOUS ORDER

What the Austrians—starting perhaps with Menger (and drawing upon Adam Smith before him) and fully blooming with Hayek—first referred to as "spontaneous order" has steadily grown fashionable in the physical sciences (a most rare example of concepts flowing from the social to the physical sciences), starting in the guise of "cybernetics" and moving to "complex adaptive systems," "self-organization," and "emergence."[16]

Spontaneous order may be thought of as the order that emerges from the interaction of disparate acting agents, in a bottom-up dynamic that emphasizes the role of the individual—not the top-down control of, for instance, state intervention. To specifically reference this internal regulation, Hayek even coined a term, "catallaxy," to replace the word "economy." Thus, spontaneous order might be viewed as haphazardly designed though purposeful organization out of what appears to be highly disorganized—the order in the flock, or the ant colony (of Douglas Hofstadter) whose hidden social coordination is like that of neurons creating a coherent mind.[17]

The concept of spontaneous order takes us, once again, back to the Daoists; Mises's protégé Murray Rothbard saw the Daoist scholar Zhuangzi from the Warring States Period of the third and fourth centuries BCE as embracing Laozi's "devotion to *laissez-faire* and opposition to state rule," and credited him with being the first to articulate the idea of spontaneous order—whereby order results automatically when things are left alone, an idea that was later developed by Hayek in the twentieth century. Sounding a decidedly Libertarian view, Zhuangzi

**Friedrich Hayek Sees Beyond the Single Tree
to the Discovery Process of the Forest Economy**

(also known as Chuang Tzu, as Rothbard calls him), "was perhaps the first theorist to see the state as a brigand writ large: 'A petty thief is put in jail. A great brigand becomes a ruler of a State.' Thus, the only difference between state rulers and out-and-out robber chieftains is the size of their depredations."[18]

Spontaneous order is interrupted (and as we have seen, often perilously) by top-town control from intervention to full-on socialism. In a system as complex as the market such attempts at outside, artificial control are doomed to fail. As we know, roundabout production requires the ambiguous and uncertain focus on a future advantage—*shi*. However, the distortions of interventionism paradoxically morph that into a focus on quick and decisive outcomes—*li*.

DISTORTION

As we can see, distortion is not merely a by-product of growth in the economy. Rather, and most important for our discussion, it is a monetary phenomenon. Specifically, the Austrians blame the business cycle on government protection of artificial credit expansion, which reaches its zenith with central banking, but existed even before the Fed created in 1913. Those who criticize ABCT based on this 1913 birthdate of the Fed miss the nuances of past monetary-based credit booms. (Rothbard's doctoral dissertation on this matter focused on the Panic of 1819.) Even the infamous "tulip mania" of 1630—considered the greatest bubble in history—when Hollanders were gripped in a craze of speculation over tulip bulbs, was caused by monetary distortion, even though there was no central bank behind the scenes. At the time, the Netherlands had a "free coinage" policy that allowed those who had silver and gold bullion from the Americas to mint their own coins. By 1630, a large increase in the supply of coins and bullion in Amsterdam far exceeded the market demand, and led to malinvestment and speculation.[19]

The market movement in tulips, therefore, was not caused by mere waves of emotion that produced a mania—mistaking the cause for the effect; it was rather an increase in the supply of money that prompted a massive (though highly localized) asset inflation, right out of the Land of the Nibelungen. We thus we plant a stake in the ground of understanding of economics and the functioning of markets: that the former view of randomness invokes state inventions, whereas the natural teleo-logical ebb and flow defers to the homeostatic process.

To clarify my view, we can contrast it with that of the American economist Hyman Minsky, who tried to lay blame for the boom and bust cycle on leverage. Simply stated, he believed that as the market goes up for an extended period of time without any corrections, the total leverage in the financial sector gradually increases, making the system ever-more tenuous. Although Minsky's narrative is accept-able as a description of certain features of the business cycle, he doesn't really give an *explanation* for the phenomenon. In contrast, the Austrians give a much more satisfactory theory of how artificially low interest rates foster an unsustainable boom (characterized by overleveraged bor-rowers invested in operating capital that will be unproductive at natural interest rates) and the inevitable bust.

This aspect of Minsky's view—the inherent instability and unpre-dictability of the crash—is one of its virtues, in the eyes of his Keynesian admirers. Indeed, there are two major trends in Keynesian thought, both descended from different themes in John Maynard Keynes's 1936 work. On the one hand, there was the straightforward, deterministic system of aggregate demand and involuntary unemployment—the stuff of text-books. At the same time, Keynes's prose contained passages describing the utter unpredictability of the market, in particular asset pricing. Here entered the famous "animal spirits," and Keynes's likening of the stock market to a casino and a game in which contestants had to vote on "general opinion," not on what the underlying reality was. In this latter worldview, Minsky's vague treatment of the boom and bust is proper, since there really *aren't* demonstrable "causes" in the way many econo-mists would like to believe (and as I show in Chapter 9).

THE SAND PILE EFFECT

Minsky's belief that the leveraged run-up is the underlying cause of crashes is similar to the notion of self-organized criticality in a dynami-cal system, the classic metaphor of which is the sand pile effect. Grain by grain the pile gets higher until it is of considerable height, and at some point will reach a critical state where just one more grain will cause a cascading collapse—an avalanche of sorts (the proverbial straw that breaks the camel's back). This basic cellular automata model has similarly been applied to forest fire models and to stock market crashes—with exceedingly limited success; indeed, it has become fashionable to look at crashes as critical systemwide landslides. However, these and Minsky's analyses miss the mark: The homeostatic market process must first be broken by intervention from outside the system in order for it to fail. Specifically, criticality is not an inherent epiphenomenon of the system, growing organically as a delicate cascading network from within. Rather, it grows from unhealthy sprouts doomed at their start from a temporary deception, a miscommunication and failure of control within the cybernetic machine.

In the popular financial jargon, a "Minsky moment" now refers to a sudden collapse in asset values, following a leveraged run-up during a period of apparent prosperity. To repeat: This description is *consistent* with the Austrian theory of the business cycle, but it leaves major questions unanswered: Why should the market's normal negative feedback mechanism suddenly fail? Sure, individual entrepreneurs can make mistakes, but what explains the *systematic* mistakes of the boom years—the "cluster of errors" as Rothbard calls them?[20]

The leading theoretical argument for the supposed efficacy of the various rounds of quantitative easing is the so-called "wealth effect," meaning that consumers go out and spend more because they feel richer when their assets (stock portfolios, houses, etc.) rise in price relative to consumer prices. It would be difficult to come up with an economic policy more at odds with Austrian capital theory—printing up new money in order to convince people that they can consume more based on their immediate asset appreciation (and never mind what happens once the cost of capital inevitably returns to normal—and the economy and MS index return to stationarity).

If the Austrians can dispense with the idea of "animal spirits" and "Minsky moments" as explanatory devices, they can also jettison another Keynesian nostrum: the so-called "paradox of thrift" in which the individual households do the rational thing by attempting to save more in light of a financial setback, yet when aggregated over the whole economy the motive becomes self-defeating since one household's spending is another household's income. According to textbook Keynesian theory, the paradox of thrift shows the role for government deficit spending to escape a slump, when the homeostatic mechanism of the market has failed. Here again, a focus on Austrian capital theory—as opposed to Keynesian income flows—shows the problem. A recession isn't simply some stroke of dumb luck, in which people have failed to spend enough; it is characterized by physical distortions in the structure of production. Racking up more government debt is hardly the cure to inadequate saving and physical investment.

No matter how noble such measures might sound on their own—particularly in the bloody aftermath of a crisis, as if the government were handing out tourniquets—these interventionist actions (like the fire suppression in the forest) only prolong the problem and postpone the restoration of health to the forest.

Distortion persists, leaving a wide swath of destruction in its wake, but ultimately it does not prevail.

DISTORTION'S MESSAGE: "DO NOTHING"

Generations of economists teach us that the market economy—like many other "spontaneous," self-regulating systems found both in nature and the social world—has an internal logic. When it moves away from a stationary point, negative feedback automatically kicks in, restoring it to a balanced state. Whether we describe it as Adam Smith's "invisible hand" or as Mises's counterbalancing of entrepreneurial forces, or we take Hayek's cue and employ the concepts of cybernetics, the crucial fact is that there are underlying laws governing the operation of the market, steering it back toward an orderly trajectory whenever it is disrupted. Left to its own natural development, the market will hit bumps in the road. Yet paradoxically, the paternalistic effort to spare us the pain of these periodic readjustments will, at best, merely "postpone" the needed fixes, making the ultimate crisis that much worse. To avoid economic depressions—just as to avoid epic forest fires—the surprising solution is to let the homeostatic system work; "Don't just do something, sit there."

In the meantime, when the economy *is* subject to top-down intervention from the government and especially the central bank, investors need to read the signs in order to protect themselves, as well as still find a way to own productive assets—as the last two chapters show in Austrian Investing (with our hero, Siegfried, becoming our mascot and model).

After all, civilization's progress—Galt's "engines of the world"—mustn't end. Believing that homeostasis will, indeed, prevail, we are steadfast in our pursuit of the roundabout.

THE *SHI* OF CAPITAL

The masters have taught us well, if only we will heed the lessons. From ancient Daoist philosophers to military strategists, an old grain trader at the Chicago Board of Trade, Austrian economists, and roundabout entrepreneurs, they have bridged their unique backgrounds with a common refrain that echoes in a single word: *shi*, with its complex and multiple meanings of strategic positional advantage, potential, disposition, configuration, influence, and propensity.

As we orient everything to *shi*, we automatically keep to the roundabout path, refusing to be led astray by distorted perceptions in a world that focuses only on today, as if it is all that matters—indeed, all there is. To embrace *The Dao of Capital*, we purposefully and intentionally raise our sights and deepen our field of focus to see that today is but one unit—a single bead in a long strand. We refuse the blinders of myopic time inconsistency, while being well aware that much of the world can see only this way. Ours, though, is the intertemporal view, a never-ending series of now moments, each connected to the next, that extend throughout our lifetime and beyond it as well.

For courage and example, we look to our array of *shi* masters who were able to wait with the cunning patience of the manipulative sage to accrue strategic advantage. Oh, these masters knew all too well how hard it was to embrace the doing/not doing of *wei wuwei*—patience as self-inflicted agony, while letting one's opponent gloat over racked-up points and small victories in the moment. The masters' feints of humility must have felt very much at times like humiliation. But the reward of being purposefully and intentionally circuitous—to be *shi* until strategic advantage coalesces into the opportunistic action of *li* within *shi*—can be found in the single pinecone loaded with seeds for dispersal on fire-cleared land, the loaded crossbow trained at last on the intended target, and the accumulation of productive capital to advance material society. We take heart in Eugen von Böhm-Bawerk's words about the roundabout, which we now apply to the imperative of being *shi*: It is "so much the better that it is often the only way!"[21] (If this lesson has not been learned as yet then, please, do so now for it will serve you well as we move on to Austrian Investing I and II; without this understanding, Chapters 9 and 10 will do you no good.)

In *shi* and the synonymous roundabout and *Umweg* we can also find the continual workings of homeostasis and the return to the equilibrium known as stationarity. Perpetual reversion is the way of the world; no matter how distortion subverts the natural process, in the end it cannot be prevented. As the *Laozi* reminds us, "We can witness their reversion. / Things proliferate, / And each again returns to its root. / Returning to the root is called equilibrium. / Now as for equilibrium—this is called returning to the propensity of things."[22] Thus, in "the propensity of things"—a seminal meaning of *shi*—we also find the Daoist definition for returning to equilibrium, homeostasis, or, in Austrian terms, stationarity.

To the great masters who have come before us we owe a tremendous debt, for they have left us a treasure trove of wisdom compressed into a diamond of great value: *shi*, the roundabout, the return to homeostasis. This is our touchstone; that is, if we choose to use it. Fortunately, in our quest to be *shi* in a *li* world, we have prototypes and guides to follow. We have the *shi* of Klipp, with his paradoxical loving to lose and hating to win, and of the military strategists Sun Wu and Carl von Clausewitz who found the greater valor in the intermediate *Ziel* as the *Mittel* (means) for achieving the desired outcome of the end goal of *Zweck* (and without the carnage of the head-on clash). In Frédéric Bastiat, we know better than to follow the bad economist (now, our archnemesis) who sees only the small apparent good while ignoring the greater evil to come—that which is unseen by the myopic but should be foreseen by those who know to look.

On the roundabout, we have the real-world example of Henry Ford who eschewed the quick profits of today and patiently invested in a more circuitous process, so that with stopwatch in hand he might be highly impatient (with greater efficiency) in his production later. And there are the mythical entrepreneurs as well, starting with that shipwrecked savage Robinson Crusoe in his lowly economy of one, hungry today but hungrily catching all the more fish tomorrow. And in economics as a Wagnerian epic, we have Siegfried, the entrepreneurial hero of Nibelungenland, who evades the evil (in the form of the magic potion of distortion) that seeks to turn him into his opposite and force him unwittingly to betray his entrepreneurial oath of *shi*.[23]

Like Siegfried, we will be confronted with temptations that could lead us into all sorts of evils, from leverage to blithely following the positive-feedback crowd into the illusion of distorted assets. Our sword and our shield against such foes have been forged by the Austrians— Menger who defeated the Historicists and their slavish attachment to empirical data, Böhm-Bawerk who quelled the Marxists by proving the end product justified the value of its means (not the other way around), and Mises, who bashed the Keynesians (though they were too self-absorbed to notice) with the unavoidable truth about distortion that torches a destructive path across the economy (felling good trees and bad).

Now, at this juncture, the philosophical part of our journey comes to an end. Next, we move to the pragmatic application of what we have learned in Austrian Investing I and II, the subject of Chapters 9 and 10. Before we move on, we face our moment of truth, when we must stand up as true believers of this gospel of Austrian theory, which in its attempts to explain the entire boom/bust cycle gives us a coherent story that ties all the pieces together. As we move from theory to practice (the first eight chapters of this book to the last two), we will utilize what I have dubbed the MS index and the Faustmann ratio, as well as Siegfried, the roundabout entrepreneur—the embodiments of all the principles that have come before.

When the MS index diverges from 1, unnaturally because returns on capital exceed the cost of capital, and myopic time inconsistency plus monetary distortion traps everyone else into chasing immediate returns, you do not have to follow the ill-fated crowd. More generally, you needn't chase the immediately seen over what should be foreseen. You can let those who listen to the siren song of *li* be dashed on the rocks of their own impatience. You can stay true to *shi*, the roundabout, in its various guises, and wait for the return to homeostasis that will prevail even in the midst of pervasive distortion. Indeed, you can become the hero of your own roundabout investing story, by avoiding the distortion and, thus, having all the more resources later for opportunistic investing.

It is your path and your choice. If you choose well, it will become your *dao of capital*.

Chapter Nine

Austrian Investing I: The Eagle and the Swan

Exploiting the Distortion with Misesian Tools

Having followed the vast, varied, and often ancient lineage of the roundabout strategy to its central economic role in the orthodoxy of the Austrian School, we are now prepared to apply the principles of the roundabout—*wuwei, shi, umweg*—to capitalistic investing. We have reached the end, of sorts, a practical and tangible conclusion of following our well-developed roundabout path in the effective deployment of capital. We have indeed turned a corner in *The Dao of Capital*, as we begin here a new discussion of an approach I call Austrian Investing.

My intention in this chapter, far more important than any action step and exceedingly more useful, is to affirm a way of thinking as introduced in the preceding chapters; to plainly recognize when distortion exists, and to assess one's attitude—and appetite—when it comes to that distortion. We ask ourselves: How are we exposed to malinvestment?

Are we, for instance, investing in what is most manipulated by, whose profitability is most dependent upon, artificially low interest rates? Beyond avoiding it, can we perhaps even benefit from it?

If this book achieves nothing else, it would more than hit its mark if readers came away with greater awareness of such distortions in the economy and the markets, which magnify the human tendency toward the direct reward of *li*, and acquired a deeper appreciation for the arduous path of *shi*. The thought process here is what matters most; it is the real takeaway, a prescription for all investors, as it culminates the overarching theme of this book: the roundabout of *The Dao of Capital* as the circuitous means toward the ends of productive capital investment, despite our biology and a system rigged against it.

In this chapter, what has previously been an *a priori*, praxeological understanding becomes a historical understanding as it turns from thought to action. Yet, we stay true to the very path prescribed in the methodological roots of preceding chapters—the great thinkers from Laozi to Bastiat, Menger to Mises: from the deductive to the inductive, from methodological individualism to the flock, developing logical constructions of human action that then conform to how we understand the day-to-day world. They taught us that much of the visible is a distraction from a hidden reality, cautioning us not to "learn" from and thus be fooled by data—and moreover by what comes first, the seen; theirs are the simple insights for the foreseen. They taught us of the multidimensionality of the world, the cross-currents obscuring cause and effect; we do not experience the governing forces. The study of "economic history," Mises said, was a "laudable thing," but the "results of such studies" should not be confused with the study of economics. Studying economic history does "not produce facts in the sense in which this term is applied with regard to the events tested in laboratory experiments. [It does] not deliver bricks for the construction of *a posteriori* hypotheses and theorems."[1]

Thus, in true Austrian style (in their early battles with the German Historical School), we start by *thinking through* our task, having embraced the principles and adopted the theories that guide our thinking. Only then are we ready to take a peek at the data (and we will still feel a bit sullied after having done so). First and foremost, this exercise is about restraint. I focus only on what matters and is worthy of testing, and include here the results of each of my scanty tests (none left on the factory floor), each one serving to further validate a thought process (rather than the other way around). For me, when testing these investment results and properties, I insist on keeping the empirical work short and sweet—such that the clock is always ticking (and is thus curbing the all too easy and common slide into a useless back-fitting exercise). I'm reminded of the roundaboutness of Henry Ford for whom years of developing methods and constructing tools were followed by only minutes in production (sometimes reduced to seconds)—the former were the means to the latter. Here, years of introspection and preparation for what became Austrian Investing are followed by mere minutes of data processing.

The difference between the Austrian approach here and what is otherwise standard in the empirical sciences (economics and finance quite erroneously considered among them) is that without our understanding developed thus far, *none* of the testing that follows would have any merit *whatsoever*. (Moreover, I would even consider our understanding valid no matter what the data show; such is the dilemma of economic science.)

HOMEOSTASIS *EN FORCE*

The simple insight that the market is a natural homeostatic, self-correcting mechanism and that monetary distortion results only in a temporary disruption of that mechanism portends some results. From this, what do we expect to see—not *require*, but *expect*? Let's take a step back and survey what we really know. Since the Misesian Stationarity index can reach a lofty level (meaning the economy can persistently deviate from stationarity) only because of monetary distortion, we should expect a very high MS index to act as a prelude to a price of title to existing capital (the stock market, the numerator in the MS index) that is unsustainably high; this follows our expectation that the replacement value of that capital (the denominator in the MS index) will be unresponsive, as further new investment is thwarted by the distortion. Savers and investors, dissatisfied with artificially low interest rates that don't reflect their actual time preferences, placate themselves by eking out yield and otherwise chasing immediate returns (which are themselves given a boost from higher immediate consumption and lower savings from artificially lower rates). They quickly devour the immediate marshmallow in front of them, scoffing at the potential rewards for waiting. The lower rates make otherwise marginal investment schemes look good, and otherwise marginal existing capital (having marginal returns) look suddenly profitable, resulting in a scramble to own it and resulting in persistent market maladjustments. The system becomes starved of capital for roundabout production, as capital is trapped in the present—consuming itself, as it were—and thus there are insufficient resources to support the ongoing illusion of economic progress.

It only stands to reason that the stock market should inevitably fall (and fall in a violent, concentrated manner) as investors are routed into immediate liquidation altogether; existing capital is priced too high relative to its ultimate profitability, and all the monetary delusions of grandeur are simultaneously revealed in a burst of highly correlated entrepreneurial error. When, in Mises's words, "the airy castle of the boom"[2] can no longer buttress itself, and either rates rise from higher factor prices or from exhausted credit, it collapses on itself in a mass liquidation of malinvestment—a stock market crash, the homeostatic process *en force*. An auspicious and cathartic rout of malinvestment should then eventually produce an exceedingly low MS index, as the fire-sale prices of titles to existing capital become unsustainably low. Capital will again begin its journey toward productive use and its pricing is reorganized by the markets as they move back toward stationarity. Savings will necessarily grow again as rates finally reflect true time preferences, balancing the desire for and timing of roundabout investment, and immediate consumption will fall. The grand homeostasis reigns.

Here we have the comprehensive Austrian setup for the ubiquitous violent twists and turns of the stock market and the economy, the events that the authorities and masterminds of the day always see as the unfortunate effects of hazardous and haphazard market forces—what have come to be routinely though erringly called black swans. And this is our setup for Austrian Investing I, whereby we swoop down like Sun Wu's bird of prey (or better yet the Austrian eagle), when the moment is ripe and from a strategic position of advantage, and exploit these otherwise unexpected booms and busts.

The Eagle and the Swan: Birds of a Different Feather

WITNESS TO THE DISTORTION

Now for some housekeeping: As discussed in Chapter 7, the MS index is very well represented by what is known as the (Tobin's) Equity Q ratio—total U.S. corporate equity divided by total U.S. corporate net worth—which is readily available online through numerous sources, and easily computable using Federal Reserve Flow of Funds balance sheet data (and it is the height of irony that the very institution at the root of the distortion, the recognition of which is the point of the MS index, provides the data necessary to calculate it).

Figure 9.1 shows the history of the MS index going back to 1901. (I have scaled it by its running geometric average, meaning it averages only data available as of each date, and thus removes any *ex post* information; this scaling is meant to smooth any historical balance sheet bias.) While we see a regular and orderly mean-reverting line cycling

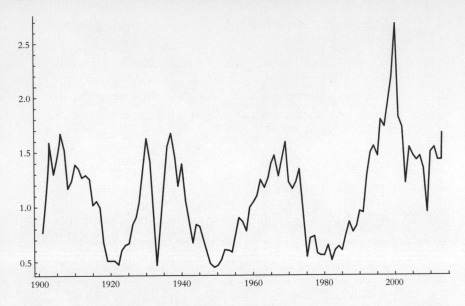

Figure 9.1   Footprints of Distortion: The Misesian Stationarity Index

through history, the story it fails to tell, I might add, is the human mis-ery and tumult and otherwise brake on civilization's march suffered over the deep credit cycles displayed.

This history depicts the clear footprints of historical monetary distortion. I regard it as pseudoevidence of Austrian Business Cycle Theory (ABCT); as academics struggle with empirically proving (a misnomer, to be sure) ABCT, I argue they have simply been looking in the wrong places.

The first obvious question to ask is: What is the subsequent effect of this distortion on the replacement value of all the capital valued in the numerator? That is, to what extent have higher expected profits in the price of title to existing capital been subsequently imputed into the source of those higher profits? Shouldn't high MS index levels above 1, for instance, logically lure profit-seeking entrepreneurs into greater capital investment, such that their successive efforts raise the replace-ment value and accumulated magnitude in the denominator (and thus offset the rise in the numerator of the MS index)? In fact, there is absolutely no statistically significant or consistent relationship between MS index levels and subsequent aggregate capital investment—visible neither in changes in aggregate capital expenditures (as a percentage of invested capital) nor in changes in aggregate corporate net worth (the denominator of the MS index). Much to the chagrin of the meddling central bankers, only the stock market is reliably affected (and only for a time) by monetary interventionism. In other words, when the central bankers try to stimulate actual physical investment by goosing asset prices with loose money, they fail to achieve their goal. (The result puzzled Tobin and other Keynesians, as mentioned in Chapter 7, and might have even surprised Mises somewhat before applying his entirely correct theory of malinvestment to Böhm-Bawerk's earlier insight on myopic time inconsistency and to real-world interest rates.)

Any alternative explanation for this history of the MS index, such as the existence of psychological "animal spirits" driving economic booms and busts, must explain how this irrationality applies only to the stock market but not to its components (that is, only to the whole but not to the sum of its parts). How are equity holders (the owners of capital—the factors of production) specifically and highly segmented from those who further build new capital—new factors of production? This is a far more dubious proposition than simply saying that assets are expensive (as apparently only certain assets are expensive).

The next and most pertinent question: What is the real effect of this distortion on the numerator (the aggregate land expectation value if this were taking place in our Nibelungenland, and the aggregate stock market capitalization in our real economy)? Let's start by examining the *total excess returns* (the return, including dividends, in excess of the one-year "risk free" treasury rate) of the S&P Composite Index (the biggest, most closely watched, and most heavily traded and well recorded capitalization-weighted U.S. stock index, a very good proxy for the total corporate equity of the MS index) following different regimes of monetary distortion since the turn of the twentieth century.

I throw each annual return data point of the S&P Composite into one of four buckets, based on the MS index at the start of each one-year period. In Figure 9.2, the first bucket (on the far left) corresponds to the lowest quartile (or lowest 25 percent) MS index readings, the second for the next higher readings, the third for the next, and finally the fourth bucket (on the far right) for the highest quartile MS index readings. I then take the average of the excess returns in each bucket to see simple expectations for each MS index level. (All returns are total

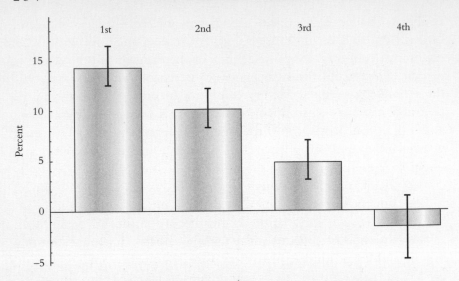

Figure 9.2   Lower Expected Returns with Higher MS Indices

S&P Composite Excess Total 1-Year Returns (Arithmetic Mean)

Bucketed by Starting MS Index Quartiles, 1901–2013

excess returns—including dividends; the error ranges around each bar, depicted by the vertical lines with hash marks at each end, are 95 percent confidence intervals of the sample statistics—found through a nonpara-metric bootstrap. This same methodology is used throughout this and the next chapter.) Based on what we now know, we would expect to see an inverse relationship: When the MS index is low, the subsequent average stock return should be high; when the MS index is high, the subsequent average return should be low. (If we *didn't* observe this outcome, it would mean that somehow investors responded to lower rates with more new capital investment, and this new investment as well as the old remained, on average, profitable after rates normalized. An impossibility!) The data cooperate; with greater than 95 percent statistical significance, my conjecture—derived from Austrian theory—is right.

What's driving these return differentials? Do stocks merely drift up at steeper rates under low MS index levels than under high ones, or is there something else going on? Of course we would expect to see the indications of severe malinvestment liquidation driving these results,

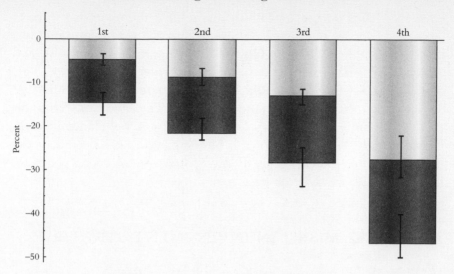

Figure 9.3   Higher Expected Drawdowns with Higher MS Indices

S&P Composite 20th and 50th Percentile 3-Year Drawdowns

Bucketed by Starting MS Index Quartiles, 1901–2013

meaning severe subsequent stock market losses (and we'll look at the concentration or speed of such losses a bit later).

In the following test I use S&P Composite Index "drawdowns"— or the amount by which our S&P returns cumulatively turn negative during any three-year window before rising again—as a measurement of stock market losses. In bucketing these drawdowns based on the MS index at the start of each period, just as I did in Figure 9.2, we start to uncover the market's dynamics.

In Figure 9.3, the lowest dark bar indicates the 20th percentile drawdown, or the realized drawdown at which 20 percent of all the data in the bucket are lower, and the light bar above the dark bar is the 50th percentile—also called the "median"—drawdown, or the realized drawdown at which half of all the data in the bucket are lower. (Error bars indicate 95 percent confidence intervals around each percentile estimate.) Going back over a century, this looks pretty bad for capital investment following high MS index levels. And for low MS index levels, there really wasn't much to worry about. Imagine that.

What a financially distorted world tells us is that the market, just like the overgrown forest, carries within it the seeds of its destructive correction; thus the inevitable bust that follows the boom is *not* (or at least *should not be*) an unexpected event. This is a very important realization, something of a death blow to the concept of systemic risk, and which will become the backbone of the Austrian Investing I rationale (and without which we would be left as mere victims of the distorted market and seemingly random shocks). The Austrians were right (before the time of this data): Just as we saw in Nibelungenland in Chapter 7, the undulations of the business cycle (as reflected in the stock market) do indeed simply follow a pattern of correcting persistent inflationary departures from stationarity.

AN INITIAL MISESIAN INVESTMENT STRATEGY

What would the assumption of the validity of this simple idea have done for an investor in the U.S. back when the Austrians first formulated the principles behind it, starting 100 or so years ago? Let's put this to the test—a tremendous century-long out-of-sample test (truly free of hindsight bias) of the deductive *a priori* Austrian capital and interest theory. Let's consider what one might do with just this robust information on the existence and effects of distortion (for which, obviously, we didn't really need the tests presented earlier). Let's become greedy capitalists, licking our chops, crossbows drawn, and wondering how we can make money from this knowledge. To start, the simplest, back-of-the-envelope strategy would be to *buy when the MS index is low and sell when it is high*.

I'll call this our *Misesian investment strategy*, in honor of the man whose approach was to avoid the systematic collapse of the 1930s. A version of this strategy has of course been identified by others before—and what investment strategy hasn't? What matters here is the conceptual thinking—the identification of the edge or, in this case, the imbalance—behind the strategy. Here, we are playing the explicit role of our pedagogical conifer, anticipating and exploiting through circumvention the roiling wildfire and resulting nutrient-rich soil.

A quick and dirty scan of the MS index chart (Figure 9.1) tells us that, say, a reading of 1.6 and, say, of 0.7 were historically generally high and low levels—so likely good places to sell and buy stocks, respectively. And when we've sold out of our stocks, we buy one-month treasury

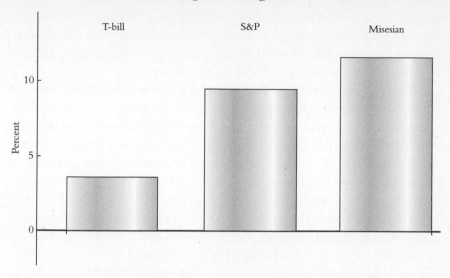

Figure 9.4   Misesian Outperformance

1-Month Treasury Bills, S&P Composite, and Misesian Investment Strategy,
Compound Annual Total Returns, 1901–2013

bills and roll them each month until we buy back into the stock market. How would that have done? (There is a good deal of *ex post* information in this strategy, because we didn't know what constituted a good MS index level at which to sell or buy until it was all over, of course. However, it turns out—not surprisingly—that's not a concern: If I instead start my test after, say, 1925—the first complete cycle—rather than 1901, and use only the information known at the time from then on, I get equivalent results. No cheating.)

As my old mentor Everett Klipp would have advised, our methodology here is exceedingly simple—again, dubiously so. But there is great beauty and effectiveness in our simplicity (see Figure 9.4).

The Misesian strategy outperforms the stock market by more than two percentage points per year. Think about what this shows. A basic "toy" strategy (with an "alpha" t-score of well over 4) based solely on an easily calculatable and logical measure of market distortion beats not only the average professional stock picker (who consistently underperforms the S&P), but also the (highly survivorship-biased) average hedge fund manager (such as from the HFRI Fund Weighted Composite

Index)—and with *far* less fanfare and risk. (And, for the record, while others have made attempts at Austrian market indicators of all sorts, none to my knowledge has either had these results nor avoided the lures of arbitrary *ex post* fitting and spurious relationships.)

The properties of the MS index offer a logical, straightforward, and highly pragmatic guide that most people can follow and understand, acting as a very simple gauge to judge one's investment theses. And yet it still seems to elude most people—after all, very few people, including professionals, get these kinds of investing results over time. The reason, as you've probably deduced by now, is that these returns are only realized in an exceedingly roundabout way; the detour beats the direct route. That is, it takes the Misesian strategy's average underperformance duration and magnitude of almost three years and 9 percent annualized to gain the advantages of investing for its eventual 2 percent cumulative outperformance. (Just imagine still waiting today after two decades to reenter the once-again booming stock market.) It painfully sacrifices immediate profits (as markets become more and more inflated by artificially low rates) most of the time for a tremendous eventual advantage (in buying after they inevitably deflate). It is investing, *weiqi*-style.

In the immediate-marshmallow world of investing, it is so hard to be the one sitting with folded arms, not taking the sweet enticement of now, and focusing instead on intermediate means for positional advantage to be exploited later. In *weiqi*, it takes great discipline to be *shi*, building only potential that may or may not ever really materialize, while one's *li* opponent racks up points and appears to be winning by a sizeable margin. Yet it is a choice that we must make, to take on the roundabout burden of the indirect, retreating now and looking foolish (or worse) to the rest of the world. (Klipp used to have a pithy phrase that embodied the difficulty of being *shi* in a *li* world, saying to be successful in trading, one had to "look like a jerk feel like a jerk." Though, what else would we expect from the man who said you had to love to lose money and hate to make it?) Given all the time we've spent in the esteemed company of Laozi and Sun Wu, Bastiat and Clausewitz, Menger, Böhm-Bawerk, Mises, and Ford, why would we not want to apply this thinking for ourselves? Not to do so would seem the ultimate foolishness, to turn our back on this archetypal strategic wisdom.

If you are wondering right now, after eight chapters of the roundabout, if the first investment strategy you are receiving basically tells you to stay out of the market for long periods of time when distortion is running high, the answer is yes. Although that may seem anticlimactic, it is anything but. To put this in the most straightforward terms, it's a really big deal—a very different and contrarian (and highly effective) way to approach investing. Just as Klipp's Paradox of "love to lose money, hate to make money" led to incredible discipline (and some healthy returns) in the trading pit, so, too, does this Misesian approach in anyone's portfolio.

The objective of roundabout Austrian Investing is not to find a way to make money now, but to position ourselves for better investment opportunities later. Or, as we might state it, we're being patient now so that we can be strategically impatient later. Whatever you decide to do as an investor, keep in mind the overarching aim of this book; it is about a way of thinking, of understanding the roundabout and the considerable strategic advantages to be gained along the patient, circuitous path. If you take away nothing else from this chapter (or even from this book) know that there is usually imminent danger in the direct approach, in ignoring the means for the ends, particularly in the market when distortion is running high. Thanks to the Misesian Stationarity index, there is a way to gauge that danger so that, no matter what your investment decisions are, you are better informed about those dangers.

Implementing this cookie-cutter Misesian strategy is extremely ambitious, even audacious (particularly for professionals), as Chapter 6 reminds us, because of that humanness about us that gives us a high immediate time preference—further magnified under monetary intervention—and makes it difficult to impossible to forego the immediate marshmallow, even though we may believe there are a great many more marshmallows to come. Think of the Misesian Wall Street investor (an oddity, to be sure) who shows no excess return during the distortion years when he owns low-yielding T-bills (and dramatically underperforms the stock market as it further runs up); he and his ilk would have mostly been weeded out by natural selection over a year or two of underperformance. No *über*-hyperbolic discounter will ever get to monetize the 2 percent outperformance of the Misesian strategy (though he would be a wealthy star if he could).

Hyperbolic discounting requires enduring a difficult wait, which is most intense in the earliest steps—from today until tomorrow, from tomorrow to the day after, and so forth. We perceive that the wait will get easier with each step, but that doesn't help us over the next step, particularly if interest rates have been manipulated all the way down to zero and everyone is piling into the stock market. As stated earlier, our sense of immediacy is made all the more acute, paradoxically, by monetary distortion—feeding an ever-shortening investment horizon. (If everyone could steel themselves against the temptation brought on by the distortion—or if humans were robotic exponential discounters, and all capital were the same homogeneous blob—then distortion likely wouldn't even happen.) To succeed, we need the fortitude of Mises who turned down a lucrative job with the prestigious Kreditanstalt bank, saying he wouldn't be part of the great crash to come. We, too, need to distance ourselves from the distortion, so that we do not become suckered in by it, which will lead to the opposite of what we intend: buying when the MS index is high and selling as it falls, which—rather than the roundabout path to capital accumulation—is the direct path to capital destruction.

There is yet another challenge in executing this Misesian strategy. It requires contrarian thinking, a not-to-be-underestimated psychological feat, to zig when the rest of the world is zagging—to step aside when the rest of the world is scrambling to buy, and to buy when the rest of the world is bailing out of positions. When the MS index goes so low it falls well below 1, then one can act like a corporate raider (particularly common around the last generational low in the MS index in the early 1980s), scooping up good assets that can then be liquidated at a profit—because in the aftermath of a malinvestment purge, title to capital is available for less than the replacement cost. Think of a low MS index for a cash-rich investor as analogous to the no longer dormant conifer seeds after their serotinous cones have opened, ready to spread throughout the fire-cleared, competitor-free land, enriched by nutrients of their vanquished predecessors.

THE EAGLE AND THE SWAN

The sudden realization of mass correlated entrepreneurial error is Austrian-speak for "stock market crash," as most if not all companies suddenly are revealed to have been priced wrong, and many are engaged in (and now looking to quickly exit) projects that one minute were considered profitable, and the next not. This is of course the retreating rout, to be followed by the counter-rout.

How can this happen (outside of the distortion described in Nibelungenland)? Everyone continues to scratch their heads over this. Many are quick to become financial ornithologists, crying "black swan!"—as per Nassim Taleb's wonderful book by the same name. (A black swan—or "tail event"—is an epochal event, big and extremely rare, or better still has never yet even happened at all. The word *tail* refers to the outermost and relatively thin tail-like appendage of a frequency distribution, or probability density function.) The first and second century CE Roman poet Juvenal is credited with coining the term *black swan* in reference to a "decent" wife—"a rare bird, as strange to the earth as a black swan."[3] (Any spousal ire over that comment should be directed at Juvenal, not at this author.) "Black swan" as the code words for an unexpected event (the discovery that not all swans were white as once believed) was promulgated in the early twentieth century by Viennese-born philosopher Karl Popper, who taught at the London School of Economics. (Popper and rival Ludwig Wittgenstein, who famously argued over sundry philosophical problems, were major forces in the intellectual prowess of early twentieth-century Vienna.)

When they occur, stock market crashes seem so irrational to most, so haphazard and unforeseeable, so black swan. But are they irrational? Are they even unforeseeable? Or do they simply stem from the distorting effects of credit expansions as the Austrians suggest? We have already seen (in Figure 9.3) that severe stock market losses (what I've called "drawdowns") follow periods of great distortion. While accumulated losses are likely the only crashes that matter (after all, it is the extent to which stock market losses accumulate that they are economically important), let's nonetheless take this a step further and look at temporally concentrated stock market losses—those that occur over a month, for instance—selling routs. (I'll actually use two-month returns in order to best capture noncalendar monthly swings.) These should be the true mark of a distorted world, since the end to the distortion is a sudden revelation as interest rates rise or credit evaporates, not a slow, orderly correction. (If it were the latter, it would presumably be correctable through ordinary entrepreneurial adjustments.)

Over the past century-plus, there have been sizeable monthly losses of 20 percent or more in the aggregate U.S. stock market, and

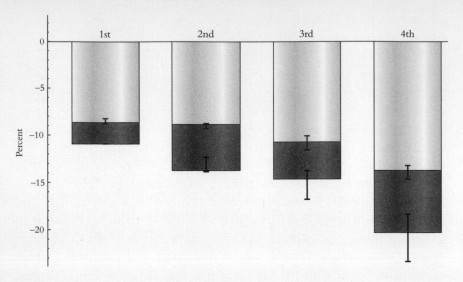

Figure 9.5   Higher Expected Two-Month Losses with Higher MS Indices

S&P Composite 2nd and 5th Percentile 1-Month Returns

Bucketed by Starting MS Index Quartiles, 1901–2013

they have occurred with exceedingly low frequency. By definition, therefore, it would seem we should be able to call such crashes in the stock market tail events. But on closer inspection, a different story emerges in Figure 9.5.

Upon bucketing two-month returns by their starting MS index quartiles (over a 3-year window of overlapping two-month returns following bucketing) and calculating the 2nd and 5th percentiles in each bucket, we see, again, that crashes follow distortion. (This is just as was done in Figure 9.3 with 20th and 50th percentiles of all the cumulative drawdowns, only here I'm looking at 2nd and 5th percentiles of all the two-month returns—meaning, in the case of the 2nd percentile, the realized two-month return at which 2 percent of all the two-month return data in the bucket are lower. Error bars once again indicate 95 percent confidence intervals around each percentile estimate.) To put Figure 9.5 into perspective, with 2 percent of two-month returns having been even worse than a 20 percent crash during the high MS index quartile (the lowest dark bar in the fourth bucket on the far right), one could expect to wait around 50 months (as the expected number of random trials needed to get an outcome with a 2 percent chance on each trial) for a greater than 20 percent two-month crash to occur when the MS index is in this highest of ranges. Clearly, 20 percent or worse crashes are not the random hundred-year flood as people generally think: They happen fairly quickly under certain conditions—a very distorted MS index—while those *conditions* have happened a handful of times over the past century; moreover, they happen much less quickly (and one would in fact still be waiting) following a low MS index. Once again, with such sound Austrian logic behind these studies, the evidence of distortion and its ramifications to investors is overwhelming: When the MS index is high *ex ante*, subsequent large stock market losses and crashes are no longer tail events at all—rather they are perfectly expected events. To Austrian eyes, these epochal losses were not unforeseeable. (More alarmingly, due to the evidence of monetary credit expansion of late visible in the MS index in Figure 9.1, as of this writing in July 2013, we have no right to be surprised by a severe and imminent stock market crash. In fact, we must absolutely expect it.)

For the record, our discussion of black swans here is confined to events as registered by the stock market. Should an asteroid come hurtling at us from the depths of space and strike us unawares, then maybe we'll chalk that one up to a black swan. However, stock market plunges that have occurred over the past century most certainly were *not* black swans or tail events. When it comes to events such as the crash of 2008, we see, instead, a bird of a very different feather (the Austrian variety).

What we have here is an induction problem of vantage point, such as Bertrand Russell's chicken that is surprised to have its neck wrung by the very farmer who has been lovingly feeding it all of its life.[4] The common epistemological problem is failing to account for the possibility of a tail until we see it. But the challenge here is something of the reverse: We account for visible tails unconditionally, and thus fail to account for when such a tail is not even a tail at all.

Perhaps the scientific and mathematical methodology (the "physics envy" of Chapter 7) of modern economics and finance is at the very source of the perception problem; a mainstream economist will typically model stock price movements such that a tail event, by definition, is bad luck. Every serious student of mathematics and finance recognizes the naïve simplicity of the Gaussian (bell curve, loosely speaking) assumptions underlying standard economics and finance models of the markets, but I am claiming here that the solution is *not* to come up with even fancier probability distributions. The deeper problem is the treatment of the return in the market as a number given to us by capricious Nature. Despite the apparent tremendous uncertainty in stock returns, they are most certainly not randomly generated numbers. Understanding tails would be tricky matters if they were (as we know from the deceptive small sample bias of power law distributions, for instance). Stock markets, however, are so much richer, grittier, and more complex than that.

Why shouldn't the price of immediacy jump to infinity along with perceived demands for immediacy? Why should anyone be expected to accommodate a burst of counterparties at prices that are strongly and suddenly believed to be in error—to accommodate the liquidation of malinvestment? After all, to assume anything else would be to assume that liquidity providers are charities.

The black swan notion is still paramount, however—I named many of my investment partnerships after it—but only because of the vantage point perception problem: Truly, the real black swan problem of stock market busts is not about a remote event that is considered unforeseeable; rather it is about a foreseeable event that is considered remote. The vast majority of market participants fail to expect what should be, in reality, perfectly expected events. Intertemporally challenged and further blinded by a myopic focus on the now, they price in only Anglo swans, missing the Viennese bird lurking conspicuously in the weeds.

CASE STUDY: PROTOTYPICAL TAIL HEDGING

We are now ready to transition from the simple Misesian investing strategy to Austrian Investing I; in so doing we return, in essence, to Marco at McElligot's Pool—although his gear to catch Thing-A-Ma-Jiggers has been upgraded considerably to highly sophisticated harpoons (put options in our case). In the second phase, Austrian Investing II, we switch from Marco to Siegfried, that intrepid Wagnerian dragon slayer and Nibelungen entrepreneur, whose activities are less susceptible to distortion and who represents the true advantage of the roundabout. When distortions and imbalances in the aggregate capital structure come to an end, by necessity, it happens so ferociously, due to the surprise of entrepreneurs across the economy as they simultaneously discover that they have all committed investment errors. Rather than entrepreneurs serving their homeostatic function of correcting mal-adjustments, the entire market must adjust itself abruptly through an essentially simultaneous liquidation. What follows in the eyes of those who couldn't see the distortion is a dreaded tail event.

If the market perceives (or rather prices) a large loss in the stock market as very unlikely, even when such perception and pricing are unwarranted, obviously tremendous opportunity exists—even if only to protect a portfolio against such deleterious losses.

The test depicted in Figure 9.5 was perhaps just a crude (though perfectly robust—they tend to go together) way of measuring the negative tail of monthly equity returns. There are endless other ways (ranging from the maximum likelihood Hill estimator to log–log regressions of *fractal dimensions*—all of which show essentially the same thicker tails under higher MS index levels). In measuring the prof-its had by tail hedging, we, in fact, now have what I would regard as the most economically intuitive and comprehendible method to mea-sure the dreaded tail. In so doing I will simultaneously thus illustrate the Austrian Investing I methodology.

I present an analysis of a simplified, prototypical tail-hedged equity portfolio. In this discussion, I move from the commentator I was in previous chapters to practitioner; tail hedging (or Austrian Investing I) is at the center of what I practice in my investment partnerships (and Austrian Investing II of Chapter 10, in combination with Austrian Investing I, is what I practice in my family office). However, while this is something of a glimpse into what I do in my funds, my actual approach is far more nuanced—as it is far beyond the scope and inten-tion of this book. It bears repeating: I am not telling anyone to run out and do this as described; even the very generic version of tail hedging is very hard and involves options that are very illiquid, which makes pricing and taking profits very difficult. Nonetheless, this part of the discussion is meant to serve as a conservative and honest case study, the purpose of which is (beyond further measuring tails) to demon-strate Austrian tools and the application of the roundabout approach through the conditional historical outperformance generated by adding extremely out-of-the-money puts to the S&P Composite Index.

To begin with a little basic knowledge for readers who are not familiar with options: A put is a derivative instrument that gives the holder the right, but not the obligation, to take a short position in the underlying security at the strike price—e.g., an equity index such as the S&P Composite. With tail hedging, the puts involved are necessarily, by definition, extremely far out of the money, meaning the strike price at which they become exercisable is very far below the current market price.

The portfolio I am testing in this study purchases 2-month 0.5 delta puts on the S&P Composite Index (approximately 30 percent out of the money, in the case of a 40 percent implied volatility) at the start of each strategy period at an assumed 40 percent starting volatility level (which is a historical median pricing level—and, in fact, within a large range, the return outperformance levels reported are surprisingly robust to this pricing level). After every month, the 2-month put options position is rolled (the existing options are sold and new 2-month puts are purchased, which resets the position every month). A historical, conservative interpolated mapping is utilized, which maps monthly index returns into concurrent monthly changes in pricing (or implied volatility) of the 2-month puts (for monthly vega profit and loss), as well as changes in the pricing spread between 1-month and 2-month puts (for monthly rolling). This mapping allows the test to include time periods before data are even available for options markets, thus providing a much greater range of market environments. Each month the portfolio spends one half of one percent on puts, and the remaining 99.5 percent stays invested in the S&P index. No leverage is employed (and, in fact, typically when the market is down by not even 20 percent the entire portfolio is actually net profitable).

Each strategy period encompasses two years of returns, and outperformance measures are annualized and bucketed into quartiles according to the MS index level at the start of each respective period. The periods tested range from 1901 (when the MS index data is first available) to the present. The outperformance mean and 95 percent confidence interval of the mean are calculated for each MS index quartile. All returns include reinvested dividends.

The case study compares the returns when tail hedging is used versus only owning the S&P to determine if and when outperformance occurs and its magnitude. As Figure 9.6 shows, with more than 95 percent statistical confidence, just as we saw in Figure 9.5 (not

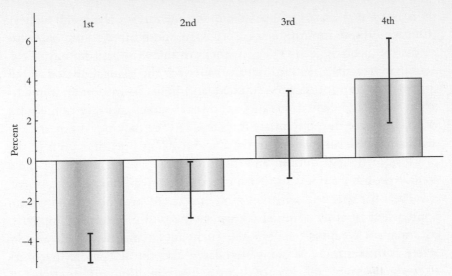

Figure 9.6   Austrian Investing I: Tail Hedging an Equity Portfolio

Annualized Outperformance of Tail-Hedged S&P Composite Portfolio (Arithmetic Mean)

Bucketed by Starting MS Index Quartiles, 1901-2013

surprisingly, since both use essentially the same monthly return data), the benefits of tail hedging are highly conditional on *levels of distortion* as evidenced by the MS index.

When the MS index is in the upper quartile (as it is as I write), there has been an approximate 4 percentage-point outperformance of the Austrian Investing I strategy (or a tail hedged index portfolio) over only owning the index (an outperformance that fades as the starting MS index level falls). Thus, there is a third choice between owning stocks or cash (as in the basic Misesian strategy) in a high distortion environment. (Indeed, when combined with the expected excess returns of equities alone shown in Figure 9.2, it is clear that a tail-hedged equity portfolio is superior to any of the investment industry's misplaced fine-tuning between equities and cash only.)

This is the roundabout Austrian capitalizing on the fact that investing in far out-of-the-money puts requires intertemporal vision, an indirect route (the likely loss in the immediate, as that one half of one percent spent on puts is lost each month without a crash) to achieving a later potential gain (the eventual profits from the puts, which are then invested in stocks whose subsequent returns will be much higher). (Of course those monthly put costs pale in comparison to the opportunity costs of being uninvested in stocks in the Misesian strategy.) Each option represents a seed in time, a chance for the giant redwood to put down roots into future fire-scorched land. What to most is an immediate sunk cost (a capital investment in what seems unlikely at the peak of the boom to be a potential future crash in the making) is potential to the savvy Austrian investor in the context of his portfolio, both in the profit from his put options and the future compounding returns (new trees) to come from investing in a resulting low MS index environment.

Clearly, expecting a market purge need not be a doom and gloom approach; it is rather a tremendously opportunistic, optimistic approach for one with capital—means—in such an environment, specifically when malinvestment is being liquidated and the MS index becomes exceedingly low. Capital is not destroyed; rather, title just changes hands at more advantageous prices to the buyer. The obvious takeaway is the benefit to investors who have access to effective tail hedging; however, seeing only that conclusion misses the far larger and more important point to understand: the source of this edge. As we know both deductively and now inductively (from Figure 9.6), the edge in the tail-hedging strategy is driven by monetary distortion. I would argue that systemic tail hedging wouldn't be nearly as important and probably not necessary at all if it weren't for the distortion.

The fact is, the many people who make predictions about the goodness of tail hedging as an asset class (something inconceivable as recently as when I launched Universa in 2007) without any thought to the environment of monetary distortion or the intertemporal effects on their investment decisions through time are missing most of the story: When the MS index is high, tail hedging further becomes expected-event hedging and provides the investing means for when the MS index is low.

THE *ZIEL* AND THE *ZWECK*: CENTRAL BANK HEDGING

I have shown that the epistemological problems of black swans and tails can be quite advantageous, both in the Misesian strategy and, most notably, in Austrian Investing I; an extreme loss in the stock market is certainly priced into much of the equity derivatives markets as an extreme tail (i.e., extremely unlikely), despite such overwhelming evidence to the contrary. I cannot fully explain why this is, just as I cannot explain why the Austrian School remains, in Mises's words, the "somewhat reluctantly tolerated outsider."[5] But, given that the two are inherently one in the same, we should not be surprised.

From the face of it, it is impossible to come to predicting or even understanding the properties of the most severe and rare events by extrapolating what we have already seen. There is a fundamental perception problem at the heart of this problem, a distributional illusion that can be shattered in an instant. Some may find this paradoxical coming from me, known as I am for tail hedging and so-called black swan investing. From my view, empirically and from an *a priori* Austrian interpretation, *black swan events have been largely insignificant in at least the last century of capital investment in the United States, including the most recent crisis.* Investors have, indeed, encountered surprising and pernicious events, but the fact is those who were surprised have been those in the extreme majority with either a blind or brazen disregard for the crucial concepts of Austrian capital theory and monetary credit expansions, and the corollary understanding of capital goods and the time structure of production. Of course, this does not mean that catastrophic, free market capitalism-destroying events—either manmade or not—*couldn't* have happened (and the manmade variety has historically been entirely related to the interventionism discussed in this book). We are dealing with the realm of entrepreneurial action within a competitive economic system and the monetary distortions that affect it. But note that during the 100-plus years of this study there was much devastating unprecedented world conflict (including two World Wars), which were still subsumed by Austrian praxeological principles when looking at equity market returns. It seems that tail hedging, as I have been explicitly practicing for about 15 years now, should be called *central bank hedging*—or, better yet, as I have coined the term, *Austrian Investing I.* (This activity over my career likely would have been much less interesting and fruitful without the insights of Mises and the cooperative actions of Federal Reserve Chairmen Greenspan and Bernanke. To which, I note with my hearty thanks, *Danke schön, meine Herren. Wir sind jetzt alle Österreicher.*)

Austrian Investing I is thus the autocatalytic process of indirect tools begetting greater tools, of profitable positions which then beget even more profitable positions—a roundabout investment process. (Puts are just as much about reinvesting cash at a market low as they are about making money on the path down to that low.) Austrian Investing I and II, which are encompassed here and in Chapter 10, respectively, both of which attain the ability to deploy capital where and when it is most productive, and then actually do it, are the destination toward which this book has been aiming all along.

Although the thought process is the important takeaway here, there are demands (and perhaps even a requirement) for investment books to provide action items. In the Misesian strategy discussed earlier, we switched between two choices, profiting from both a full equity position when the MS index was low, and avoiding drawdowns with a full cash position when the MS index was high. This 100 percent treasury bill position provided a roundabout position of advantage in a future period to be deployed as potential investments in *titles to capital* (i.e., equities) when the price of that capital is much lower (and thus its subsequent productivity and returns are much higher). The use of puts in Austrian Investing I is but a logical (and even more effective) progression from our simple cash position—a somewhat more refined *shi* strategy. This is the ultimate game of *tuishou*—where yielding to the initial rout is an intermediate step (of *zouhua*) toward the counter-rout of buying cheap title to productive capital and following (or *niansui*) the market back again to stationarity; as effective as the option trade is, it is but the prelude, an intermediate waypoint toward an even greater edge, an attack and counterattack. In the option trade is the temporal coordination of capital with its most advantageous and opportune use.

The put options that comprise our tail hedge serve not only to provide even more liquid capital in a rout for reinvestment, but also allow a large (and even full) investment in stocks during the distortion. (Think of it as a fast-growing angiosperm with the serotinous cones of a conifer.) It seems the stock versus cash decision of the basic Misesian strategy (and of virtually all asset allocation decisions, and a good bit of academic research) is entirely misplaced with the availability of other such Austrian tools.

The positioning of puts is the Thing-A-Ma-Jigger harpoon of Marco, the advanced tools, building blocks, or intermediate links—the

Clausewitzian *handeln* "leading up to the effectual principle, but never as that principle itself."[6] While generating profits from the hedge is its aim, its *Ziel*, that is not the intended end. The profits are but the first stage of this roundabout investment scheme; the second is what is done with those profits within a world in which distortion has suddenly been burned away. Thus, the put positions are the *Mittel* for the *Zweck* of *highly productive capital investment*, the superior technical productivity of means employed toward ends.

THE ROUNDABOUT INVESTOR

Admittedly, investing based on MS index levels to take advantage of distortion is not roundabout in the Böhm-Bawerkian sense of things; Eugen von Böhm-Bawerk did not discuss distortion. But it is roundabout in the Austrian sense, because of its alignment with *Umweg* (and its Daoist counterpart, *shi*), in that our investment goal is to *maximize our investment edge at some particularly advantageous intertemporal points in the future*. Thus we are using time—or, more specifically, roundaboutness—to attain higher capital productivity. Although our case study shows the importance of tail hedging, as we look at it on its own merit, we remind ourselves that we cannot confuse it with the *Zweck*, the end goal in itself. For me, the hedge is a *Ziel*, an intermediate objective, a waypoint of advantage along a roundabout path known as Austrian Investing. With this perspective, we can also see a link between Austrian Investing I and the basic strategy presented earlier in this chapter of avoiding the market when the MS index is high and exploiting the market when it is low. The commonality of the two strategies—one to pinpoint when to avoid the market and the other to exploit the distortion—is the importance of preserving and generating capital to be deployed opportunistically later, when the moment is right. Thus, tail hedging is, indeed, *shi*, becoming the means and setup for strategic positional advantage—a fully loaded crossbow (with extra arrows in the quiver) to be fired later when the vulnerable target appears. As such, tail hedging is a tool that allows us to actually exploit the distortion and not succumb to it.

Now, in the next chapter, we see what real investment in capitalistic production is all about as we gain a full appreciation of what is so special about this process. And so from Austrian Investing I, insulating ourselves from the trap of distortion and even profiting from it, we move on to Austrian Investing II, which is grounded in the wisdom of Böhm-Bawerk's roundabout and a straightforward lesson, thanks to the Austrians, of how to invest in such a manner. We take a page out of the Austrian classics as we accumulate the means of production and heed the entrepreneurial charge. Thus, as investors, we become fully Austrian in thought—and action.

Chapter Ten

Austrian Investing II: Siegfried

Exploiting the Böhm-Bawerkian Roundabout

The roundabout route—leading first to an intermediate point, a *Ziel*, from which to launch the next campaign in pursuit of the destination, the *Zweck*—is the road map for Austrian Investing. On the first leg of the journey, as I laid out in Chapter 9 with Austrian Investing I, we focused on the distortion in the financial markets, indicated by the telltale sign of an MS index significantly higher than 1. Recall that this signal tells us that the physical structure of production of the real economy has been, through monetary sleight of hand coerced away from stationarity, and is poised to snap back again as the forces of negative feedback become ever stronger. Once we have identified such a scenario, we can exploit our knowledge (elusive to most, and known only through study of Austrian theory) through two basic responses: We either can keep our capital on the sidelines in reserve (what I have called the basic Misesian strategy), or we can enter positions that opportunistically generate capital when its deployment is most effective (the more sophisticated complement of tail hedging, and what I call Austrian Investing I)—*shi* strategies all.

Now, in this chapter, we are ready for the second part, where we seek out opportunities that are aligned with the true Böhm-Bawerkian round-about of the Austrian *Unternehmer*. Rather than gauging the stationarity (or lack thereof) of the market as a whole, in Austrian Investing II I zoom in on individual firms and their exceedingly heterogeneous capital, moving from the macro to the micro, which is only fitting for an investment philosophy bearing the name Austrian. In so doing, we deploy all the tools we have amassed thus far to scout out and capture those rare round-about investments that will make us truly Austrian investors.

As always, we are guided by the Austrians' principles of parsimony and fidelity to reality. That is, they say only what they can say in simple tautological language (as opposed to the convoluted mathematical models of the mainstream)—with the fewest inputs, if you will—which leaves them extremely constrained. By restricting themselves to qualitative but necessarily true statements, the Austrians often come under fire, even today, as being quaint or medieval, yet they avoid the false precision that plagues the smartest guys in the room who built impressive and clever computer models of the financial markets that seemed to predict just fine . . . until they didn't. Needless to say, this hyperprecise modeling approach (which characterized Long Term Capital Management and other strategies cooked up by the mathematical experts) is diametrically opposed to our uniquely Austrian methodology.

Just as I stated in Chapter 9, only the *thinking* behind Austrian Investing can validate it. An investment strategy that seemed to work on the historical data can famously disappear (assuming it was not a spurious mirage in the first place), as soon as analysts become aware of it—this is one of the central findings in the efficient markets literature. But in this book I have used deductive Austrian reasoning to explain systematic forces of *disequilibrium*, and our logic also explains why other (presumably non-Austrian) investors, having a distinct humanness about them, will leave the proverbial money on the table. Our look at the data indicates not the truth of the underlying theory, but rather it shows us the *magnitude* of the potential gains—the historical data show us the *importance* of our theoretical deductions.

Roundabout investing (a very apt synonym for Austrian Investing) is all about the temporal structure of productive capital. As we recall from the slow-growing (at first) conifers and Henry Ford's capital structure extending from raw materials to automobiles, production by its very nature takes much time. Roundabout production, therefore, cannot focus myopically on the immediate profit; rather, it invests teleologically, building the indirect means—the positional advantage—toward the ends of profits that will not materialize in the near term. In fact, as we will see, it is all the better for us that such evidence is hidden from the rest of the investing public who focus on the seen, and impatiently gobble today's marshmallows. Their impatience makes them blind to future potential, tomorrow's profits that are yet unseen but can, if we know where and how to look, be foreseen. Indeed, Austrian Investing II, like Austrian Investing I, is all about the straightforward plan of attack comprised in this book: being patient now in order to be strategically impatient later.

SIEGFRIED, THE DRAGON SLAYER

The telltale sign of what we are seeking is *highly productive capital*. From a Böhm-Bawerkian perspective, we know that the most productive capital is also the most roundabout capital. In a *physical* sense, the result is obvious; Böhm-Bawerk taught that we can always find technological ways of producing more output with our inputs, if only we are willing to wait longer. Yet I want to go further and claim what is *not* so obvious, perhaps even to Austrian readers: The most *profitable* capital structures will tend to be very roundabout as well.

I am focusing here on the Austrian model of capital and production that we have understood in teleo-mechanisms from the conifer to the caterpillar and the strategy of Robinson Crusoe, acquiring later-stage advantages of efficiency through present-stage disadvantages—roundaboutness. In this book, I have developed a code word for highly productive roundabout capital, a name that embodies the best of the Böhm-Bawerkian approach: *Siegfried*. As we recall from our parable of Nibelungenland in Chapter 7, there is something special about Siegfried, "joyous in victory," slayer of dragons, entrepreneurial hero, which allows him to provide the best products to consumers with great efficiency (as his trees and pastures and goat herd flourish, thanks to his exquisite *Wunderhorn* playing). Like Henry Ford, with time Siegfried amasses a roundabout capital structure to make products that people want to buy, when they want to buy them. Therefore, we know that the mark of a true Siegfried is a *high return on invested capital* (ROIC)—best calculated by dividing a company's EBIT (operating earnings before interest and tax expenses are deducted) by its invested capital (the operating capital required to generate that EBIT). Wisely, Siegfried continually reinvests his profits into his business—becoming increasingly more roundabout—instead of pocketing the profits by paying out high dividends to himself (or just accumulating cash). He is driven to act by what he sees as *false prices* on his factors of production—his capital and other costs are just too low relative to the prices at which he can subsequently sell his finished products. (To put it simply, his enterprise can transform dollars spent on inputs into dollars earned from customers at a much higher rate than he could earn by lending the money out.) A true entrepreneur, Siegfried finds those false prices to be, in Mises's words, "intolerable"; when he sees them, he has to act, which ineluctably makes him become increasingly roundabout (as he is continually building new roundabout capital from square one) and, therefore, even more efficient in the future. While driven by his ends—profitability—he takes aim on his means—the tools of higher order capital goods.

Siegfried's Idyll

Most important of all—what truly makes Siegfried a Siegfried—is that he is not all that sensitive to interest rates; his profitability is not terribly contingent upon marginal movements in everyone's time preferences or the central bank's imposition of artificial interest rates. Of course, Siegfried is not perfect. When there is a big credit collapse and a liquidation of assets, following a period of monetary distortion, Siegfried will see a decline in his ROIC (even he lost a little in 2008). But his capital likely remains profitable and productive, well above his cost of capital, even if the central bank should suddenly and sharply raise interest rates in the thick of a boom. After such a surprise move by the central bank to "take away the punch bowl," the Günthers of the world will be crushed, as their bloated enterprises were utterly dependent on the artificially cheap credit of the boom. They will be forced to scale back operations, or fold altogether. In contrast, Siegfried will be okay, as his business model remains fundamentally sound. In the mass liquidation of the Günthers, the crashing prices of various business inputs may cause Siegfried to regret some of his purchases made at the height of the boom, but that will be a luxurious position compared to many of his peers.

Siegfried is akin to the conifer, as he willingly turns his back on the fray of fast growth (that often exists only because of the artificial fertilizer of distortion), and thus is overlooked by those who have no way to appreciate what he is constructing. (They are mesmerized by the fast, but likely unsustainable, growth of the angiosperm hares.) With an intertemporal perspective, Siegfried cedes what looks like the prime places stampeded with competitors who race for the win, and instead he happily retreats (*Wunderhorn* in hand) to the rocky places, where the growing is hard at first (as he foregoes his profits today to build his tools of later efficiencies). Yet to perseverance and tenacity and an intertemporal view come the payoffs, rewarding those who are not obsessed with today and, instead, have a depth of field perspective. Yes, Siegfried will grow more slowly now (so slowly that he may not appear to be growing his profits at all) as he amasses his roundabout capital structure, but when the time is ripe, he will emerge with the greatest advantages (and when the field of competition is cleared by the wildfire that destroys unhealthy, malinvested growth, he is still standing, even ready to advantageously invest more). His slow but deliberate roundabout growth has given him the structure he needs to accelerate later on, to kick into high gear and outperform the rest—the tortoise-that-morphs-into-a-hare and then surpasses the mere hare.

To move from our fable to an operational strategy for the real (non-Wagnerian) world, note that Siegfried qualifies as our investment ideal because of the first (of two) criterion: *high ROIC*, which prompts him to keep reinvesting profits into his capital structure to become even more efficient and eventually grow. This pattern explains why we should expect a strong correlation between above-average returns and a roundabout capital structure (even though such a connection is not usually made even among Austrian writers); and this expectation is confirmed by data: High ROIC firms show consistently and significantly greater increases in their invested capital compared to non-high ROIC firms. Academic Austrians tend to view above-average returns—what they would call *pure profit* as opposed to mere interest earnings—as due to superior entrepreneurial vision, while capital roundaboutness is handled in a separate, equilibrium analysis of interest rates. Yet I claim that in the actual market, we should expect these two Austrian concepts to overlap substantially. Consider: The entrepreneur who foresees a profit opportunity in the distant future, and who patiently reinvests earnings into his business year after year in anticipation, has a much greater opportunity for (eventually) posting an enormous ROIC than entrepreneurs who are engaged in short-term projects. (The fewer the rings spanned on Böhm-Bawerk's *Jahresringe*, the more commoditized the business.) Thus, while there may be no *direct* cause-and-effect relationship between capital roundaboutness and above-average returns, once we think through the actual forces governing them, we come to expect an observed, *ex post* correlation between the two.

As Austrian investors (by which I mean capitalistic investors seeking to accumulate productive capital—as opposed to the more common mere gambler-investors seeking to exploit changes in prices on title to capital), we have two basic choices of roundabout paths. One path is to go the Siegfried route ourselves, as that other ideal Austrian entrepreneur, Henry Ford, did when he doggedly amassed factors of production to build his own self-contained, ever-deeper, and more productive capital structure. We, too, could mimic Siegfried and bring together our own factors of production in such a way that allows us to be similarly roundabout in our production as we discover and exploit what, to us, are false prices. The high ROIC of our Siegfried means that (relative to his competitors) he is very good at taking investment dollars and transforming them into earnings; the ratio is much better than the going price of capital. This, of course, requires something special, a great insight, and an unwavering belief in what is perhaps merely a promising hunch—the *Verstehen* of Chapter 7. (One might think of this as the burden of the angel investor.) While important and sometimes even lucrative, this is beyond the scope of this book.

Yet as Austrian investors, there is another option open to us: to identify a metaphorical Siegfried and own a piece of him—that is, we can use our funds *to buy title to some of his existing operation*. We can thus exploit what are false prices only to Siegfried by acquiring and then stepping into his shoes. Yet this route has an additional variable, which makes us take pause: Unfortunately, we should presume that it will cost us dearly to get in. The baseline assumption of efficient capital markets would be that other investors are just as keen as we are, and that the price of stock in a Siegfried would already reflect the tremendous economic advantage indicated by his high ROIC (which is of course public knowledge).

Yet for whatever reasons—and I will give my own thoughts and evidence shortly—this is *not* always the case. In other words, in the real financial markets we often encounter high ROIC Siegfried firms where these superior efficiencies at turning invested and reinvested capital into future earnings are apparently *not* priced in. Back in Chapter 5, in our discussion of forestry development I explained a concept that we can now fully deploy: In addition to casting our net for firms with a high ROIC, we are *also* looking for firms with a *low Faustmann ratio*, meaning a low market capitalization (of common equity) over net worth (or invested capital plus cash minus debt and preferred equity) ratio. In Chapter 5, I explained that this Faustmann ratio is driven by the degree to which the ROIC exceeds the cost of that capital, so clearly one might expect high Faustmann ratios (where the whole is greater than the sum of its parts—or the sum of the factors of production) to accompany high ROICs. (When we make this more realistic and allow for the reinvestment of profits into more land—and thus eventual growth in those profits—this robust relationship remains.) Stating it in Nibelungen terms, we want to acquire ever-more roundabout Siegfrieds while they are priced like breakeven Johanns, or even struggling Günthers.

The ultimate *end* for the Austrian investor is the same as for any other investor: profit. Yet the *means* are entirely different; here, they are the central focus. The Austrian investor doesn't lunge in *li* fashion immediately for the goal; he doesn't set out directly to find firms with immediately rising profitability, or firms to hold while others also pile in immediately, or firms with immediate dividend yields, or even underpriced firms per se. Rather, his *first* task is to find highly roundabout, productive firms—ones with high ROIC—that possess the circuitous means of economic profit. Then, to these Siegfrieds he applies a second filter, or screen, and looks for firms with a low Faustmann ratio. This two-pronged approach would strike most investors as quixotic, simplistic, and even contradictory. By this point in the book, though, the reader should understand that such a commonplace attitude is precisely what will deliver remarkable rewards to the roundabout Austrian investor.

This strategy is neither easy nor automatic; we certainly won't find these companies on a "Siegfried Stock Watch List," and they likely won't be making headlines. Some tricky analyses of financial statements are necessary, and we will have to resist, once again, that very humanness about us. Strangely, Siegfrieds are often the quiet, hidden, and even scorned treasures in the world of investment, because they often appear to be doing nothing much of anything at all, not progressing, even regressing—except for one very important thing: We can be confident that the incentives are there for them to diligently and roundaboutly reinvest capital. Thus, our goal is to identify precisely those firms that—in light of Austrian economics—we expect to *eventually* progress (or grow their EBIT) and thus deliver (perhaps after a large lag) a substantial return on investment in ownership of the firms.

To drive home the rationale behind this Austrian approach, it might help if I note that neither of these screens *in isolation* is enough to warrant our attention. For example, a firm with a high ROIC but a correspondingly high Faustmann ratio will be expected to experience its roundabout earnings growth; that is true. It might make sense as investors to take our funds and buy the same factors of production—at the same false prices—in order to copycat such a firm. But its high Faustmann ratio means we don't want to *invest in* that firm by buying shares of its stock.

On the other hand, suppose we encounter a firm with a relatively low Faustmann ratio that also has a low ROIC. Armed with Austrian insights, we pass on such a firm. Yes, the low Faustmann ratio might lead us to believe that the financial markets are, for some reason, underpricing the productivity embedded in the physical capital assets of the firm. Yet the firm's low ROIC makes us pause. If management perceives that the operation cannot earn a higher return on reinvested earnings than the going rate of interest, we can hardly expect them to plow the profits back into the business (and, even if they did, it would be economically destructive malinvestment). Without more information, we should worry that this firm will provide no entrepreneurial profit, will thus not progress, and worse yet will even regress.

Now that I've spelled out why either criterion in isolation is inadequate, we can more fully appreciate why the two operating *in tandem* is just what the Austrian *Doktor* ordered. A firm with a high ROIC will naturally engage in high rates of reinvestment in the business—the managers almost cannot help themselves, as this is a simple matter of putting available funds to work in an outlet with a proven track record and over which they have exquisite control. Armed with our knowledge of Böhm-Bawerkian capital theory, we have a general presumption that such a firm *eventually* will be reappraised by the market as more efficient than its peers, as the accumulated roundaboutness eventually manifests in greater economic profit.

How then does the second criterion—a simultaneously low Faustmann ratio—come into play? Here we draw on Böhm-Bawerkian *subjective value* theory. The simple fact is that many investors—including and even *especially* professional asset managers—suffer from extremely concentrated time preference, or what the literature calls *hyperbolic discounting*, discussed extensively in Chapter 6. *Now* we have an explanation for why the asset markets may be undervaluing—dinging—our productive little Siegfried, despite its bright future. The various equity analysts and investment managers may have concluded that this particular Siegfried will not see its earnings grow any time soon enough. (If the reader wants a real-world explanation for why this tends to be, even among highly productive firms, consider the fact that a sustained program of high capital expenditures would make a firm more roundabout, but would also depress future earnings for some time as the income statements are saddled with higher depreciation expenses.) Of course, in any specific case, the actual reason for an apparent undervaluation could be something quite legitimate, such as a pending lawsuit or regulatory ruling. Yet if we aim to find simple, axiomatic (Austrian) rules of thumb for identifying stocks likely to return superior returns, our two criteria—rooted in the Böhm-Bawerkian treatment of capital theory and subjective value theory—are remarkably robust. The high ROIC flags for us firms that are likely to experience earnings growth, while the relatively low Faustmann ratio further segregates those firms where other investors apparently underappreciate this lucrative prize, lying as it does just beyond the horizon—and at the end of a round-about route. It might be, of course, that for any particular firm, the insiders know something we don't; but in the aggregate, it might also be simply that most investors have a more immediate horizon, a much shallower depth of field, than we do.

Austrian Investing II is indeed the sibling to Austrian Investing I. These Austrian *Kinder* are both essentially angling to accomplish the same roundabout task: to continually and cumulatively own highly pro-ductive capital. One might say that Austrian Investing I went about this *longitudinally*, by exploiting opportunities available intertemporally across time; and one might say that Austrian Investing II is now going about this *cross-sectionally*, by exploiting opportunities available at the same point in time—a handful of Siegfrieds found each month, for instance. (Our pedagogical conifers, in their retreat to the rocky places in order to ultimately outgrow their neighbors and intermittently take their land,[1] similarly employ both cross-sectional and longitudinal strat-egies, respectively.) This, too, is a highly intertemporal strategy. As was the case in Austrian Investing I, here in Austrian Investing II we find that as we wait—in this case for EBIT to grow and the stock price to subsequently rise—we actively construct the very means of our sub-sequent superior profits. *Produktionsumweg* requires an intertemporal exchange of payment now for the tools of higher productivity later; to be soft now in order to be hard later; to retreat in this moment in order to advance all the more imperiously later on. And we know that the Böhm-Bawerkian opportunities of Austrian Investing II (like the Misesian opportunities of Austrian Investing I) are hidden from the eyes of less discerning investors—they see in these Siegfrieds only Johanns or Günthers. Or, to switch our metaphor for a moment, the vast major-ity of investors encounter a hungry Robinson Crusoe whom they see is catching fewer fish, which seems to make his operation unattractive, and they want no part of it. However, the savvy minority of investors—appreciating Austrian insights—can see beneath the surface, and rec-ognize when Crusoe is hungry *not* because of sloth or ineptitude, but because he is currently investing his resources into building a boat and a net. The Austrian investor sees the fish jumping offshore, and realizes that Crusoe's inability to catch them is merely a temporary condition, as Crusoe is preparing himself for the big catch further downstream.

CASE STUDY: BUYING THE SIEGFRIEDS

We are now ready to observe our scorned Siegfrieds in action in the real world. (Our laboratory is the Compustat database of reported financial data, as well as historical stock price and dividend data, going back to the 1970s.)

Let's start by looking at the Siegfrieds and confirming that they do, in fact, tend to remain Siegfrieds. (After all, if Siegfrieds were to quickly deteriorate into Johanns, then certainly our presumption of their ever-advantageous roundaboutness would be mistaken.) On theoretical grounds, we *expect* a firm with high ROIC to remain in such standing, as its managers will continue to reinvest in the firm (why *wouldn't* they?), and this will only further solidify their positions of competitive advantage.

The data match up with our theoretical deduction. It turns out that high ROICs have been sustainable.[2] In Figure 10.1 we see that

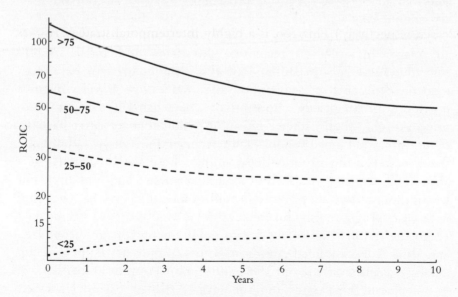

Figure 10.1   Siegfrieds Stay Siegfrieds

Rolling 10-Year ROIC (Median), All Stocks

Bucketed by Starting ROIC Quartiles, 1970–2013

the Siegfrieds (the top line)—defined here as firms realizing 75 percent or higher ROIC at the start of each 10-year period—have tended to persist as Siegfrieds—or have retained their elevated ROIC by the end of each 10-year period.

To be clear, I acknowledge that there is nothing *guaranteeing* this result, and no doubt we can find individual firms with high ROICs one year that lapse into low ROICs in the future, or even go bankrupt. This is even assured by the preeminent *regression fallacy*, whereby an extreme value generated by random noise in a data series is consequently reversed when the noise abates—and assigning meaning to that reversal is a mistake. (Mistaking the deliberately roundabout swerves described in this book for randomness is a similar, though inverse, error.) Yet in the real world the type of farsighted entrepreneurs who continually reinvest earnings are the very people poised to seize profit opportunities that have eluded others, and they are ahead in the capital-configuration race, so that *in the aggregate* we expect a persistence in high ROIC. The statistical result is even more reasonable once we consider that certain intangible assets (such as the rewards of research and development, or brand-name recognition, or the leadership skills of an owner) will very often show up in the measured return on tangible capital.

We can see that being a Siegfried comes with tremendous advantage. In order to reap that advantage and more specifically the advantages of Böhm-Bawerk's insights, my aim here is to turn these insights into portfolios, as it were. Now I will construct portfolios of Siegfrieds, choosing the best handful every month, using a highly robust screen (meaning wild numbers don't have an undue affect, as I equal weight each purchase): Each month I purchase the lowest Faustmann ratio firms among those with recent ROICs above 100 percent (with further screening for size and liquidity), and I turn them over as they eventually fail to meet our criteria (checking each year). (I ignore fishy financial values as well as sectors like banks.) I start the test in 1978, solely due to requirements for sufficient available data. (I use a spliced combination of Compustat's Point in Time database, available starting in 1987, and its non-Point in Time database; as is apparent, these results don't materially change if I restrict myself just to the more timely Point in Time data.)

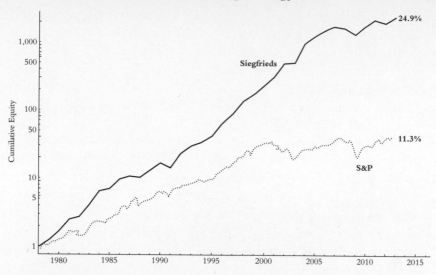

Figure 10.2 Siegfrieds versus the "Average Johanns" of the S&P

The Siegfried Strategy's Cumulative Performance Alongside the S&P Composite Index

Figure 10.2 shows this simple portfolio's results (specifically the cumulative equity in the strategy, starting at $1 in 1978) through time, compared to the S&P Composite Index.

Needless to say, these are tremendous results (like Austrian Investing I, beating most—if not in this case all—peers), in the simplest of non-optimized screens (another basic toy strategy) built only on economic logic and focusing on just ROIC and the Faustmann ratio. However, again, these data say nothing of the validity of the Böhm-Bawerk arguments on roundaboutness; the data show us only the displayed *magnitude* of importance.

Now, let's investigate what's going on under the hood here. Put simply, why are there highly productive firms (ROIC over 100 percent is an outrageously big number) so scorned that they have such low Faustmann ratios to meet our thresholds? It turns out, as Figure 10.3 shows and as we anticipated, among the Siegfrieds (operationally defined in Figure 10.3 as companies with ROICs above 50 percent—in order to provide enough data for comparative significance), those with the lowest (1st quartile) Faustmann ratios (the dark line at the bottom)

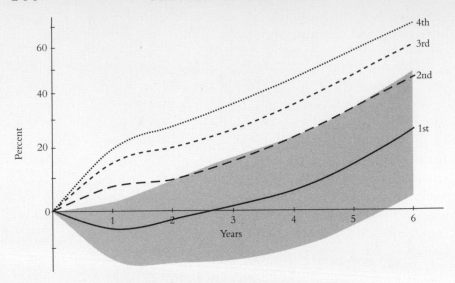

Figure 10.3　Roundabout EBIT Growth

Rolling EBIT Growth (Arithmetic Mean), All Stocks with ROIC >50%
Bucketed by Starting Faustmann Ratio Quartiles, 1978–2013

have seen their subsequent EBITs take a temporary turn for the worse (and the shaded 95 percent confidence region around the mean EBIT changes for the lowest Faustmann ratio bucket indicates the rigor in this statement). In fact, the statistically significant differences between each progressive Faustmann bucket would suggest that the market is actually pricing these differences in. As the EBIT paths diverge at one year, and as guidance and analyst forecasts seem to predict this far out in the future fairly well, this should not be surprising at all; what should be surprising, at first, is how fooled the market tends to be over the subsequent one-to-two-year bend in the road. When you consider that these divergences are essentially—even entirely, with high statistical significance—accounted for by spurts of fixed and intangible capital spending, this is all the more surprising. These first-quartile Siegfrieds are merely becoming more roundabout—sacrificing today for growth tomorrow—and paying the price today.

As we know, roundabout production—bearing the costs of capital investment—typically results in an immediate hit on profits (particularly from noncapitalized investment such as research and development).

Our constant refrain sounds again: We live in the seen (what is available to us), and we extrapolate the seen such that we are deceived as it curves (minor leaguers hit linearly extrapolated fast balls, major leaguers hit curve balls); the roundabout is hard, and we are not biologically cut out for it. Thus, the stock market tends to be about immediate bets (or expectations) on distant outcomes—yet all that matters to the bettors tends to be the immediate outcomes. That is, among high ROIC firms, stock valuations and the resulting Faustmann ratios seem to anticipate future profits in the short run so accurately that they miss the curves and the changeups. It is a doctrine of investing that stocks follow their earnings—that, in the words of Peter Lynch, "It's the earnings that waggle the wiggles" in the stock market (so "what's the sense of wasting time on sluggards?"[3])—and naturally the near-term earnings are all we see. (As it turns out, stock market investors are less savvy than the hoary forestry investors of ages past, who overcame the dreaded *axiom of the axe* and saw the faster and more profitable tree growth just around the corner.) The market focuses on immediate profits and growth thereof—immediate progress—all the while treating the productivity of the means of those profits as homogeneous. This is the penalty assessed by the myopic market as the price of *Produktionsumweg*. The premium goes to the marshmallows produced today, while punishment is meted out on Siegfrieds that devote their profits to becoming more efficient in marshmallow production tomorrow. (No wonder Henry Ford tried to avert equity partners and considered typical Wall Street investment to be a sideshow.) Contrary to my central tenet from Hazlitt's *Economics in One Lesson* (from Chapter 1), the markets truly look at just the immediate rather than at the longer effects of capital and production processes; these are the two games always at play, with so little competition in the latter.

Figure 10.3 is reminiscent of Figure 2.1 depicting growth rates of conifers and angiosperms in Chapter 2. It is the quintessential Böhm-Bawerkian roundabout. Turn Figure 10.3 ninety degrees counterclockwise, and we see my favorite image of literally "going right in order to go left." (That is, the 1st-quartile Faustmann ratio firms see *lower* EBIT for about the first two years, in contrast to the immediate growth of firms with higher Faustmann ratios.) And when one considers what's driving this detour to the right, it becomes clear that this is indeed "going right in order to then better go left." (Of course all the other quartile firms have already engaged in the roundabout, and are thus already headed left—and of course the market fully appreciates them by then.) In the tyranny of first consequences, in the market's systematic scorn for this circuitous path through the indirect means of economic growth, lies the very edge of Austrian Investing II. (The best investment approach may even be to search out such high ROIC companies where forward profits are expected to take this detour—a very difficult thing to do; the good news is we don't have to, as the market seems to be already systematically doing it for us.)

The next question to ask is: Just how insulated are our Siegfrieds from the booms and busts of distortion demonstrated in the previous chapter? Since a Siegfried, by definition, is a farsighted visionary—who can better anticipate future market conditions than his peers, and who has spent years building up a roundabout capital structure accordingly—and whose ROIC far exceeds his cost of capital (and his investment plans are thus generally insensitive to movements in rates), we should expect that he is more protected than the Johanns and certainly the Günthers from engaging in malinvestment. Let's see what actually happened in the data.

Siegfrieds aren't perfect; they are still exposed to the cluster of errors of distortion—just not as much as everyone else in the market. When the average stock does really well or poorly (as denoted in Figure 10.4 by the S&P Composite gaining or losing more than 20 percent in a year, respectively), so too, relatively—with over 95 percent confidence—does the Siegfried strategy (as seen in the conditional mean annual returns—the light bar—and 20th percentile drawdowns—the lowest dark bar—in Figure 10.4). Thus the Siegfried strategy benefits from low MS index regimes (when the S&P Composite has high subsequent returns, as per the previous chapter) and is somewhat hurt by high MS index regimes (when the S&P Composite similarly has low subsequent returns). Overlaying the same intertemporal strategy of the previous chapter—of facilitating opportunistic capital deployment following the routs of distortion—on the present strategy will confer even greater advantages.

It truly pays to take a roundabout route toward roundabout capitalistic production. That is, our Austrian *Kinder*—Austrian Investing I and II—get along well together; the former well hedges the latter, and the

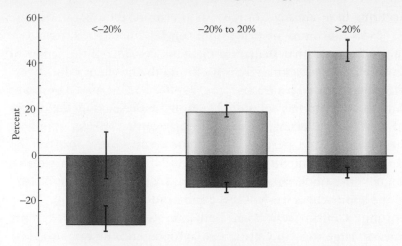

Figure 10.4 Siegfrieds and the Effects of Distortion

Siegfried Strategy Mean Annual Returns and 20th Percentile Drawdowns
Bucketed by S&P Composite Annual Returns (over the Same Period)

latter is the superior deployment of capital to which the former serves. In Austrian Investing is a cohesive whole of intertemporal opportunism and the roundabout acquisition and construction of the factors of production; indeed, from the strategic framework and logic accumulated through the entirety of this book comes an effective framework for investors of all stripes and means.

VALUE INVESTING: AUSTRIAN INVESTING'S ESTRANGED HEIR

Austrian Investing I and II should both sound somewhat reminiscent of what has come to be known as value investing. Indeed, Austrian Investing can be seen as value investing's intellectual forerunner, not only drawing on insights older than value investing but, more significantly, providing clarity and focus to its underpinnings and ultimate systematic source of return. Although their paths cross at times, value investing does not strictly follow *The Dao of Capital*. There are significant differences, largely in the thinking behind the strategies—most specifically Austrian Investing's deliberately roundabout approach rooted in a firm understanding of its edge (no "mystery" as claimed by value investing's founder), in its pursuit of Siegfried opportunism.

Thus, we can say that Benjamin Graham, considered the father of value investing and security analysis itself, and the horde of value investors who have followed his treatises are, in effect, an estranged brood of Austrians—an unwittingly splintered faction. Understanding the differences should help us refine, focus, and improve the broader approach of value investing, and perhaps coax some to the orthodoxy of the Austrians. Such adjustments to what is already an ingrained approach, as well as a better understanding of the real source of information and edge in the approach, as we will see, can be most productive.

Benjamin Graham was born Benjamin Grossbaum—the family name means "large tree" in German, so apropos since he came so close to the archetypal conifer strategy—in London in 1894. (The surname was changed on account of the German prejudice surrounding the Great War.) The family moved to New York when Graham was a year old and enjoyed a comfortable lifestyle, until the father died in 1903 and his porcelain business began to fail. His mother turned the family home into a boarding house, and then borrowed money to trade stocks on margin, which left the family in poverty after the crash of 1907. After attending Columbia University on scholarship, Graham became a clerk in a bond trading firm, then an analyst, a partner, and finally principal of his own firm.

A Keynesian interventionist, particularly regarding the inadequacy of consumption during economic downturns, Graham extolled a commodity-based currency that was very similar to the so-called Ford-Edison money (of Chapter 5). And, like Keynes, he was blindsided by the great market crash that came at the end of the roaring 20s. (Ludwig von Mises, we recall from Chapter 7, had little company in predicting the Great Depression.) Graham, the "dean of Wall Street," lost nearly 70 percent of his largely arbitrage portfolio in 1929–1932. This would become a most formative experience for him—likely responsible for much of his value investing principles that would evolve. This was a purely inductive lesson, establishing value investing's legacy of remembering the Depression—though without ever recognizing the distortion that caused it. Graham's opening line of *Security Analysis* (from Horace, though it could be right out of the *Laozi*)—"Many shall be restored that now are fallen and many shall fall that now are in honor."[4]—tells the paradoxical story of the monetary-fueled market swings we saw in Chapter 9, and in that it is a pretty good, though overly simplistic, approximation of Austrian Investing I. (There is perhaps no better illustration of his central "margin of safety" principle in action than Figure 9.3.) In Graham's metaphor of the bipolar "Mr. Market" is a sound, though proximate, approach to avoiding the (ultimately Austrian-explained) traps of distortion and entrepreneurial "incompleteness of the imaginations."[5] (Had he heeded the Austrians, he no doubt would have diagnosed the real causes of Mr. Market's personality disorder.)

There is much common ground between value investing and its Austrian predecessor. Certainly value investing is as close as we come to it in practice today, having become a popular intuitive approach (though I would argue that a small percentage of the value practitioners truly share the original focus laid out by Graham in his authoritative texts *Security Analysis* in 1934 and *The Intelligent Investor* in 1949—the same publication year as Mises's English-language version of *Human Action*). One might say that Graham gave the practice of investing a rigor, logic, and entrepreneurial orientation not commonly seen before, and in that he was very Austrian (as Graham famously noted, "Investment is most intelligent when it is most businesslike"[6]).

Perhaps Graham's greatest insight was to stay out of the shadows of securities markets, ignore the sideshows, and instead focus entirely on the entrepreneurial action itself—the business, the capital. A diligent researcher of stocks, he had a laser focus on capital as the tangible asset and the thing that is ultimately owned in a stock. We can see this in the MS index and the Faustmann ratio, as well as Graham's price to book ratio (or P/B, which simply compares a firm's equity to its total net depreciated book assets); all three ask: What is the whole relative to the sum of its parts? (It is not clear whether Graham ever read Faustmann or the Austrians directly; though he was fluent in German, he admitted to being unschooled in economics.) In his P/B approach, alone, Graham had good results. After adding a litany of quantitative screens—from debt restrictions to long-term earnings and dividend growth and stability to price to earnings (P/E) ratios (spelled out in his book, *The Intelligent Investor*)—over his long career as an investor he did quite well. (His multi-ingredient, quantitative stock portfolio recipe is the stuff of modern-day financial engineers.)

We might say, however, that traditional value investing has been something of a misnomer: Traditional value stocks (defined by low P/B and P/E ratios) have been shown to have statistically similar revenue growth as traditional growth stocks, and have had lower ROIC than growth stocks.[7] This is yet another instance of naïvely treating all capital as the same, as a homogenous blob. Consider that P/B and P/E ratios are utterly incommensurable unless we assume all firms have the same basic capital structure. In reality, firms have different degrees of roundaboutness and hence variability in their ROIC; indeed, investors must always delve deeper into the *means* of economic profit—certainly a central message of this book.

Between Austrian Investing and value investing is again the difference between depth of field and the telescopic long term. The latter is about waiting patiently over a long interval, as if for a far-off coupon at the very end—the plodding tortoise, or Marco sitting with his rod. The former is about patience now in gathering the factors of greater potential coupons to come—the accelerating tortoise–hare, or Crusoe. Both require discipline and patience, but Austrian Investing is concerned with the intertemporal process at work, rather than just the endpoint.

Interestingly, the man who is most closely associated with value investing today, Graham's one-time pupil and perhaps one of the most successful investors in history—Warren Buffett himself—once had a close brush with the Austrian School via his father, Howard Buffett. In a letter from 1962, Howard wrote to Austrian economist Murray Rothbard seeking a copy of his book *The Panic of 1819* for his son Warren "who is a particularly avid reader of books about panics and similar phenomenon."[8] It is apparent that, despite the son's later vocal criticisms of much of what could be considered Austrian orthodoxy, his basic investing actions are more closely aligned with it than he would ever admit. (Most have forgotten how unpopular—and even ridiculed—Warren's yielding, *zouhua*, and very Misesian cash position was in the late 1990s.)

Over the years, value has sprouted many variations on the Austrian/Grahamian theme. In 1992, Eugene Fama and Kenneth French formalized a value factor, which was basically Graham's *P/B* measure.[9] Another approach, called "The Magic Formula" by Joel Greenblatt, combines our traditional ROIC screen with a simple EBIT relative to enterprise value screen.[10] And there is a similar screen known as "Quality," whereby high gross profits-to-assets (which avoids penalizing high capital investment) and low P/B ratios are selected.[11] These cover the variation gamut (though there are certainly countless subvariations on these, including their intersection, such as perhaps the approach of Buffett), and in fact triangulate or cross-verify the Austrian Investing II approach. All introduce noise by assuming additional degrees of freedom: too many to name (in the case of Graham's intricate screens), heterogeneous capital productivity (in the case of Fama-French's sole P/B parameter), heterogeneous EBIT growth rates (in the case of Greenblatt's growth-sensitive P/E parameters), and heterogeneous capital depreciation and thus productivity (in the case of Quality's depreciation-free gross profit parameter). But as much as they might approximate this approach, they fail to necessarily isolate what matters: *roundabout capital and its price*. So we should expect these variations to capture some of the Siegfried portfolios, some of their edge, but with some added noise, evident in lower returns resulting from lower information content in the screening methods used, as well as inconsistencies across a range of portfolio construction methods employed.

To see if this expectation holds, I tested the performance of these portfolios: In my experiment, I own 40 stock positions for one year, and I stagger how many I buy in each monthly mini-portfolio in different ways, as well as limit how large each mini-portfolio as well as each position may swell before constraining it. Such variation and somewhat arbitrary portfolio construction techniques result in essentially different portfolio constituents, and thus nicely reveal a degree of luck and inconsistency in some of these results—as well as remove much of any ability to optimize (thus keeping the author honest). All portfolios share the same screens, ranging from tradability (size) constraints and general noise constraints. I start the tests in 1978, as before (which, once again, doesn't impact the relative results). Figure 10.5 shows the range of performances found, as well as the mean performance across this range.

Here we see a literal stair-step up from the naïve capitalization-weighted S&P Composite up to our most pure and archetypal Austrian approach (the Siegfrieds portfolio). It is not an evolution, as the top step came first in the historical development of these approaches, and the others sporadically branched from each other; but it is nonetheless a refinement, of both the methodology and most importantly of the thinking behind them. The point is that we have a methodology that separates

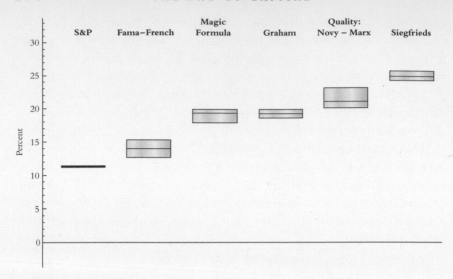

Figure 10.5 Stair-Stepped Refinement

Various Annualized Portfolio Returns (Mean and Range), 1978-2013

the wheat from the chaff, focusing on what matters and ignoring what doesn't. In this, and to its credit, the value approach has come very close. But focusing the mind does so much more than just adding an additional 5 to 10 percentage points to what some smart investors are already doing pretty well. Most importantly, it provides a logical and sound basis for understanding the *why*. The rigor and appeal of Austrian Investing is in the intuitive logic of its principles; even before we test, we know why our edge exists. For most value investors, even when they see the edge that their approach provides, they do not comprehend it—typically relying on mere nebulous long-term price mean reversions, and Graham famously called it "one of the mysteries of our business, and it is a mystery to me as well as everybody else"; they thus remain susceptible to being swept away by the next seemingly attractive investment scheme and distorted environment to come along (as even Graham himself was in the late 1920s).

Truly, the why is all that matters when we are faced with our profound intertemporal constraints amid investment results that appear, to the Phineas Gages among us, unacceptably inconsistent, even recklessly irresponsible. Understanding that we are investing in a means to subsequently greater profitability, not greater profits themselves, we see that we must take the detour in order to gain the intertemporal edge of greater tools. Such thinking clears our field of view, giving it that all-important *depth*.

When considered as a somewhat noisy and tweaked version of Austrian Investing, perhaps value investing's mystery can be put to rest: Production that leads to entrepreneurial profit is an exceedingly roundabout process, which takes time and capital, and thus patience in acquiring the indirect means of that process; we should not expect such entrepreneurial profit to be easy or even desirable as it starts the process (and made even less desirable by monetary distortion). To those who understand and can thus suffer through the process go the spoils of capitalism.

A *ZWECK* FINALLY ATTAINED

In Austrian Investing I and II we have finally reached the destination, the *Zweck*, of *The Dao of Capital*. When brought together, Austrian Investing I and II are nested roundabout strategies, the first used to deploy the second—the Grand *Shi* strategy of the Daoist sages; each is a *Mittel* to a higher *Zweck*, culminating in maximally productive capital investment and reinvestment, a progressing economy and civilization. The strategies are quintessentially Austrian, with Austrian Investing I relying on concepts developed by Mises, and Austrian Investing II relying on concepts developed by Böhm-Bawerk. However, as stated in Chapter 9, Austrian Investing I is very difficult; for most investors, the only applicable takeaway will be to avoid the stock market when distortion elevates the MS index. Fortunately, *The Dao of Capital* does not require that investors simultaneously employ Austrian Investing I and II. Both Austrian Investing I and II can be pursued even as stand-alone strategies—as each on its own beats the vast majority of professional results—to exploit distortion (which also includes the basic Misesian strategy of Chapter 9) and to identify and invest in mispriced productive capital.

As a devotee of the Austrian School all my adult life, and having had the pleasure of delving more deeply into the texts during the writing of this book, I can say without question that the influence of the men from Vienna has been profoundly meaningful—the source of any success that I have achieved as part of the market process. It has been my intention in these pages to share this knowledge and, in the last two chapters in particular, to provide a practical application and takeaway of what we have learned.

No matter what action you take as an investor, once again, what is far more important to consider is the thinking behind this methodology. Are you *shi* in your approach, taking the roundabout and teleological means-end path? Or are you *li*, focusing only on the immediate end, the returns of today? It is not for everyone; if it were, the advantages would be lost. But it remains an important ideal for every investor, no matter how they perceive the ticking of the clock. All can stand in the company of Bastiat and Menger, Böhm-Bawerk and Mises (and Laozi, Sun Wu, Clausewitz, and, of course, Klipp) to gauge their approach. The relevant question to always ask, then, is: How far are you from the Austrian ideal? Let this one query serve as your compass and your map as you continue on your own path, along *The Dao of Capital*.

Epilogue
The Sisu of the Boreal Forest

The conifer, as the *leitmotif* of this book, conjures up the essential lesson of the roundabout, going right with its slow yet steady development at first until, finally, reaching a stage of maturity at which it can go left with accelerating growth that outpaces its competition. The slow-then-fast pace allows the conifer to build and configure its structures, amassing the necessary capital, such as thick bark, a high canopy, and more efficient foliage. This pattern of development requires tenacity and persistence—the necessary ingredients of the roundabout.

The intertemporal world of the boreal forest and its strategies of survival stretch back epochs through twists and turns, growth and decline, and internal battles for survival among competing plant species and voracious herbivorous dinosaurs. In contrast, humans, who made their appearance on the planet much later, remain overwhelmingly anchored in the realm of the present, made all the worse by our inherent wiring around time preference, so that we value (indeed, overvalue) today's marshmallows more than the prospect and potential of many more to come. Our societal attention deficit disorder steals our focus away from the protracted path, toward our shallow depth of field; thus, we become prone to making short-sighted, even disastrous mistakes with decisions that undermine the ability of our forward selves (our look-ahead trees) to act opportunistically.

Like the conifer, we need perseverance to equip ourselves to triumph over (and from) falling behind while never being fazed by it, even to the point of loving to lose and hating to win—Klipp's Paradox, which started us off along *The Dao of Capital*—because of the sheer grit it engenders and the prominence of indirect and sometimes costly means it allows. To be roundabout is to expect adversity (as opposed to just the false binary choices of failure and success). It is a prerequisite of the circuitous nature of progress itself, such as we found at the *weiqi* board, where the *shi* strategist pursues positional advantage for later potential, which until the end of the game, appears to be a losing strategy; all the while the *li* opponent goes for the more comfortable direct assault in hopes of a quick and decisive victory. The great artists and entrepreneurs (and economists) have well understood that anything worth doing takes time—and so have their polar opposites, the military strategists, thus giving us the spectrum of the very creators and destroyers of civilization. Each in his own way has followed the common thread of intertemporal exchange (as explained in Chapter 3), the patient pursuit of an intermediate state, the efficacy of which furthers the realization of a desired final state. And so, achievement of one's eventual *Zweck* only comes after much effort, moving from *Ziel* to *Ziel*, along with a good deal of waiting, even to the point of testing the limits of one's perseverance.

Both encourager and sustainer, such tenacity maintains our resolve along the indirect route from intermediate means to eventual ends, a journey we know is nearly impossible—the circuitous road least traveled—because of that very humanness about us. To overcome our human nature takes stamina, the ability to stay focused on and committed to a goal or objective, like the roundabout conifer that moves beyond the reaches of its competitors and hunkers down among the rocks through survival adaptations such as symbiosis with helpful fungi, all the while waiting for the opportune moment to make its move into the fertile areas after wildfire. The epitome of *shi*, the conifer exemplifies the cunning of Sun Wu's guerilla warriors, battling across a temporal depth of field. We, too, must possess qualities that are best captured in a word that comes from deep within the boreal forest (where else?) of Finland—*sisu*.

THE WORLD LEARNS *SISU* FROM THE VICTORIOUS FINNS

In the early months of World War II, not long after Ludwig von Mises's escape from the Nazis, deep within the north woods of the taiga, another battle was waged—the 100-day Winter War of 1939-1940, during which outgunned Finnish forces fended off the much larger Soviet army, in what is perhaps the best example of *shi* in modern warfare. (Neutral Finland was unluckily caught between the two equally evil and totalitarian clashing powers of Stalin and Hitler, and was thus an immensely valuable path between the two for whichever could seize it first.) Although much is often made of the underdog story, we must recognize that the Finns' victory was not some inexplicable event; rather, it was the result of a carefully executed strategy right out of the *Sunzi* and *Vom Kriege*. As we will see, the former is evident in the use of *shi*, as nimble Finnish troops on skis avoided direct clashes and instead maneuvered into position within the snowy, forested terrain in order to gain the upper hand. Influence of the latter is found in the very conduct of the war, particularly by the Finns who attacked key focal points along the advancing Soviet lines and, thereby, fractured a large opponent into much smaller pieces that could be surrounded, attacked, and defeated.

The Red Army, too, had its share of Prussian-German influence, but Joseph Stalin had tried to purge it from the Soviet forces by imprisoning or executing many senior officers. Thus, the forces that invaded Finland were typically led by less-experienced midlevel officers who at times acted as if they were following fighting manuals written for a different time and place, such as assuming that troops would be able to ski without ever being trained for fighting and firing weapons in snow. The Soviet's unified military doctrine allowed for no flexibility in field command; they adhered to the strict dogma of decisive engagement without question or alteration.[1]

Among these many influences and factors that led to the Finnish victory, we cannot underestimate the importance of *sisu*. Difficult to translate—a linguistic trait shared with *shi*—*sisu* has been compared to having guts, moxie, courage, toughness, tenacity, stubbornness, strength of will, and determination. *Sisu* is perhaps best thought of as gritty perseverance, making it a natural complement to the strategic positional advantage of *shi*. Inherent in *sisu* is intertemporal endurance—not gritting one's teeth in a difficult moment, but rather possessing fortitude that sustains along an arduous path, from one seemingly insurmountable challenge to the next.

Sisu permeates the identity of the Finnish people, capturing their national character long before they were an independent nation, with a gritty perseverance rooted in the land and history. Flat forested tundra, pitted with lakes and marshes, this isolated land is plunged into Arctic darkness for a significant portion of the year, making even daily life a test of endurance at times. Overlaying such will to survive is centuries of having been a battleground for the Swedes to the west and the Russians to the east. Finland was part of the Kingdom of Sweden until it was captured by the Russians in 1809 and made into the Grand Duchy of Finland, which was then slowly assimilated into Russia. During the Russian Civil War of 1917, Finland seized the opportunity to declare its independence, and held off the Russian threat with forces under the command of General Carl Gustaf Mannerheim, a staunch anti-Bolshevist who had been in the court of Tsar Nicholas II. The Treaty of Tartu, signed in 1920, formally established peace between Finland and Russia, yet even then the lingering tensions foreshadowed another war to come. The strategic advantages against the threatening Nazis, such as the Gulf of Finland, and large nickel deposits discovered in the former Petsamo region (later ceded to the Soviets) baited the Russian bear; Stalin wanted Finland back.

Russian propaganda in late 1939 provided the cover for aggressive, overt military action: "Imperialists" were said to be planning to use Finland to stage an invasion of the Soviet Union (even though Finland, at the time, had a population of about 3.7 million and the USSR's was nearly 180 million). The first shots of the war on November 26, 1939, were supposedly fired from Finnish observation posts into Soviet territory. Yet, historians believe the "Mainila shots" (named for a nearby village) could not have been fired by the Finns because Mannerheim had ordered all guns withdrawn from these outposts to avoid such an incident from happening.[2]

Posturing that it had been provoked, the Soviets rolled into Finland in tanks, mimicking the German *blitzkrieg*, which had proven effective in the heart of Europe where there were well-defined centers of supply and communication to be targeted. The Finnish forest, however, offered no such targets, only natural obstacles that thwarted such cumbersome military operations. The Soviets further burdened themselves with truckloads of propaganda material and brass bands to celebrate what was anticipated to be a swift and decisive victory, but without winter uniforms and supplies for a prolonged campaign. (What better illustration of *li* can we imagine than a direct assault with plans for a celebration before it even has begun?)

Sisu and *shi* would become an unbeatable combination. Although the Red Army was greater in number and in weaponry, the Finns gained strategic tactical positions by combining the speed and agility of small, targeted forces. White-clad bushwhacking troops, guerilla soldiers on skis, used the terrain to their advantage, becoming like the "good general" of the *Sunzi*, who calculates "in advance and with accuracy every factor, so that the situation develops in a way as beneficial as possible to him," even to the point that "victory is then simply a necessary consequence."[3] Finland had on its side *hsing* (positional advantage)— the boreal forest itself—that came from deep knowledge of its unusual terrain. As we recall from Chapter 3, the positional advantage of *shi* overlaps the concept of *hsing*, so that *shi* is the greater superiority gained through *hsing*. The *hsing* of troops is compared in the *Sunzi* to the positioning of pent-up water in a mountain stream, the potential (*shi*) of which is eventually opportunistically unleashed as it gushes downward carrying boulders and logs in a powerful, yet effortless surge, overcoming everything in its path. Thus, the sage acts by "positioning himself upstream from its full deployment."[4]

The Finns used means that were far removed from ends—in time and space—and often exceedingly indirect, by blocking roads, conducting ambushes, and antagonizing an overstretched enemy until conflict becomes a war of nerves, which allowed the Finns and their *sisu* to exploit the advantages of the roundabout path. At all times, the Finnish forces avoided attacks against a strong enemy on open terrain, particularly one with such superior weaponry and air power. Instead, the Finns fought in the coniferous forests from which their victorious strategies were distilled—of fortitude to endure, persevere, and ultimately triumph, but only through time with positional advantage obtained intertemporally. The Finns gave ground strategically in order to command a more favorable position—*weiqi* played out on a snow-covered battlefield. The Finns staged tactical retreats, feigning the rout and luring the enemy into position. Then the Finns would emerge as if from nowhere, having amassed a strategic position unseen by the enemy, and stage a strong counterattack, including raids behind Soviet lines. The Finns' attacks targeted key focal points—Clausewitz's center of gravity or *Schwerpunkt*, in the pursuit of intermediate aims—thus weakening their enemy.

While the Finns used the *hsing* of the forest for offense and defense, the Soviets were thwarted by it—literally. The Red Army strategy depended upon open terrain on which to maneuver; they even brought mostly flat-trajectory field guns that proved useless since they could not shoot over trees (though captured by the Finns, those field guns were used quite handily against the former owners as they retreated).[5]

In harmony with their turf and fighting for their homeland, the Finnish army moved with the skill of *tuishou* ("push hands"), the objective of which is to exploit imbalance within one's opponent, which will make the ultimate rout all the more effective. With cold, snow, and the terrain on their side, the Finns effectively turned the force of their opponent against itself. Rather than engage the Soviets directly, the Finns yielded—even to the point of letting the Red Army advance at times along strategic roads—while subzero temperatures did damage to Soviet weapons, causing them to malfunction. Bogged down in snow and immobilized by cold, the Red Army could not retreat, no matter the cost (another foolhardy and highly destructive example of *li*).

The *shi* of the Finns' nonengagement allowed them to spare lives and conserve ammunition, particularly in what the Finnish commanders called the *motti strategy*, so named for the quaint *mottis* of cut and stacked wood still often found along roads through the forest. The strategic meaning of the term has since become an encircling maneuver (perhaps the closest Finnish word for *weiqi*, or "encircling game"). Encirclement was at the very core of the Finns' strategy, wherein these (not so quaint) *mottis* were composed of dead enemy soldiers. Under orders never to give up any captured ground, but unable to advance further, the Soviet forces became stationary units, the disastrous consequences of which meant the surrounding Finns could watch as the Red Army soldiers starved or froze to death.

Along with *shi*, *sisu* provided an enormous edge, emboldening the Finns to face incredible odds, such as when they carried satchels loaded with TNT to within a few meters of Soviet tanks (and sometimes right up to the tanks themselves), risking detection as well as death from the blast. Such sneak attacks required grit and patience, for the opportune moment to strike (Sun Wu's bird of prey). Thus, a 30-ton tank could be destroyed by a pack of explosives carried by a soldier on skis.

As the world looked on, the Winter War quickly took on mythic proportions. Today, the battle of Suomussalmi in January 1940 is considered a military classic of what can be achieved in true *shi* fashion when troops that are well commanded use strategic advantage against a much larger adversary. The Soviets advanced along two roads in the wilderness, intending to capture the city of Oulu, a major railroad connection with Sweden, and effectively cutting Finland in two. The Finns, though outnumbered and outgunned, prepared a brilliant plan. Finnish Colonel Hjalmar Siilasvuo utilized the unique strengths of the Finnish JR-27 regiment that had no heavy weaponry—not even a single antitank gun. What the JR-27 did have was a cadre of loggers from small towns who knew the forest and how to cross-country ski. The timing and ferocity of their guerilla attacks even unnerved the opponent at times, making the Red Army believe it was facing superior Finnish fighting forces (and certainly not ill-equipped foresters on skis). Such a strategy calls to mind Clausewitz's *Vom Kriege* and the advantages that "cannot be regarded as the destruction of enemy's forces, but only leading up to it certainly by circuitous road, but with so much the greater effect."[6]

When the Soviet troops advanced to the small town of Hyrynsalmi, the JR-27 was waiting for them, with a blaze of bullets that blocked their advance. The Finns then fractured a much larger enemy into smaller pieces that could then be destroyed in retreat. The Red Army suffered thousands of casualties at Suomussalmi, compared to a few hundred for the Finns, and left behind large caches of tanks, artillery, guns, ammunition, and other supplies. In testament to *sisu*, Suomussalmi was Finland's most monumental victory of the war—a perfectly executed rout.

When the Winter War ended after 16 intensely fought weeks—punctuated by a savage bombing raid by the Soviets that was nothing more than retaliation for having been humiliated in battle—Finland emerged victorious and unconquered. (However, in peace negotiations, Finland had to give up significant territory—what Stalin called just enough ground to bury his dead.) The takeaway here for us goes beyond the herculean efforts of the Finns in a war that is too often regarded as little more than a side note in the long narrative of World War II destruction. The Winter War serves as a powerful example of the effectiveness of the roundabout military strategy of Sun Wu and Clausewitz, of indirect over direct, *shi* over *li*, achieving intermediate gains over grabbing immediate territory, and most of all, *sisu* as the gritty perseverance without which such undertakings are virtually impossible.

SISU—OF CHARACTER AND CHARACTER-BUILDING

The story of the Winter War, of the fortitude of *sisu* over military power alone, is central to the stories Finns tell of themselves, like the nineteenth century epic poem *Kalevala*, which captures the ancient stories and mythology of Finnish culture (such as Tapio, god of the forest, and Kalevanpoika, a giant-hero who cut down forests—their heroic, Nordic Siegfried). *Sisu*, though, like *shi*, does not apply only to martial or even investment strategy, but also much more broadly to living one's life with purpose and tenacity. It is also a reminder of inner strength that enables one to carry on in spite of difficulty and obstacles, speaking as it does of character—and character building. (A typical Finnish monument to *sisu* is a lonely mound of rocks in Lapland, piled slowly and steadily, one by one—perseverance in the making.) My wife, who is of Finnish descent, can often quell complaint in our young children with one word—*sisu*—delivered as a loving reminder to look within themselves for what they need to persevere and, ultimately, prevail.

The benefit of *sisu* is becoming increasingly understood today, particularly among psychologists who recognize the advantages it bestows. Angela Duckworth salutes grit in children as a dominant predictor of their future success, describing "gritty individuals" who make slow and steady progress over time despite temporary setbacks as being "tortoise-like."[7] (This description should surely call to mind those accelerating "tortoises," the tenacious conifers.)

Capitalism, as we know from the Austrians, is perhaps the grittiest of arenas; it requires enduring current disadvantage in order to achieve a later superior advantage—the essence of roundaboutness. We can think of *sisu* and grit as precisely the lower time preference described by Eugen von Böhm-Bawerk, overcoming "our anxiety in the present," which arises over "the satisfaction of wants that will not emerge till the future." The pleasures or pains we will experience later must dictate what we will need now to facilitate or mitigate them. Yet, we are ill-equipped to process such projected feelings because of what Böhm-Bawerk called "the incompleteness of the imaginations we form to ourselves of our future wants," and thus "we will not take the necessary trouble" to give adequate consideration to our future, and particularly "our far-away future wants."[8]

The gritty tenacity of *sisu* is our only saving grace. It is what got us out of the primordial ooze, out of the caves, out of our day-to-day hand-to-mouth existence (and, in many cases such as the Finns', out of the menace of totalitarianism), and toward the autocatalytic world of capitalistic production. There is of course an element of patience in grit, but not as an abstract quality; it is not just about waiting, but rather it is purposeful, teleological, the means to work through a process and toward something. And being tenacious is not about thinking or acting "long term" (my constant refrain); rather, it is intertemporal and roundabout, thus becoming a kind of litmus test. If a strategy does not require grit, then it is aligned with neither the roundabout nor capitalistic progress that got us to where we are today. We mustn't forget this, and mustn't allow ourselves to be sidetracked by the sideshows of capitalism (the securities markets)—and rather stand down from that game, and choose for ourselves which game we play.

Without the ability to forego immediacy, civilization would be doomed to follow the Phineas Gages who are ruled by their appetites in the now. Perseverance, when coupled with an intertemporal depth of field, enables us to create and configure tools by which our civilization progresses. Thus the words used throughout this book—*shi* and *Umweg*, and now *sisu*—unlock nothing less than the fate of humanity. Yet few appreciate the roundabout, because we only see the final product or result, the end of an interval and process, and not the means, the winding path that produced it.

Fortunately, we do have role models who have blazed the roundabout trail, great strategic thinkers, decision makers, and actors from throughout history, in every society and in every era—Daoists, militarists, economists, industrialists—the heroic Siegfrieds of *The Dao of Capital*. Across centuries and thousands of miles, on battlefields and through the sweep of the great boreal forest, they demonstrate passionate commitment to universal principles for the teleological pursuit of means toward ends. Drawing from the lives and lessons of these greats, I hope I have given readers a strategic framework by following its roots from natural history to the Warring States of China and Europe, to modern economic thinkers.

The concept of a framework, as opposed to a formula, is an important one. Even Austrian Investing, rather than providing precise instructions, is meant to be scaffolding for the roundabout process from which anyone's degree of capitalistic investment can be better understood and gauged. We can think of such investing as a work in progress, rather than focusing on disparate results. Thus, we heed the stoic's (and Bastiat's "good economist's") call to get neither too excited about our victories nor too disappointed by our defeats. (I know from much experience, pretty much without exception, that you can always tell an ultimately good trader from a bad one by this simple test—it is equanimity, *sisu!*) When the game is played correctly, the results are but indirect *Mittel* to our *Zweck*.

For investors, the roundabout of Austrian Investing, as laid out in Chapters 9 and 10, requires tenacity, which bestows an edge that even seemingly sophisticated Wall Street investors, who may have certain order flow and market intelligence advantages (both of which skirt what is or should likely be legal), cannot match. Wall Street's institutional myopia keeps it playing in the shadows rather than being able to see what is really going on because of insatiable appetites for the immediate. Gritty *sisu*, however, allows one to feed upon such insatiableness in the market; as noted in Chapter 1, my mantra is inspired by a baseball pitcher's creed, who earned his "living from the hungriness of hitters."[9] Striving to satisfy only immediate profits, however, is truly, in the words of Henry Ford, putting the "cart before the horse."[10] This quintessential entrepreneur of the twentieth century understood intuitively that it was all about evermore roundabout means, patiently and laboriously accumulated, followed at last by impatient pursuit of ends in the final stages of production.

From this perspective, we might even see capitalism, itself, as a *Ziel*, a way station along the path toward a much bigger *Zweck* (a far grander *shi* strategy). We may be making nets and boats with the intention of catching more fish, but what we are actually doing, over many forward slices of time, is advancing society. The Austrians understood this, especially Mises, who saw in capitalism an expression of the freedom of the individual to act according to free will and self-determination. Thus in his stand for capitalism, Mises also stood for freedom. How symbolically fitting was it that, in the wee hours of the morning as I completed a late-night writing session, the very top volume of a stack of books on my desk—no less than 10 high—suddenly toppled and hit a memento I keep as the symbol of the ultimate victory of capitalism and freedom: a large chunk of the fractured and defeated Berlin Wall. The falling book was Mises's *Human Action*, and its impact further cleaved the Berlin Wall.

Such images become inspiration for the exceedingly difficult journey of the roundabout. We carry these things mentally as intellectual and emotional talismans, and sometimes even physically. I make it a point—perhaps as a gambler's tic, though, like my old Adam Smith necktie, also a constant reminder—to pick up a conifer cone whenever I see one. This happens every day outside my door, whether redwoods in Southern California or the even more roundabout tribes at the cusp of the boreal forest (in Michigan). It is as ordinary an object as anyone could imagine. And yet, it is extraordinary—profundity in the quotidian—a living embodiment of the tenacity developed from the prehistoric age when the late-coming angiosperms barreled into the prime areas like so many sprinting hares and drove out the slow-growing (at first) conifers in a rout to the rocky places. (As we recall from Chapter 2, by the end of the Cretaceous period, 65 million years ago, nine out of every ten vascular plant species were angiosperms.) But let those angiosperms grow impatiently, hogging sunlight and choking off competitors even from within their own species; the conifers can wait, a phalanx of patient capital-producers with time on their side.

As an adult, just as when I was a child, the outdoors is my preferred milieu, particularly in the company of craggy old conifers; in this, I am not alone. As Finland has become known as "the land of Sauna, Sisu, and Sibelius," all three are even combined in the latter's country estate, *Ainola*, a log villa deep in the coniferous wooded lake region north of Helsinki. (For the record, Jean Sibelius is probably still the world's most underappreciated composer.) Others, the likes of von Karajan as well as myself, have tried to emulate Sibelius's refuge in a country retreat, similar to the summer retreats of the great Austrian composer Gustav Mahler. (One can hear the echoes of their boreal forest home in their sweeping idyllic music.)

The forest is a source of endless teachings. When I was a boy in Michigan, Hemingway's boyhood northern woods was the ideal child's domain, where rocks, logs, and lakes became fortresses, outposts, and the terrain from which to wage campaigns of exploration and conquest. (Sun Wu and Clausewitz would have been proud.) For my friends and me, it was all in good fun; little did we know we were actually pursuing an important *Ziel* as we exercised our bodies and minds, learned skills, and deployed our imaginations—all essential to our development. When left to their own desires, children can be naturally roundabout insofar as pursuing the intermediate objectives of play, and with a great deal of gusto, even though it does not produce anything (tree forts and airplane models notwithstanding). Yes, children will grab for the immediate marshmallow, but when it comes to development, nature tricks them with the enticement of play that is part of the roundabout accumulation of cognitive abilities, creativity, physical attributes such as strength and balance, and interpersonal relationships, all of which will later bear fruit as the skills and aptitudes deployed by a forward self—the adult. Because their prefrontal lobes are undeveloped, children are blind to their long-term goals (although their parents tend to have better than 20/20 vision in such matters). Thankfully, children are thus inclined, otherwise they might look askance at play and dismiss it as a worthless objective, while trying to cram for SAT examinations starting at the age of six. (I agree with the conclusion of Paul Tough who in his book *How Children Succeed*, cited research that shows what matters most in a child's development "is not how much information we can stuff into her brain in the first few years," but rather noncognitive qualities that include self-control, curiosity, self-confidence, and grit.[11] To that list I would add, of course, in summary, *sisu*.)

Intuitively, we would all want our children to have greater capacity for the roundabout and the gritty perseverance of *sisu*, thus equipping them for life well beyond anything material or even the advantages gained through a superior education. With *sisu* and *shi* come the ability to withstand the direct assault and remain indirect in one's outlook and actions, to never go for the immediate but seek, instead, intertemporal opportunism. We would further give them the ability and tolerance for deliberate exploration and discovery (what we might think of as production) through a prolonged period of ambiguity and uncertainty, along with a general lightness of spirit, plus the subsequent sweat of exertion.[12] These are the lessons that nature teaches us; to learn them we must be in nature's classroom. Even for a child, it is nearly impossible to miss the fact that every conifer bears countless cones (which for kids are quite handy missiles to launch at friends—perhaps helping with seed dispersal). And within each of those cones are innumerable seeds. Pretty soon it becomes clear that to cradle a cone in one's hand is to hold an entire forest. (What became a fond childhood memory was brought back to me in Klipp's folksy wisdom that, "Anyone can see the pinecones in the tree. None can see the trees, none can foresee the forest in the pinecone.") And, as a youngster, seeing some of those conifers in out-of-the-way places, such as along windswept hills overlooking Lake Michigan, I couldn't help but wonder why they were growing there. Surely there were better places. In time, that question would be answered, with a deep appreciation for the false humility of the conifer/sage that only appears to retreat. Even in the midst of the rout, the conifer is merely waiting, outliving its neighbors and becoming poised to take over their living space.[13]

The conifer's eventual *Zweck* is not achieved by rushing headlong into the fray, but rather by enduring the uncomfortable places on the rocks. Such discomfort becomes bearable because there are advantages to come over time—longevity is an attribute of the species. A secondary roundabout strategy of the conifer, of course, gives the advantage to its offspring sown from wind-borne seeds or, in some conifers, serotinous cones scorched and opened by wildfire. The conifer's gritty nature allows it to persist where others cannot. No wonder then that ancient Daoist Chinese scholars depicted the pine growing on the rocks as the symbol of stalwart tenacity.[14] Such images long ago painted on bamboo and silk scrolls still remind us today of the endurance known as *sisu*, of the conifer and nature's compelling logic, that out of what appears to be disadvantage and devastation comes opportunistic conquest. This is the very model of organic efficacious growth in our world.

All that wisdom—indeed, the summation of every word on these pages—is contained in a deceptively mundane object that weighs but a few ounces and through which, in the words of William Blake, you "hold infinity in the palm of your hand": a humble pinecone. Worth nothing, neither rare nor unusual, it is like the *Dao* itself, failing to catch the eye or interest; to most, its meaning remains unseen. Yet to those who know what they are beholding, it is nothing less than a marvel. In the pinecone is a visible reminder of a practical discipline, the tenacious, unyielding pursuit of intermediate means as strategic advantage for achieving the ultimate ends—a quest only possible for those who dare to take the roundabout route.

Notes

FOREWORD

1. Murray N. Rothbard, *An Austrian Perspective on the History of Economic Thought*, 1995, Edward Elgar Publishing Ltd.
2. Ralph Raico, *Classical Liberalism and the Austrian School*, 2012, The Ludwig von Mises Institute, Auburn, AL.
3. Ludwig von Mises, *Planning for Freedom*, 1974, Libertarian Press, South Holland, Illinois.
4. Ludwig von Mises, *Human Action*, 1998, The Ludwig von Mises Institute, Auburn, AL.

INTRODUCTION

1. *Walter Legge: Words and Music*, Alan Sanders, ed., 1997, Routledge, New York.
2. Gia-Fu Feng, trans., Lao Tsu, *Tao Te Ching*, 1972, Alfred A. Knopf, New York.
3. Murray Rothbard, Preface to *Theory & History* by Ludwig von Mises, 1985 (reprint 2007, Ludwig von Mises Institute, Auburn, AL).
4. Gia-Fu Feng, Lao Tsu, *Tao Te Ching*.

CHAPTER ONE

1. Roger T. Ames and David T. Hall, Daodejing *"Making This Life Significant": A Philosophical Translation*, 2003, Ballantine Books, New York.
2. Laozi and Philip J. Ivanhoe, *The Daodejing of Laozi*, 2003, Hackett Publishing Co.
3. Ames and Hall, *Daodejing*.
4. Bertrand Russell, *Uncertain Path to Freedom: Russia & China 1919–1922*, 2000, Routledge, London.

5. Ames and Hall, *Daodejing*.
6. Paul Carus, Lao–Tzu, *Lao-Tze's Tao-teh-King*, originally published 1898, The Open Court Publishing Company, Chicago.
7. Ames and Hall, *Daodejing*.
8. Murray N. Rothbard, *An Austrian Perspective on the History of Economic Thought*, 1995, Edward Elgar Publishing Ltd.
9. Paul Carus, *The Canon of Reason and Virtue: Being Lao-tze's Tao Teh King*, originally published 1913; 1954, The Open Court Publishing Co., Chicago.
10. Ibid.
11. Ames and Hall, *Daodejing*.
12. Gia-Fu Feng, trans., Lao Tsu, *Tao Te Ching*, 1972, Alfred A. Knopf, NY.
13. François Jullien, *The Propensity of Things: Toward a History of Efficacy in China*, 1999, Zone Books.
14. Ames and Hall, *Daodejing*.
15. Ibid.
16. Laozi and Ivanhoe, *The Daodejing of Laozi*.
17. Tsung Hwa Jou, *The Dao of Taijiquan: Way to Rejuvenation*, 1989, Tuttle Publishing, North Clarendon, VT.
18. Gia-Fu Feng, *Tao Te Ching*.
19. Chen Xin, *The Illustrated Canon of Chen Family Taijiquan*, 2007, INBI Matrix, Maroubra, Australia.
20. Yang Jwing-Ming, *Tai Chi Theory and Martial Power*, 1996, Ymaa Publication Center, Second Edition.
21. Gia-Fu Feng, *Tao Te Ching*.
22. Ellen Chen, *Tao Te Ching: A New Translation with Commentary*, 1998, Paragon House.
23. Chen Man Ch'ing, *Chen Tzu's Thirteen Treatises on T'ai Chi Ch'uan*, 1985, North Atlantic Books, Berkeley, CA.
24. Ames and Hall, *Daodejing*.
25. Carus, *The Canon of Reason and Virtue*.
26. Gia-Fu Feng, *Tao Te Ching*, (1989, introduction copyright by Jacob Needleman).
27. Chen, *Tao Te Ching*.
28. William Falloon, *Charlie D.: The Story of the Legendary Bond Trader*, 1997, John Wiley & Sons.
29. Gia-Fu Feng, *Tao Te Ching*.
30. Carus, *Lao-Tze's Tao-teh-King*.
31. George F. Will, *Men at Work: The Craft of Baseball*, Macmillan, 1990.
32. Theodor Geisel, *McElligot's Pool*, 1947, Random House, NY.
33. Henry Hazlitt, *Economics in One Lesson*, 2012, The Ludwig von Mises Institute, Auburn, AL.
34. Ibid.

35. Richard Osborne, *Herbert von Karajan: A Life in Music*, 2000, Northeastern.
36. Ludwig von Mises, *Human Action*, 1998, The Ludwig von Mises Institute, Auburn, AL.
37. Ibid.
38. Ibid.
39. Ibid.
40. Ibid.
41. Ibid.
42. Ibid.
43. Gene Callahan and Roger W. Garrison, "Does Austrian Business Cycle Theory Help Explain the Dot-Com Boom and Bust?" *The Quarterly Journal of Austrian Economics*, Summer 2003, 6(2), pp. 67–98.
44. Ludwig von Mises, "Why Read Adam Smith Today," Introduction to *The Wealth of Nations* by Adam Smith, 1953, Henry Regnery.

Chapter Two

1. Gia-Fu Feng, trans., Lao Tsu, *Tao Te Ching*, 1972, Alfred A. Knopf, NY.
2. Ibid.
3. Roger Ames, *Sun-Tzu: The Art of Warfare*, 1993, Ballantine Books.
4. Hans-Geor Moeller, *Daoism Explained: From the Dream of the Butterfly to the Fishnet Allegory*, 2004, Open Court.
5. Aljos Farjon, *A Natural History of Conifers*, 2008, Timber Press, Portland, OR.
6. Jay E. Anderson, Marshall Ellis, Carol D. von Dohlen, and William H. Romme, "Chapter 4: Establishment, Growth, and Survival of Lodgepole Pine in the First Decade," *After the Fires: The Ecology of Change in Yellowstone National Park*, Linda Wallace, ed., 2004, Yale University Press.
7. W. J. Bond, "The Tortoise and the Hare: Ecology of Angiosperm Dominance and Gymnosperm Persistence," *Biological Journal of the Linnean Society*, 1989, 36:227–249.
8. Ian D. Lunt, Heidi C. Zimmer, and David C. Cheal, "The Tortoise and the Hare? Post-Fire Regeneration in Mixed Eucalyptus-Callitris Forest," *Australian Journal of Botany*, 2011, 59, 575–581.
9. W. J. Bond, "The Tortoise and the Hare."
10. Farjon, *A Natural History of Conifers*.
11. Ibid.
12. Ibid.
13. Gia-Fu Feng, *Tao Te Ching*.
14. Roger T. Ames and David T. Hall, *Daodejing "Making This Life Significant": A Philosophical Translation*, 2003, Ballantine Books, NY.
15. Ibid.

16. Anderson et al., "Establishment, Growth, and Survival of Lodgepole Pine in the First Decade."
17. Aljos Farjon, *A Natural History of Conifers*.
18. Ibid.
19. Ames and Hall, *Daodejing*.
20. Ibid.

Chapter Three

1. Ralph Peters, Introduction, *The Book of War: Sun-Tzu's "The Art of War" & Karl Von Clausewitz's "On War,"* 2000, Modern Library, Random House.
2. François Jullien, *A Treatise on Efficacy: Between Western and Chinese Thinking*, 2004, University of Hawaii Press.
3. Roger Ames, Sun-Tzu: *The Art of Warfare*, 1993, Ballantine Books.
4. Ibid.
5. D. C. Lau and Roger Ames, *Sun Bin: The Art of Warfare: A Translation of the Classic Chinese Work of Philosophy and Strategy*, 2002, State University of NY Press.
6. François Jullien, *The Propensity of Things: Toward a History of Efficacy in China*, 1999, Zone Books.
7. Ibid.
8. Roger T. Ames, *The Art of Rulership: A Study of Ancient Chinese Political Thought*, 1994, State University of NY Press.
9. Gia-Fu Feng, trans., *Lao Tsu, Tao Te Ching*, 1972, Alfred A. Knopf, NY.
10. Ames, Sun-Tzu.
11. Jullien, *A Treatise on Efficacy*.
12. Ames, *The Art of Rulership*.
13. Arthur Waldron, "The Art of Shi," *The New Republic*, June 23, 1997.
14. Ames, Sun-Tzu.
15. Ibid.
16. Carl von Clausewitz, *On War*, trans., Michael Eliot Howard and Peter Paret, 1976, Princeton University Press.
17. Ames, Sun-Tzu.
18. Nicholas D. Kristof and Sheryl WuDunn, *Thunder from the East: Portrait of a Rising Asia*, 2001, Vintage.
19. Jullien, *The Propensity of Things*.
20. Ames, Sun-Tzu.
21. Ibid.
22. Gia-Fu Feng, Lao Tsu, Tao Te Ching.
23. Ames, Sun-Tzu.
24. Jullien, *A Treatise on Efficacy*.

25. Patricia Buckley Ebrey and Anne Walthall, *Pre-Modern East Asia: A Cultural, Social and Political History*, vol. 1: To 1800, Third Edition, 2013, Wadsworth Publishing.

26. Ames, Sun-Tzu.

27. Office of the Secretary of Defense, Annual Report to Congress, "Military Power of the People's Republic of China," 2006.

28. Jullien, *A Treatise on Efficacy*.

29. Jullien, *The Propensity of Things*.

30. Ibid.

31. Peter Shotwell, "Appendix VII, The Use of Shi and Li in Weiqi and American Politics: Some Notes on a Forbes Opinion Article by Mark Spitznagel," 2012.

32. David Lai, "Learning from the Stones: A Go Approach to Mastering China's Strategic Concept, *Shi*," Strategic Studies Institute, May 2004.

33. Henry Kissinger, *On China*, 2011, Penguin Press.

34. Peter Paret, *Clausewitz and the State: The Man, His Theories, and His Times*, 2007, Princeton University Press.

35. B.H. Liddell Hart, *Strategy: Second Revised Edition*, 1991, Plume.

36. Ibid.

37. Paret, *Clausewitz and the State*.

38. Hew Strachan, *Clausewitz's On War: A Biography*, 2008, Grove Press.

39. Paret, *Clausewitz and the State*.

40. Ralph Peters, Introduction, *The Book of War*.

41. Ibid.

42. Hart, *Strategy*.

43. Ibid.

44. Ibid.

45. Capt. Kenneth L. Davison, Jr., USAF, "Clausewitz and the Indirect Approach: Misreading the Leader," *Airpower Journal*, Winter 1988.

46. Carl von Clausewitz, *On War*, trans., James John Graham, 1873, N. Trübner.

47. Ibid.

48. Michael Howard, *Clausewitz: A Very Short Introduction*, 2002, Oxford University Press.

49. Strachan, Clausewitz's *On War*.

50. Ibid.

51. Jullien, *A Treatise on Efficacy*.

52. Ibid.

53. Lt. Col. Antulio J. Echevarria II, "Clausewitz's Center of Gravity: Changing Our Warfighting Doctrine—Again!" 2002, Strategic Studies Institute.

54. Clausewitz, *On War*, Howard and Paret.

55. Jullien, *A Treatise on Efficacy*.

56. Echevarria, "Clausewitz's Center of Gravity."

57. Clausewitz, *On War*, Graham.
58. Ibid.
59. Strachan, Clausewitz's *On War*.
60. Howard, Clausewitz.
61. Ibid.
62. Clausewitz, *On War*, Graham.
63. Ludwig von Mises, *Human Action*, 1998, The Ludwig von Mises Institute, Auburn, AL.

Chapter Four

1. Mark Skousen, *The Making of Modern Economics: The Lives and Ideas of the Great Thinkers*, 2009, M.E. Sharpe, Armonk, NY.
2. Frédéric Bastiat, *The Bastiat Collection*, 2007, Ludwig von Mises Institute, Auburn, AL.
3. Skousen, *The Making of Modern Economics*.
4. François Jullien, *A Treatise on Efficacy: Between Western and Chinese Thinking*, 2004, University of Hawaii Press.
5. Bastiat, *The Bastiat Collection*.
6. Ibid.
7. Ibid.
8. Skousen, *The Making of Modern Economics*.
9. Bastiat, *The Bastiat Collection*.
10. Ibid.
11. Ibid.
12. Skousen, *The Making of Modern Economics*.
13. Ibid.
14. Bastiat, *The Bastiat Collection*.
15. Ibid.
16. Ibid.
17. Gérard Bramoullé, "Frédéric Bastiat: Praxeologist Theoretician," *Journal des Economistes et des Etudes Humanies*, vol. 11 [001], no. 2, art. 8.
18. Ibid.
19. Jörg Guido Hülsmann, "Carl Menger: Pioneer of 'Empirical Theory,'" excerpted from *Mises: The Last Knight of Liberalism*, 2007, The Ludwig von Mises Institute, Auburn, AL.
20. Bramoullé, "Frédéric Bastiat: Praxeologist Theoretician."
21. Thomas J. DiLorenzo, "Frédéric Bastiat: Between the French and Marginalist Revolutions," published in *15 Great Austrian Economists*, 1999, Randall G. Holcombe, ed., The Ludwig Von Mises Institute, Auburn, AL.
22. Ludwig von Mises, *The Historical Setting of the Austrian School of Economics*, 1984, The Ludwig von Mises Institute, Auburn, AL.

23. Bramoullé, "Frédéric Bastiat: Praxeologist Theoretician."
24. Ibid.
25. Bastiat, *The Bastiat Collection*.
26. David King, *Vienna, 1814: How the Conquerors of Napoleon Made Love, War, and Peace at the Congress of Vienna*, 2008, Harmony Books.
27. Eugen Maria Schulak and Herbert Ünterkofler, *The Austrian School of Economics: A History of Its Ideas, Ambassadors, & Institutions*, 2011, The Ludwig von Mises Institutes, Auburn, AL.
28. Carl Menger, *Principles of Economics*, 2007, The Ludwig von Mises Institute, Auburn, AL.
29. Timothy Lenoir, *The Strategy of Life: Teleology and Mechanics in Nineteenth Century German Biology*, 1989, University of Chicago Press, Chicago, IL.
30. Thomas Nagel, *Mind and Cosmos: Why the Materialist Neo-Darwinian Conception of Nature is Almost Certainly False*, 2012, Oxford University Press.
31. Lenoir, *The Strategy of Life*.
32. Stephen Wolfram, *A New Kind of Science*, 2002, Wolfram Media.
33. Lenoir, *The Strategy of Life*.
34. Ibid.
35. Ibid.
36. Ibid.
37. Joseph T. Salerno, "Carl Menger: The Founding of the Austrian School," published in *15 Great Austrian Economists*, 1999, Randall G. Holcombe, ed., The Ludwig Von Mises Institute, Auburn, AL.
38. F. A. Hayek, "Carl Menger," Introduction to *Principles of Economics*, Carl Menger, 2007, Ludwig von Mises Institute, Auburn, AL.
39. Bruce J. Caldwell, ed., *Carl Menger and His Legacy in Economics*, 1990, Duke University Press.
40. Schulak and Ünterkofler, *The Austrian School of Economics*.
41. Hayek, "Carl Menger."
42. Menger, *Principles of Economics*.
43. Ibid.
44. Gilles Campagnolo, *Carl Menger: Discussed on the Basis of New Findings*, 2011, The Ludwig von Mises Institute.
45. Menger, *Principles of Economics*.
46. Ibid.
47. Jörg Guido Hülsmann, "Carl Menger: Pioneer of 'Empirical Theory,'" excerpted from *Mises: The Last Knight of Liberalism*, 2007, The Ludwig von Mises Institute, Auburn, AL.
48. Menger, *Principles of Economics*.
49. F. A. Hayek, "Carl Menger."
50. Skousen, *The Making of Modern Economics*.

51. Ludwig von Mises, *Memoirs*, 2009, The Ludwig von Mises Institute, Auburn, AL.
52. Ibid.
53. Ibid.
54. Skousen, *The Making of Modern Economics*.
55. Ibid.
56. Menger, *Principles of Economics*.
57. Hülsmann, "Carl Menger."
58. Murray N. Rothbard, *The History of Economic Thought*, lecture on Menger and Bohm-Bawerk, 2010, The Ludwig von Mises Institute, Auburn, AL.
59. Mises, *The Historical Setting of the Austrian School of Economics*.
60. Ludwig von Mises, *Human Action*, 1998, The Ludwig von Mises Institute, Auburn, AL.
61. Carl Menger, *Investigations into the Method of the Social Sciences*, 1985, NY University Press, NY.
62. Caldwell, ed., *Carl Menger and His Legacy in Economics*.
63. Menger, *Investigations*.
64. Schulak and Ünterkofler, *The Austrian School of Economics*.
65. Ibid.
66. Ibid.
67. Israel Kirzner (author) and Louis Rukeyser (narrator), *Early Austrian Economics: New Importance for the Consumer*, 2006, Blackstone Audio.
68. Schulak and Ünterkofler, *The Austrian School of Economics*.
69. Greaves, Bettina Bien, *Austrian Economics: An Anthology*, 1996, Foundation for Economic Education.
70. Ludwig von Mises, *Theory & History: An Interpretation of Social and Economic Evolution*, 2005, Liberty Fund.
71. Mises, *The Historical Setting of the Austrian School of Economics*.
72. Ludwig von Mises, *Planning for Freedom: Let the Market System Work*, 2008, Liberty Fund.
73. F. A. Hayek, "Introduction," published in *The German Question* by Wilhelm Roepke, 1946, George Allen & Unwin Ltd., London.
74. Joseph Schumpeter, "Carl Menger," *Ten Great Economists: From Marx to Keynes*, 1969, Oxford University Press, NY.

Chapter Five

1. François Jullien, *A Treatise on Efficacy: Between Western and Chinese Thinking*, 2004, University of Hawaii Press.
2. Jullien, *A Treatise on Efficacy*.
3. Mary Paley Marshall, *What I Remember*, 1947, University Press, Cambridge.

4. Eugen Maria Schulak and Herbert Ünterkofler, *The Austrian School of Economics: A History of Its Ideas, Ambassadors, & Institutions*, 2011, The Ludwig von Mises Institutes, Auburn, AL.

5. Eugen von Böhm-Bawerk, *The Positive Theory of Capital*, 1930, G.E. Stechert & Co., NY (photographic reprint of 1891 edition).

6. Ibid.

7. Ibid.

8. Ibid.

9. Ibid.

10. Mark Skousen, *The Making of Modern Economics: The Lives and Ideas of the Great Thinkers*, 2009, M.E. Sharpe, Armonk, NY.

11. Böhm-Bawerk, *The Positive Theory of Capital*.

12. Heinz D. Kurz, "Schumpeter and Marx: A Comment on a Debate," *Industrial and Corporate Change*, 2012, Oxford University Press.

13. Eugen von Böhm-Bawerk, *Capital & Interest*, 1890, Macmillan & Co., NY.

14. Guillermo A. Navarro, "Re-Examining the Theories Support the So-Called Faustmann Formula," *Recent Accomplishments in Applies Forest Economics Research*, 2003.

15. Ibid.

16. Christian Bidard, *Prices, Reproduction, Scarcity*, 2011 (Reissue), Cambridge University Press.

17. Böhm-Bawerk, *The Positive Theory of Capital*.

18. Ibid.

19. Bernard Bailyn, Robert Dallek, et al., *The Great Republic: A History of the American People*, Vol. Two, Fourth Edition, 1991, Wadsworth Publishing.

20. Ibid.

21. Ibid.

22. Steven Watts, *The People's Tycoon: Henry Ford and the American Century*, 2005, Random House, Vintage Books.

23. Thomas P. Hughes, *American Genesis: A Century of Invention and Technological Enthusiasm (1870–1970)*, 2004, University of Chicago Press.

24. Henry Ford and Samuel Crowther, *Today and Tomorrow*, 1926, Doubleday & Co.

25. Henry Ford, *My Life and Work*, 1922, Doubleday & Co.

26. Watts, *The People's Tycoon*.

27. Ibid.

28. Peter J. Boettke, ed., *The Elgar Companion to Austrian Economics*, 1994, Edward Elgar Publishing.

29. Ford, *My Life and Work*.

30. Watts, *The People's Tycoon*.

31. Ford, *My Life and Work*.

32. John Kay, *Obliquity: Why Our Goals Are Best Achieved Indirectly*, 2010, Penguin Books.

33. Ford and Crowther, *Today and Tomorrow*.
34. Ibid.
35. Ibid.
36. Ibid.
37. Ibid.
38. Ibid.
39. Ibid.
40. Richard S. Tedlow, *Giants of Enterprise*, 2003, First Harper Business.
41. Jim Powell, *FDR's Folly: How Roosevelt and His New Deal Prolonged the Great Depression*, 2003, Three Rivers Press, NY.
42. Ford and Crowther, *Today and Tomorrow*.
43. Ibid.
44. Andreas Kluth, *Hannibal and Me: What History's Greatest Military Strategist Can Teach Us About Success and Failure*, 2013 (Reprint Edition), Riverhead Trade, NY.
45. Earl Weaver (with Terry Pluto), *Weaver on Strategy*, March 2002 (Revised Edition), Brassy's, Inc., Dulles, VA.

CHAPTER SIX

1. François Jullien, *The Propensity of Things: Toward a History of Efficacy in China*, 1999, Zone Books.
2. Ibid.
3. Eugen von Böhm-Bawerk, *The Positive Theory of Capital*, 1930, G.E. Stechert & Co., NY (photographic reprint of 1891 edition).
4. Ibid.
5. George Loewenstein and Jon Elster, eds., *Choice over Time*, 1992, Russell Sage Foundation, NY.
6. Eugen von Böhm-Bawerk, *Capital & Interest*, 1890, Macmillan & Co., NY.
7. Loewenstein and Elster, *Choice over Time*.
8. Ibid.
9. Böhm-Bawerk, *The Positive Theory of Capital*.
10. Ibid.
11. Ibid.
12. Ibid.
13. Ibid.
14. Milan Kundera, *Immortality*, 1991, Grove Press, NY.
15. Daniel Kahneman, *Thinking, Fast and Slow*, 2011, Farrar, Straus & Giroux, NY.
16. George Loewenstein, Daniel Read, and Roy F. Baumeister, eds., *Time and Decision: Economic and Psychological Perspectives on Intertemporal Choice*, 2003, Russell Sage Foundation, NY.

17. Ibid.
18. Ibid.
19. Antonio Damasio, *Descartes' Error: Emotion, Reason, and the Human Brain*, 1994, Penguin Books, NY.
20. Ibid.
21. Loewenstein, Read, and Baumeister, *Time and Decision*.
22. Janet Metcalfe and Walter Mischel, "A Hot/Cool System Analysis of Delay of Gratification: Dynamics of Willpower," 1999, *Psychological Review*, vol. 106, no. 1, 3–19.
23. Böhm-Bawerk, *The Positive Theory of Capital*.
24. Ibid.
25. Loewenstein and Elster, *Choice over Time*.
26. Richard Thaler, "Some Empirical Evidence on Dynamic Inconsistency," 1981, *Economic Letters*, 8, 201–207.
27. Böhm-Bawerk, *The Positive Theory of Capital*.
28. Paul Samuelson and William D. Nordhaus, *Economics*, 1989, McGraw-Hill, NY.
29. Shane Frederick, George Loewenstein, and Ted O'Donoghue, "Time Discounting and Time Preference: A Critical Review," June 2002, *Journal of Economic Literature*, vol. XL, pp. 351–401.
30. Douglas Rushkof, *Present Shock: When Everything Happens Now*, 2013, Penguin Books, NY.
31. Edward M. Hallowell, *CrazyBusy: Overstretched, Overbooked, and About to Snap! Strategies for Handling Your Fast Paced Life*, 2007, Ballantine Books.
32. Loewenstein, Read, and Baumeister, *Time and Decision*.
33. Richard Louv, *Last Child in the Woods: Saving Our Children from Nature-Deficit Disorder*, 2008, Algonquin Books, NY.
34. Böhm-Bawerk, *The Positive Theory of Capital*.
35. Howard Rachlin, *The Science of Self-Control*, 2000, Harvard University Press, Cambridge, MA.
36. Frédéric Bastiat, *The Bastiat Collection*, 2007, Ludwig von Mises Institute, Auburn, AL.
37. Hal Hershfield, Daniel Goldstein, et al., "Increasing Savings Behavior through Age-Progressed Renderings of the Future Self," November 2011, *Journal of Marketing Research*, vol. XLVIII, S23-S37.
38. Ruth Krauss, *The Carrot Seed*, 1945, Harper & Row Publishers Inc., NY.
39. Max Weber, Peter Baehr, and Gordon Wells, *The Protestant Ethic and the "Spirit" of Capitalism and Other Writings*, 2002, Penguin Books, NY.
40. Böhm-Bawerk, *The Positive Theory of Capital*.
41. Simon Grondin, ed., *Psychology of Time*, 2008, Emerald Group Publishing Ltd., Bingley, UK.

Chapter Seven

1. Israel M. Kirzner, "Reflections on the Misesian Legacy in Economics," *The Review of Austrian Economics*, vol. 9, no. 2 (1996): 143–154.
2. Ron Paul, *Mises and Austrian Economics: A Personal View*, 1984, Ludwig von Mises Institute (Terra Libertas edition 2011).
3. Jörg Guido Hülsmann, *Mises, the Last Knight of Liberalism*, 2007, The Ludwig von Mises Institute, Auburn, AL.
4. Mark Skousen, *The Making of Modern Economics: The Lives and Ideas of the Great Thinkers*, 2009, M.E. Sharpe, Armonk, NY.
5. Hülsmann, *Mises*.
6. Ludwig von Mises, *Memoirs*, 2009, The Ludwig von Mises Institute, Auburn, AL.
7. Ibid.
8. Ibid.
9. Ibid.
10. Hülsmann, *Mises*.
11. Ludwig von Mises, *Planned Chaos*, 2009, The Ludwig von Mises Institute, Auburn, AL.
12. Margit von Mises, *My Years with Ludwig von Mises*, 1976, Arlington House Publishers, New Rochelle, NY.
13. Hülsmann, *Mises*.
14. Alma Mahler, *Memories and Letters*, 1968, University of Washington Press.
15. Margit von Mises, *My Years with Ludwig von Mises*.
16. Eugen Maria Schulak and Herbert Ünterkofler, *The Austrian School of Economics: A History of Its Ideas, Ambassadors, & Institutions*, 2011, The Ludwig von Mises Institutes, Auburn, AL.
17. Hülsmann, *Mises*.
18. Ludwig von Mises, *Human Action*, 1998, The Ludwig von Mises Institute, Auburn, AL.
19. Henry Hazlitt, "The Case for Capitalism," reprint of *Newsweek* column, September 19, 1949.
20. Murray Rothbard, Preface to *Theory & History* by Ludwig von Mises, 1985 (reprint 2007, Ludwig von Mises Institute, Auburn, AL).
21. Mises, *Memoirs*.
22. Ibid.
23. Peter Boettke and Frederic Sautet, "The Genius of Mises and the Brilliance of Kirzner," *The Annual Proceedings of the Wealth and Wellbeing of Nations*, January 5, 2011, vol. 3, pp. 31–44.
24. Ludwig von Mises, *The Epistemological Problems of Economics*, Third Edition, 2003, The Ludwig von Mises Institute, Auburn, AL.
25. Mises, *Human Action*.
26. Paul Krugman, "To Much Talk about Liquidity," *New York Times* blog, May 17, 2013.

27. Peter Klein, "Entrepreneurs and Creative Destruction," Chapter 9 of *The 4% Solution: Unleashing the Economic Growth America Needs*, 2012, Crown Publishing.

28. Peter Klein, "Risk, Uncertainty and Economic Organization," in *Property, Freedom & Society: Essays in Honor of Hans-Hermann Hoppe*, 2009, Ludwig von Mises Institute, Auburn, AL.

29. Mises, *Human Action*.

30. Ibid.

31. Ibid.

32. Israel Kirzner, "Lifetime Achievement Award Acceptance Speech," Society for the Development of Austrian Economics, November 2006.

33. Mises, *Human Action*.

34. Ibid.

CHAPTER EIGHT

1. John Papola, Foreword to *A Tiger by the Tail: The Keynesian Legacy of Inflation*, Friedrich Hayek, 1972, The Institute of Economic Affairs (reprinted 2012, Laissez-Faire Books).

2. Murray N. Rothbard, *America's Great Depression*, Fifth Edition, 2000, Ludwig von Mises Institute, Auburn, AL.

3. W. J. Bond and J. E. Kelley, "Fire as a Global 'Herbivore': The Ecology and Evolution of Flammable Ecosystems," *Trends in Ecology and Evolution*, vol. 20, no 7., July 2005.

4. Mark Buchanan, *Ubiquity: Why Catastrophes Happen*, 2002, Broadway Books.

5. Mark Spitznagel, "Christmas Trees and the Logic of Growth," *Wall Street Journal*, December 22, 2012.

6. Ludwig von Mises, lecture, New York Economics Club, 1945, Ludwig von Mises Institute.

7. Peter J. Boettke and Frederic Sautet, "The Genius of Mises and the Brilliance of Kirzner," *Annual Proceedings of the Wealth and Well-Being of Nations*, vol. 3, pp. 31–44, 2011.

8. Norbert Wiener, *Cybernetics: Control and Communication in the Animal and the Machine*, 1965, MIT Press.

9. Ibid.

10. Ibid.

11. Friedrich Hayek, "Competition as a Discovery Procedure," Marcellus Snow, trans., *The Quarterly Journal of Austrian Economics*, vol. 5, no. 3, Fall 2002.

12. Friedrich Hayek, *The Unfinished Agenda: Essays on the Political Economy of Government Policy in Honour of Arthur Seldon*, Institute of Economic Affairs, 1986.

13. Ibid.

14. Friedrich Hayek, "Competition as a Discovery Procedure.

15. Ludwig von Mises, *Human Action*, 1998, The Ludwig von Mises Institute, Auburn, AL.

16. Paul Cantor and Stephen Cox, *Literature and the Economics of Literature*, 2010, Ludwig von Mises Institute, Auburn, AL.

17. Douglas R. Hofstadter, *Gödel, Escher, Bach: An Eternal Golden Braid*, 1999, Basic Books.

18. Murray N. Rothbard, *Economic Thought Before Adam Smith*, Edward Elgar Publishing, 1995.

19. Doug French, "The Dutch Monetary Environment During Tulipmania," *The Quarterly Journal of Austrian Economics*, vol. 9, no. 1 (Spring 2006).

20. Murray N. Rothbard, *America's Great Depression*, Ludwig von Mises Institute.

21. Eugen von Böhm-Bawerk, *The Positive Theory of Capital*, 1930, G.E. Stechert & Co., NY (photographic reprint of 1891 edition).

22. Roger T. Ames and David T. Hall, *Daodejing "Making This Life Significant": A Philosophical Translation*, 2003, Ballantine Books, NY.

23. John Deathridge, *Wagner: Beyond Good and Evil*, 2008, University of California Press.

Chapter Nine

1. Ludwig von Mises, *Human Action*, 1998, The Ludwig von Mises Institute, Auburn, AL.

2. Ibid.

3. Juvenal (Niall Rudd, translator), *The Satires*, 1991 (reprint 2001), Oxford University Press, Oxford, UK.

4. Bertrand Russell, *The Problems of Philosophy*, 1912, Home University Library.

5. Bettina Bien Greaves, ed., *Austrian Economics: An Anthology*, 1996, Foundation for Economic Education

6. Carl von Carl von Clausewitz, *On War*, translators, Michael Eliot Howard and Peter Paret, 1976, Princeton University Press.

Chapter Ten

1. Aljos Farjon, *A Natural History of Conifers*, 2008, Timber Press, Portland, OR.

2. Tim Koller, Marc Goedhart, and David Wessels, *Valuation: Measuring and Managing the Value of Companies*, Fifth Edition, 2010, John Wiley & Sons, Hoboken, NJ.

3. Peter Lynch, *One Up on Wall Street: How to Use What Your Already Know to Make Money in the Market*, Second Edition, 2000, Simon & Schuster, New York.

4. Benjamin Graham and David Dodd, *Security Analysis: The Classic 1934 Edition*, 1996, McGraw-Hill, New York.

5. Eugen von Böhm-Bawerk, *The Positive Theory of Capital*, 1930, G.E. Stechert & Co., NY (photographic reprint of 1891 edition).
6. Benjamin Graham, *The Intelligent Investor: The Definitive Book on Value Investing*, Revised Edition, 2006, Collins Business.
7. Bin Jiang and Timothy Koller, "The Truth about Growth and Value Stocks," *McKinsey on Finance*, 2007.
8. Letter to Murray Rothbard from Howard Buffett, July 31, 1962, available from Ludwig von Mises Institute, Auburn, AL.
9. Eugene F. Fama and Kenneth R. French, "Common Risk Factors in the Returns on Stocks and Bonds," *Journal of Financial Economics*, 33 (1993) 3–56.
10. Joel Greenblatt, *The Little Book That Beats the Market*, 2005, John Wiley & Sons, Hoboken, NJ.
11. Robert Novy-Marx, "The Quality Dimension of Value Investing," December 2012 (Revised March 2013), University of Rochester, Working Paper.

Epilogue

1. Robert Karnisky, "*On War* and The Winter War," 2007, thesis submission, Florida State University.
2. William Trotter, *A Frozen Hell: The Russo-Finnish War of 1939–1940*, 2000, Algonquin Books of Chapel Hill, Chapel Hill, NC.
3. Roger Ames, *Sun-Tzu: The Art of Warfare*, 1993, Ballantine Books.
4. François Jullien, *A Treatise on Efficacy: Between Western and Chinese Thinking*, 2004, University of Hawaii Press.
5. Trotter, *A Frozen Hell*.
6. Carl von Clausewitz, *On War*, translators, Michael Eliot Howard and Peter Paret, 1976, Princeton University Press.
7. Angela Lee Duckworth and Lauren Eskreis-Winkler, "True Grit," *Observer*, May/June 2013, Association for Psychological Science.
8. Eugen von Bohm-Bawerk, *The Positive Theory of Capital*, 1930, G.E. Stechert & Co., New York (photographic reprint of 1891 edition).
9. George F. Will, *Men at Work: The Craft of Baseball*, Macmillan, 1990.
10. Henry Ford and Samuel Crowther, *Today and Tomorrow*, 1926, Doubleday & Co.
11. Paul Tough, *How Children Succeed: Grit, Curiosity, and the Hidden Power of Character*, 2012, Houghton Mifflin Harcourt Publishing Company, New York.
12. Denise Shekerjian, *Uncommon Genius: How Great Ideas Are Born*, 1990, Penguin Books, New York.
13. Aljos Farjon, *A Natural History of Conifers*, 2008, Timber Press, Portland, Oregon.
14. Wucius Wong, *The Tao of Chinese Landscape Painting: Principles & Methods*, University of Michigan (reprint 1991, Design Press).

Acknowledgments

or the journey of this book and bringing it to a conclusion, I wish to thank the following:

My wife, Amy, for her love and companionship; my children, Edward and Silja, for the immeasurable joy they bring (with such exuberance I had to do much of my writing in the middle of the night); my brother, Eric, a wonderful writer and the funniest guy I know, for his encouragement; Dad, in memory (*vitae summa brevis*), and Mom, for their steadfast support and belief along my roundabout road; Gramma Spitznagel, in memory, my first and best investor.

Everett Klipp, in memory, for taking a prying 16-year-old under his wing and giving him *shi*.

Ron Paul, for keeping Austrian economics alive and spreading the word to the next generation (his own grand *shi* strategy)—may he be known through the ages.

Team *Dao of Capital*: Robert Murphy, for his friendship and keeping an "Austrian" eye on things; Tim Foley, for his exquisite illustrations; Patricia Crisafulli, for shepherding the process; Roger Ames, my resident, patient Sinologist; Aljos Farjon, my conifer expert; Qichen Guo, Jwing-Ming Yang, and Yilun Yang, my teachers; Chitpuneet Mann and Harry Tam, for their invaluable research (even accommodating my sometimes crazy hours); Brandon Yarckin, for all his help; Jim Frolik and Jeff O'Connell, for their good counsel. (My thanks to all for their expertise; any errors or unorthodoxy in interpretation are mine alone.)

Nassim Taleb, who always reminds me of the importance of skepticism, for showing me tenacity in thought. Victor Niederhoffer, for teaching me the simple wisdom in canes, trees, and the gentleman's game of squash.

My publisher, John Wiley & Sons, with gratitude to Evan Burton for persisting in convincing me to do this book; Emilie Herman, for her careful reading and care of the manuscript; and Vincent Nordhaus and Tula Batanchiev as well.

George Viksnins, for his "Austrian" economics class at Georgetown University that started it off for me.

Eric Spencer, Damir Delic, Daisy Pham, Annelise Sarver, and Trysha Daskam, for all their help, as well as all the dedicated employees at Universa.

The Ludwig von Mises Institute for the wealth of information on Austrian economics and making the works of the masters widely available.

Lastly, Chairmen Bernanke and Greenspan, for being my dependable source of investment returns.

About the Author

MARK SPITZNAGEL is the founder and president of *Universa Investments*, an investment advisor that specializes in equity tail-hedging—or profiting from extreme stock market losses as a means to enhancing investment returns. In addition to hedge fund investing, Spitznagel's 20-year investment career has ranged from independent pit trader at the Chicago Board of Trade (the youngest local in the bond pit) to proprietary trading head at Morgan Stanley in New York. He received an M.S. from New York University (at the Courant Institute of Mathematical Sciences) and a B.A. from Kalamazoo College. Spitznagel also owns and operates *Idyll Farms* in northern Michigan.

Spitznagel pledges all personal profits from the sale of *The Dao of Capital* to charity.

Index